THE INTERNET CONSUMER BIBLE

The Internet Consumer Bible

Tess Read, Calum Chace and Simon Rowe

RANDOM HOUSE
BUSINESS BOOKS

© Tess Read, Calum Chace and Simon Rowe 2000
All rights reserved

Tess Read, Calum Chace and Simon Rowe have asserted their rights under the Copyright, Designs and Patents Act, 1988, to be identified as the authors of this work

First published in 2000 by Random House Business Books,
Random House, 20 Vauxhall Bridge Road, London SW1V 2SA

Random House Australia (Pty) Limited
20 Alfred Street, Milsons Point,
Sydney, New South Wales 2061, Australia

Random House New Zealand Limited
18 Poland Road, Glenfield,
Auckland 10, New Zealand

Random House (Pty) Limited
Endulini, 5a Jubilee Road, Parktown 2193, South Africa

The Random House Group Limited Reg. No. 954009

Papers used by Random House are natural, recyclable products made from wood grown in sustainable forests. The manufacturing processes conform to the environmental regulations of the country of origin.

ISBN 0 7126 7197 8

Companies, institutions and other organizations wishing to make bulk purchases of books published by Random House should contact their local bookstore or Random House direct:
Special Sales Director
Random House, 20 Vauxhall Bridge Road, London SW1V 2SA
Tel 020 7840 8470   Fax 020 7828 6681

---

www.randomhouse.co.uk
businessbooks@randomhouse.co.uk

Typeset in Bembo and Trade Gothic by
MATS, Southend-on-Sea, Essex
Printed and bound in Great Britain by
Biddles Ltd, Guildford and King's Lynn

Contents

Preface *by Vint Cerf and Bob Kahn* ... ix

Foreword ... xi

Authors' Note ... xiii

1. Getting Started ... **(1)**

Accessing the internet ... 2

Finding stuff on the world wide web ... 9

Email ... 14

Newsgroups ... 19

Security ... 20

2. Lifestages ... **(27)**

Births and young children ... 28

Education ... 33

Job hunting ... 45

Dating, marriage and divorce ... 54

Silver surfing	62
Death	66
3. Shopping	**(71)**
Buying online	72
Homes	82
Gardening	89
Cars	94
Clothes	100
Groceries	107
4. Entertainment and Leisure	**(115)**
Travel and holidays	116
Radio, TV and films	127
Music	135
Restaurants	143
Nightlife	149
Sport	152
Genealogy	157

Weather	163
5. Organising your life	**(167)**
Money	168
Health	186
Getting around	201
Politics and Government	208
The law	215
Religion	220
News	226

Preface

The internet, past, present and future

As we enter a new millennium, the internet is revolutionising our society, our economy and our technological systems. No one knows for certain how far, or in what direction, it will evolve. But no one should underestimate its importance.

The internet is a dynamic organism that can be looked at in myriad ways. It is a framework for numerous services and a medium for creativity and innovation. Most importantly, it can be expected to evolve.

How the US Defense department sparked the internet

In 1969, the US Defense Advanced Research Projects Agency (DARPA) commissioned Bolt Beranek and Newman (BBN) to design and implement a wide-area computer network called the ARPANET. Bob Kahn worked at BBN as the senior architect on the project. Vint Cerf worked at UCLA as a graduate student in Professor Leonard Kleinrock's Network Measurement Laboratory where he helped design the ARPANET's host-to-host computer protocols.

At the time, the methods of internetworking (that is, interconnecting computer networks) were primitive. Two organisations could interconnect by agreeing to use common equipment, but failing that, each network stood on its own with no interaction between them – a far cry from today's internet.

After the successful demonstration of the ARPANET in 1972, Vint Cerf became a professor at Stanford, and Bob Kahn became a senior manager at DARPA. Working together, we created an architecture for interconnecting independent and heterogeneous networks. This was the genesis of the internet as we know it today.

To work properly, the architecture required a global addressing mechanism (or internet address) to enable computers on any network to communicate with computers on any other network in the federation. Internet addresses fill essentially the same role as telephone numbers in telephone networks.

For a long time, the federal government did not allow organisations to connect to the internet to carry out commercial activities. In 1988, the commercial MCI Mail electronic mail system was granted permission to connect to the internet. Commercial pressure to alleviate restrictions on interconnections with the National Science Foundation (NSF) net developed by universities began to mount.

Congress passed legislation allowing NSF to open the NSFNET to commercial usage and by 1995 many commercial networks were in operation and provided alternatives to NSFNET for national level network services. Today, approximately 10,000 Internet Service Providers (ISPs) are in operation, roughly half of them in North America.

The internet and the world wide web

The growth of web servers and users of the web has been remarkable, but some people are confused about the relationship between the world wide web and the internet. The internet is the global information system that includes communication capabilities and many high level applications. The web is one such application has and electronic mail is another. Today, over 60 million computers connect to the internet, and about 3.6 million web sites are estimated to be accessible on the net. Virtually every user of the net has access to electronic mail and web browsing capability, and these two functions dominate the use of the internet for most users.

Where do we go from here?

In the next ten years, the internet is expected to get much bigger than it is today. It will be more pervasive than the older technologies and penetrate more homes than television and radio. Many of the devices connected to the internet will be internet-enabled appliances (cell phones, fax machines, household appliances, hand-held organisers, digital cameras, etc.) as well as traditional laptop and desktop computers.

As we struggle to envision what may be commonplace on the internet in a decade, we are confronted with the challenge of imagining new ways of doing old things, as well as trying to think of new things that will be enabled by the internet, and by the technologies of the future.

Vint Cerf and Bob Kahn, co-designers of the internet

Foreword

The surfing metaphor for browsing the internet is a good one. The world wide web can be as intimidating as the surf at The Pipeline on the north shore of Hawaii, but if you know how to master the waves it can be equally as exhilarating, with none of the danger.

The only real danger is being left on the beach as millions of users join the exciting world of convenience, discovery and enjoyment that the world wide web offers. In the UK alone 19.5 million people are now using the internet, to do everything from shopping to gossiping. And that number is growing by eight million every year. Not learning to master the internet would be like not learning to drive a car, use a telephone or switch on the television would have been when those technologies changed the world. For the impact of the internet is no longer just a business issue, it will affect almost every aspect of our daily lives. And it will do so far more quickly than the phone or TV did. It has taken only five years for the internet to reach nearly a third of our homes – it took the TV fifteen years to reach the same level of acceptance.

The real question, then, is not if, but how? This book offers an easy-to-use and informative way to catch the next wave and realise your full potential as a seasoned surfer. It will show you:

- How to navigate and use the millions of web sites that exist

- How to search quickly, and find exactly what you are looking for

- How to save money – not just when getting online, but also on practically everything you buy or use

- How to personalize the information available so it is relevant to your needs and preferences

- How to separate hype from substance and fact from fiction

- How to find fun, excitement, answers and ideas.

In short, this book gives you the information and insights that you need to get the most out of your time on the web, and just as importantly, how to enjoy it. Which is why we at Metrius were happy to provide the research that forms the foundation of the book's findings and recommendations.

Our company, a subsidiary of KPMG Consulting with offices in Europe and North America, was founded with the sole intention of helping companies develop an integrated, people-focused approach in all their internet-related activities. Metrius and the consultants who helped research this book have extensive experience helping companies like Motorola, Swatch, Virgin, Sony and Compaq make their digital businesses people-friendly. Like everyone using the web, we are still discovering new ideas and better ways of managing information. This book offers you the opportunity to benefit from everything we have learned to date.

Separating the hype from the substance of the internet can be a daunting task, even for the professionals among us. Read this book and you will have the best information and web sites at your fingertips, so that you can join the millions of people who are already enjoying the very real benefits of the web. As daunting as it may at first appear, this is one wave you cannot afford to miss.

Clive Pinder

CEO, Metrius.

Authors' Note

What can the internet do for you? How can it save you money, save you time, make your life easier? Our aim in writing this book was to answer these questions.

In the next twelve months, many more people in this country will have 'proper access' to the internet at home. By that we mean unmetered broadband access, and by *that* we mean that you can stay online for as long as you like for free, with web pages loading fast, even if they have lots of moving graphics.

The arrival of unmetered broadband access will mean that you can explore the internet without frustratingly slow websites or expensive phone bills. You could find a better mortgage for your house; get a better job; check the performance tables for schools around the country; listen to American, French or Japanese radio stations and download the best music they play; or track down that poem whose first line and author you have forgotten.

This book is designed to help you do all these things, and much more. It gives you a map to explore the highways and byways of this exciting, misunderstood and curious world. Rather than write about what just happens to exist on the internet, we've set out to write about what you will want from it. We've written about what sites we find useful and interesting, and tried to describe how best to do the things that you will want to do there. We've also examined the limitations of what is on offer and how things may develop.

The internet changes quickly. Everything in this book is as true as we can make it at the time of writing. Over the coming months, some good sites will go bad, some bad sites will improve, and many new sites will appear. If you find that any information in the book is out of date please let us know at **www.consumer-bible.co.uk**. We will do our best to incorporate any corrections in subsequent editions of this book.

Our thanks are due to many people, but in particular we would like to thank Vint Cerf and Bob Kahn, Clive Pinder, Kavita Copas and Simon Kwiesinski at Metrius, Nick Hadlow, Daniel Davies and Clare Smith at Random House.

Simon Rowe

Tess Read

Calum Chace

London and Oxford, October 2000

Site ratings

At the end of each chapter we have included a set of ratings for sites which are either good (in our view) or important. One star means the site is weak, five stars mean it is heroically good. We have not tried to be laboriously scientific about this; our system is a subjective and intuitive mixture of design, content, and user-friendliness.

1 Getting Started

Accessing the Internet

What you'll need

To begin surfing the internet you don't actually need to buy anything. The number of public sector places where you can get online, such as libraries, is increasing. There are also commercial internet cafes such as Easyeverything, at **www.easyeverything.com**, which has branches around the world, including five in London and one in Edinburgh. One pound buys between 20 minutes and 6 hours online, depending on how busy it is. If you've never used the internet before (or even a computer), don't worry, the instructions about how to get online are very clear and easy, at about ten words long.

However, if you want to be surfing frequently, and assuming you cannot spend your working hours exploring the net, you will want to get connected at home. There are a number of ways to do this, but by far the most common currently is using a PC. You will need a number of things:

1. A computer. Around 95 per cent of the world's desktops are PCs – personal computers – running Microsoft Windows. The remaining 5 per cent are Apple Macs (including iMacs).

The debate over the merits of Windows and Macintosh operating systems becomes largely irrelevant when using the net. The iMac/iBook is probably the easiest computer to set up and operate. However a PC will probably offer better price/performance ratio, and there are far more software titles for PCs than for Apples.

Most new computers have the power and capacity to run the required software to get online. Any Pentium-class PC should be more than adequate, and even many PCs which are ancient by internet standards (for instance, those with a 486 processor) would be capable of getting connected, although sites containing animation may run slowly, if at all. The old adage holds true: buy the best you can afford.

2. A modem, or modem-like device. A modem is the hardware your computer needs to be able to connect to the internet. The current standard speed of modems is 56Kbs. If you are lucky enough to have access to a digital line (ISDN2/Home Highway/ Business Highway) then you need the digital equivalent of a modem, a Terminal Adapter or ISDN router.

3. Browser software. This allows you to view and interact with the information found on the web. The most common browsers are Microsoft's Internet Explorer and Netscape's Navigator which are both available free of charge. A new computer will almost certainly come with one of these two programs pre-installed. If not, most setup disks from ISPs (see below) will include the latest versions. Once you are online, you can download updates and new releases from **www.microsoft.com** and **www.netscape.com** respectively for free. There is little to choose between them: some people think that Microsoft is the evil empire, but on the other hand there are a few sites which work less well with Netscape. You can of course operate both, simultaneously if you like, and see which you prefer.

4. An ISP (Internet Service Provider) account. ISPs provide your connection to email and the internet – and other net services. You dial into your ISP, and it connects you with the world.

ISPs and connection charges

Until recently, users had to pay their ISP a monthly fee, and some still make a charge, often £10–15 per month. On top of this you pay for local call charges – that is, for the call from your phone to the ISP. Two recent developments are bringing the costs down.

Free ISPs

'Free' ISPs have sprouted like mushrooms, following the lead of Dixons's partially-floated subsidiary Freeserve. Under Freeserve's original model, you still have to pay for call charges, so you may feel constrained from surfing freely because you are running up your phone bill.

The downside of free ISPs is that they do not guarantee permanent connection, 24 hours a day, 365 days a year. Most get pretty close, but a lot of people were put out recently when Freeserve reduced its capacity over a weekend without giving notice. If constant connectivity is absolutely mission-critical to you, it may be worth paying an ISP which guarantees it, but it will be expensive. Otherwise you may be best advised to save your money and sign up with one or more of the free ISPs. These are now widely available; you can pick up free CD-Roms for free ISPs from numerous retailers, such as Oxfam or HMV.

Unmetered access

During 2000, unmetered access (where there are no phone charges for being online) has made a tentative appearance, with services currently available from Freeserve, World Online, and cable company NTL, among others.

These companies launched their products in the belief that Oftel, the government's regulator of telecoms, would force BT to 'unbundle the local loop' (i.e. give competitors access to your home phone) and speedily introduce Flat Rate Internet Access Call Origination, better known as FRIACO. With FRIACO, a wholesale product, BT leases ports to ISPs rather than charging per user. ISPs are then able to offer unmetered access profitably.

BT executives argue that they are working on this unbundling as fast as possible, but it is hard to find anybody who believes them. According to many people, BT is abusing a monopoly position and slowing down the internet revolution in the UK. Surprisingly, it has managed to give this impression while at the same time experiencing a serious slide in its share price.

Until unbundling happens, the providers of unmetered access are making a loss because they buy phone time by the minute and sell it for a standing charge – and a low one at that. Unmetered Freeserve Time, for instance, costs £10 a month, and even that is rebated against the cost of national and international calls which they sell at lower-than-BT prices. However, Freeserve has recently stopped offering this service to new customers.

A number of ISPs have been highly embarrassed by this situation. NTL has drawn flak for making it hard for users to sign up, AltaVista's MD lost his job when a feisty online IT news service called The Register forced him to admit that AltaVista did not actually offer the service they said they did. Even the big ISPs, with plenty of money to invest ahead of BT's roll-out, are terminating contracts with heavy users whom they accuse of 'abusing' the service.

When deciding whether it is cost-efficient for you to subscribe to unmetered access you need to work out how much time you will use the internet each month. Then double it: most people find that when they have unmetered access they surf far more than they expected. Then work out the cost of local calls for this time. You need to factor-in the standing charge per month for unlimited access (for example, £10 for Freeserve) and the fact that you may find you need an extra telephone line.

Subscription ISP services

People who make the curious decision to subscribe to AOL or Compuserve pay a monthly charge to get access to AOL's exclusive news and information. Presumably the reassurance of dealing with the world's largest ISP helps account for this behaviour.

Helplines

A factor to bear in mind in choosing between ISPs is that there is a huge disparity in the cost of calls to help lines, and the service you can expect from those lines. Most of the free ISPs have extremely high rate call charges for their help lines, around 50 pence per minute. Subscription ISPs usually have cheap rate help lines. But:

Helplines can be profit centres for free ISPs, so they make sure they have enough staff to deal with your call instantly. The helplines of subscription-based ISPs such as Compuserve are notoriously difficult to get through to.

Most calls to help lines are fairly short because the staff are usually well-trained and familiar with the set of difficulties you may be having.

If you are able to load up a CD-Rom, and can find your way around Control Panel within the My Computer function, you are unlikely to need to phone a helpline very often.

Checklist for choosing an ISP:

- How highly does it score in the ever-growing number of internet-related magazines for reliability of connection?

- If it charges, how long are you committing to pay for?

- Does it pay compensation for poor quality service?

- Will it offer ADSL, and if so, when? (See below)

- Do you want to create your own personal web presence? Or use your ISP as a storage service, so you can access your files from all over the place? If so, an ISP that offers free web space is worth looking at.

o   Does the ISP offer technical support? How much does it cost? And is it actually available?

Television-based internet access

Standard television – cable company NTL offers a TV-based internet service for £10 per month, with a £10 connection fee, provided that you spend £10 per month on phone calls.

Digital television – access is also becoming available over new digital cable services. The advantage of this is that you don't use your phone line to connect, so there are normally no connection charges, and the access is usually fast.

NTL's digital TV internet service is free to digital cable subscribers. The connection speed ranges from between 512kbs to 1.6 Mbs. The service is relatively limited at present, allowing access to approximately 100 web sites.

Ondigital also offers internet access to their digital television subscribers, but it does use the phone to connect, thus incurring telephone charges. Connection is limited to standard 56kbs access speed. The service requires an additional (free) box to the iDTV setup box, and there is a five pound per month charge.

Fast access / Broadband

The things holding back the usefulness of the world wide web (and which sometimes make it seem like the world wide wait) are the cost of the equipment, the cost of being online, the time it takes to dial in, and the speed with which pages download.

The last of these is about bandwidth. Having lots of bandwidth is like having big fat pipes to receive the flow of text, graphics, animations and sounds – fast. ADSL and ISDN are the main two technologies to know about.

ADSL (Asymmetric Digital Subscriber Line) is a technology providing high bandwidth over existing telephone cables. Video, music and interactive TV should all be receivable using ADSL. Another advantage of ADSL is that you can still use the phone while surfing the net. ADSL download rates are generally 512Kbps, about ten times the speed of a standard modem.

ADSL is coming, but not especially fast. By September 2000, 35 per cent of BT exchanges had been converted to offer ADSL services. About 50 per cent are due to be equipped by mid-2001, with 70 per cent coverage by the end of the year. ADSL may not be available to the 15 per cent of British households that are more than 3.5 km away from their exchange (bad news if you live in Scotland); performance degrades significantly at distances greater than this.

If you get ADSL, you will be sharing your link with as many as fifty other users, so at busy times the service may not be much faster than a 56k dial-up modem. It is also expensive at the moment. Prices should drop from the current average of £40 per month when more companies offer it.

ISDN (Integrated Services Digital Network) is a digital internet connection available to home users. At the time of writing, combining BT's Home Highway, a version of ISDN, with, say, Freeserve's unmetered access can be one of the best deals for internet access. (although Freeserve has stopped offering this service to new customers). You connect to an ISDN line through a Terminal Adapter (TA) rather than a modem.

BT Openworld runs over standard phone lines with additional home hardware. Similar to ADSL, it provides a permanent internet connection up to ten times as fast as a standard 56k modem. BT charges £150 for installation plus £39 per week. There are no call fees on top.

NTL's cable modems offer download speeds (where you receive data from the ISP) of 512Kbps, four times faster than the average ISDN line. The price is currently £40 per month with no call charges, plus £149 for a modem and £25 for installation. The service does not use your phone line.

Mobile internet

The ubiquitous mobile phone is currently undergoing some major changes. The first of these is the advent of WAP (wireless access protocol) phones. WAP-enabled phones allow you to connect to the so-called 'mobile internet'. Despite the hype, and what BT in particular wants you to believe, it is not the internet, and it lacks the richness of the net. Despite this, the mobile net does point the way to what could be the future of the internet.

In October 2000, the four UK mobile phone operators (namely Vodafone, BT Cellnet, Orange and One 2 One) had between them 34 million subscribers, which translates to roughly half the UK population. These four plus a few others bid a total of £23bn for the UK's five UMTS (Universal Mobile Telecommunications Service) licences, which will pave the way for so-called 3G (third generation) mobile services. UMTS networks, expected to be in place by 2002-3, will allow for fast wireless access to some form of the internet – considerably faster than WAP.

Finding stuff on the world wide web

A **website** is a collection of web pages on a computer somewhere in the world. The files can contain text, pictures, sound, video or computer programmes. A website can have a few pages, or a great number of pages. You move from one page to another, and from one website to another by way of the links on the site.

Uniform Resource Locator (URL) is the address of a website, such as **www.bbc.co.uk**. This phrase is the precise address of the website on the internet and will take you directly there, just like keying in the correct digits to reach a phone number. If you get a letter wrong in the address, you will not connect to the correct site, just as if you put a wrong digit to a phone number you will not connect to the right number. Alternatively, you can find a site by using search engines (see below), which is like finding a telephone number by phoning Directory Enquiries.

The bit of a URL after the last dot indicates which country the site resides in. Hence '.uk' is a site in the UK, '.fr' is in France, and so on. The only exception is America, which is a pity, since around half of all the websites in the world are American. Other suffixes indicate what type of organisation has built the site: '.com' or '.co.uk' indicates a commercial site, '.org' or '.org.uk' indicates some kind of non-profit status, '.gov' means government, '.edu' denotes an educational establishment.

Search Engines and Directories

Although a listing of major sites (such as those given throughout this book) is a useful starting-point for surfers, the fluidity and sheer size of the internet means that sooner or later you will need to use search engines and directories. Simply put, the difference between the two is that a search engine allows its database of web pages to be searched, whereas a directory classifies web pages into categories and subcategories.

Search engines help you find things on the internet. They are by no means foolproof yet, and IT people think they will improve dramatically over the next few years, but they are an essential tool for using the internet. If you use a search engine properly you can easily find the telephone number of the Australian High Commission, the full text of that poem by Ogden Nash, and a million other things.

Who are they?

Some of the most used search engines are those on **www.yahoo.com**, **www.altavista.com**, **www.google.com**. But things are not as they seem: Google actually writes the software for the search engine provided on Yahoo!, having recently replaced another company, Inktomi. Some of the best search engines in the world are produced by the British firm Autonomy, which famously made its founder Mike Lynch Britain's first internet billionaire.

How do you use a search engine?

It is very easy. You simply type in the URL of a search engine, (i.e., its address, like **www.google.com**) in the address line near the top of your browser screen. The homepage of the search engine will then load and you enter your query in the box marked "Search".

Search engine databases are constructed either by teams of humans merrily surfing away, or by automated 'crawlers' or 'robots' – clever pieces of software that search out information from around the web. Search engines don't actually search the internet 'live' but search a pre-constructed database. (This is why they are so fast.) The quality of a search engine is determined by the database's coverage of the internet, coupled with the amount and quality of information stored about each site.

Which one is best?

As is the nature of the internet, the comparative performances of individual search engines vary over time – see the end of this chapter for our ratings of the current offerings. A good starting point for research is the computer category on most directory pages. For example, under Hotbot's 'Computers and internet' category is a 'Searching the Net' subcategory. IT publisher Ziff-Davies posts reviews of search engines at **http://www.zdnet.com/searchiq/**.

As well as the general ones that attempt to lay the whole of the internet at your feet, there are more specialised search engines for particular audiences. For example, **www.thelaboroflove.com/websearch/links/index.shtml** is dedicated to parenting and parenthood and **www.allacademic.com/** is a search engine for free online academic resources.

Getting even more specialised, many websites have their own site-specific search engines. **www.microsoft.com** is a quick way of locating technical information about Microsoft products from anywhere on the company's site.

An example of a directory is the Open Directory Project, found at **http://dmoz.org/**. Its aim is to provide a more comprehensive directory of internet resources than search engines can manage. The project is undertaken by volunteer editors, subject-matter experts who decide whether a site should be included in the directory. The Open Directory is made available to a number of 'mainstream' search engines.

Search Engine Syntax

Search engines list the pages they find for you according to their relevance to the query you entered. Using search engines (developing 'search strategies') is something of an art form, and a search engine's website will give information on how to get the best out of it.

The rules an engine uses to interpret your search query are called its syntax. Most use similar rules and the following rules are found in pretty much all engines.

Enclosing two or more words in quotes indicates the search engine should search for the complete phrase as opposed to the individual words.

Including the + symbol immediately before a particular word indicates that that word should definitely be returned in the search results.

Including the – symbol immediately before a particular word indicates that that word should definitely not be returned in the search results.

Search Engine Tips

- Be specific. If you are looking for information on Apple computers, try searching for the phrase 'Apple computers' as opposed to 'Apple' or 'computers'
- Only use words which are relevant to your search
- Check for typos in your search query

- Phrases often return better results than keywords

- Make use of the pre-defined categories that are included on most search engines' home pages

- Get to know the query syntax of individual search engines. Most engines provide a syntax help section or advanced search page

- Most large search sites have numerous national versions. Be aware that the .com version, for example **www.yahoo.com**, is likely to be US-based, while the UK version **http://uk.yahoo.com** may well deliver more relevant results

- Remember that different search engines cover different amounts and areas of the web. If one doesn't return the results you require, try another.

If your search generates lots of seemingly irrelevant sites, this doesn't mean your search engine is useless. Many web sites put a lot of words in the sections the search engines look at which are not relevant to what the sites do, but which make them more likely to be picked up by a search engine, and so more likely to be seen by the unsuspecting public. Some seem to enter the whole of *Roget's Thesaurus*.

Meta Search Engines

A meta search engine searches a number of search engines simultaneously. **www.copernic.com** is a good example of a meta search engine, claiming to aggregate the output of some 80 search engines. Another meta search engine is **www.dogpile.com** which uses Altavista, Infoseek, Excite, Yahoo, and Webcrawler as well as its own database. A comparison of meta search engines can be found at **www.lib.berkeley.edu/TeachingLib/Guides/internet/MetaSearch.html**.

Another useful research tool is Gurunet, found at **www.gurunet.com**. After a small program has been installed on your computer, you can 'alt-click' on any word on any document and a pop-up window will give detailed information, be it a stock chart and history on a company or a dictionary definition of the selected word.

Finding People

The web also provides a number of great resources for finding people and places. Infospace, at **www.infospace.com/uk/**, bills itself as 'The Ultimate Directory' for finding people, places and things. Like other similar sites, it is strongly focused on North America, and a search for your old school friend Albert Einstein will tend to find a lot of namesakes, but not necessarily the person you're looking for. Similar services are available at **www.people.yahoo.com** and **www.bigfoot.co.uk**. Other portals such as Lycos and Excite also have facilities for searching for email address, but they do not appear to work as well as Yahoo.

There are also several directories of email addresses, but since only a small minority of email users bother to register, these searches are very long shot. If the free searches do not work, you could go to one of the online search organisers such as **www.peopletracer.co.uk**. or **www.missing-you.net**. Peopletracer claim 90 per cent success rate and charges £100 on average. Much more tantalising is a website that lists missing heirs: **www.bureauofmissingheirs.com**.

Portals

Internet portals bring together information from other sources, as opposed to producing the information themselves. Most portals try to make themselves your first port of call (your browser's homepage) by providing additional functionality. For instance, **www.my.yahoo.com** allows you to customise what you see on your own personal 'My Yahoo' page by selecting information that is easily accessible through Yahoo's categories, including local, national and international news, selected sports information, weather and personal stock information.

The arrival of WAP has led to the creation of portals for mobile phones. **www.mviva.com**, a portal from AOL and Carphone Warehouse, is currently available in the UK, France and the Netherlands. Services range from diary and mail to share dealing and restaurant search facilities. The services are currently basic, but the introduction of 2.5G (generation 2.5) GPRS (general packet radio service) towards the end of this year and 3G UMTS (universal mobile telecommunications service) around 2002-3 will give mobile phones faster, permanent connections and will open the door to a glut of new mobile applications.

A tip for browsing

Once you've found a site you like, you may find that moving from one page to another takes a little time. And when you jump from one site to another, it takes a little longer. A good trick to avoid becoming too frustrated is to open two or more browsers at the same time, and read one while the other is loading.

Remembering and organising stuff once you've found it

Having found a site, how can you avoid losing it again? Both Netscape's and Microsoft's browsers allow you to 'file' sites you might want to return to. Netscape calls these filed sites 'bookmarks', while Microsoft calls them 'favourites'. Both browsers allow you to organise your bookmarks in folders.

As an alternative to storing your bookmarks locally, i.e. on a specific computer, there are a number of sites that will store your bookmarks for you, including **www.myhotlist.com/** and **www.mybookmarks.com/**. Portals such as **www.my.yahoo.com** also offer bookmark hosting services. Online bookmark sites offer the advantage of being accessible anywhere from any internet-enabled device.

In addition to offering an online bookmark service, **www.mypassword.net/** offers an online password remembering service.

Desktop and Organiser Services

In the attempt to be first port of call, sites are starting to offer what would traditionally be thought of as desktop software. The site **www.visto.com** gives you email, calendar, contacts, file storage, tasks and bookmarks, everything you would expect to find in an information manager program such as Outlook, Express.

EMAIL

The world wide web (invented by a Briton named Tim Berners-Lee, by the way. when he was working at CERN in Geneva) is just one of the applications that reside on the internet. The other two main ones are email (probably still the application that accounts for most time spent online) and newsgroups.

To use email you will need a connection to the net, an email address, and either a dedicated email program, such as Outlook Express, or a browser (for web-based mail services such as Hotmail). By opening an account with an ISP you will usually have automatically acquired an email address. Most search engines have freely available email accounts.

Email is also available to digital TV subscribers. Ondigital offer Onmail free to digital subscribers, the only cost involved being local call charges while online. Email is typed using a standard television plus a special remote control keyboard. Unfortunately users must be online to type messages. Email is also available through Sky Digital and digital cable services.

Email is now available using WAP phones. The service is expensive as emails can only be written while online.

Is email reliable?

These days it is more likely that a postal letter will go astray than an email. If an email that you sent is not delivered – perhaps because the addressee has changed ISP, or their server is broken – you will be notified by your ISP. Generally the ISP will try sending the message a few times before it gives up. However, although email is reliable it is not guaranteed to be delivered, and you also can't be certain that an email you receive is from the purported sender unless it is signed with a special encrypted digital signature.

Netiquette

Netiquette is the polite usage of internet communication applications, especially email. Email is a form of communication different from either traditional letters or the phone, so new rules of conversation are evolving. Emails tend to be short, and it is polite to reply to them promptly, in as brief a manner as possible. Experienced users do not reply to emails that do not absolutely require replies. Email boxes get full enough of emails without unnecessary ones being added.

There is debate about whether emails should obey the normal rules of grammar and punctuation. Some people feel that a lack of punctuation suits the medium, and so they actively promote a bowdlerised form of English called 'weblish'. However, abandoning the basic rules of grammar and punctuation makes your emails harder for your audience to read, and making people work unnecessarily hard is simply rude. It also leads to misunderstandings, and there are enough of those in the world already. (The authors of this book are deeply divided over this issue but the writer of this chapter has arranged to have the last word!) A convention that everybody agrees on is that typing emails in capitals is the online equivalent of shouting. It is best avoided.

If you receive an email whose style or content irritates you, count to ten before firing off an angry response. Ask yourself whether the sender meant to annoy you, or could there be a misunderstanding? Often the best response to an apparently rude email is a phone call.

Spam

Spamming is bulk mailing people you don't know with a view to making money or spreading an idea. There is only one rule here: don't do it. It's antisocial, and you may get 'flamed' (insulted), or you may get really unlucky and mail a clever hacker who decides to unleash a vicious virus on you.

If you receive spam, on the other hand, the best thing to do is ignore it. That way the sender does not know you got it and is likely to just go away. If you reply, asking them to desist, they know you're there and may pester you longer. Of course, if you are that clever hacker . . .

You may also want to disguise your email address so that spammers who use software to cull addresses automatically from newsgroups (see below) don't catch you. You do this by adding some clearly superfluous words; for instance, **author@bible.co.uk** might become **go.away.spammer.author@bible.co.uk**. Someone who really wants to communicate with you will find it easy to peel away the protective layer. You can also set up a special email account for newsgroup correspondence, such as **thisisnotmyrealname@yahoo.com**.

Extending your email vocabulary

Smileys or 'emoticons' can add a touch of feeling to email. Here are some of the most common.

:-) *smile*

:-(or :(*frown*

: / *hmm* . . .

;-) *wink*

:-| *keeping a straight face*

:-o *surprise*

Some more recherché emoticons include:

8-) *the writer wears sunglasses*

:-{) *the writer has a moustache*

@:-) *the writer wears a turban*

And some downright bizarre ones include:

:-F *a buck-toothed vampire with one tooth missing*

★:o) *a clown*

+-:-) *a cleric*

@= *pro-nuclear*

Many email sophisticates (the so-called 'digerati') sneer at the use of icons as 'old hat'. But who cares what they think? It can be a good idea to include a smiley when employing irony in an email which you are sending across cultural boundaries (e.g. to Americans).

As well as icons, email encourages the use of acronyms, including:

OIC *oh I see*

IMHO *in my humble opinion*

IMNSHO *in my not-so-humble opinion*

YMMV *your mileage may vary* (i.e., this is my personal experience, not a universal law)

ISTR *I seem to recall*

HTH *hope this helps*

OTOH *on the other hand*

LOL *laugh out loud*

TAH *take a hint*

LMAO *laugh my a— off*

BTDT *been there done that*

These and many more smileys and acronyms can be found at **http://www.wellweb.com/WELLNESS/smiley.htm**. If you really want to show off, visit the guide to hacker terminology at **http://www.lysator.liu.se/hackdict/split2/main index.html**. It includes such choice snippets as: '*angry fruit salad* n. A bad visual-interface design that uses too many colors. This term derives, of course, from the bizarre day-glo colors found in canned fruit salad.'

Email housekeeping

If you change your email address (perhaps because you move jobs or you change ISPs) you may want to use a free email forwarding service like **www.iname.com** or **www.netforward.com**. Iname also provide email addresses for surfers who want a more distinctive address, such as **@London.com** or **@catlover.com**.

In the same way that the files in your computer need diligent organisation so too do your emails. In addition to the standard folders of Inbox, Sent Items, Deleted Items, it is wise to create your own folders. Most email programs and web-based accounts allow this. The strategy you adopt will be personal to you and could well mirror the way you organise your desk and desktop. One good plan is to have a number of archive files into which you move emails you want to keep from your inbox, and to keep the number of mails present in your inbox down to a manageable size.

Another good strategy is to have a number of different email accounts for different purposes – one for your personal emails and another for your work ones, for instance. You might also want another account for mailings from newsletters.

Alternatively, most email programs and web-based mail accounts allow you to filter incoming mail into different folders, according to the identity of the sender, or the subject heading.

Distribution lists

A distribution list is a collection of email addresses which you have grouped together because you mail all its members together frequently. Common groups include the people you are working with on a particular project, or those you like to irritate by sharing the latest email joke with them.

Auto reply

Your email program will allow you to type in and activate or deactivate an automatic reply to all incoming emails. This is useful for letting people know that you won't be able to reply while you are away for a period of time.

Signatures

Your program will probably also allow you to automatically assign a signature to the end of your mails, or your contact details.

Email law

Despite what many people think, the internet is not some kind of Wild West where the law of the land does not apply. For example, you should take care to avoid libelling individuals or organisations. The laws covering copyright and intellectual property also apply (although they are often flouted).

Internet law is in flux, and unfortunately the government is confused. On the one hand it wants to make the UK the 'best place in the world for e-business'; on the other hand it passes controversial and damaging pieces of legislation like the Regulation of Investigatory Powers Act. Known as RIP (splendid irony – you couldn't invent this stuff!) it allows employers to snoop on their employees' emails and phone calls to check that they are work-related.

That being said, the great majority of people will continue to use email routinely without getting into legal difficulties.

Newsgroups

A great way to get answers to lots of tricky questions is to visit a newsgroup. Newsgroups are not part of the web, but they are part of the internet. Collectively, they make up the Usenet. Briefly, a newsgroup is a place where people post questions and get answers. There are tens of thousands of them, covering every imaginable topic, from online investing to alien abductions. The best way to start searching the newsgroups is to visit **www.dejanews.com**.

Before you start contributing to a newsgroup conversation (known as a 'thread'), take time to catch up with what has been written before. This is called 'lurking'. Many newsgroups also have a 'faq' or Frequently Asked Questions document which is posted every month or so. The faq will give a good idea as to the purpose of the newsgroups and what is considered acceptable or unacceptable behaviour. All newsgroups also have a charter which describes the intentions of their founders.

If you see a comment in a newsgroup that you want to reply to, you can post your reply on the newsgroup and also reply by email to the original poster. This means the poster doesn't miss your reply in the morass of other postings, but also allows other people to watch the thread develop.

Newsgroups are often ahead of the traditional news media with information and advice about products, ideas and trends. Smart companies are taking advantage of this and using the services of companies such as Infonic Ltd (**www.infonic.com**) to keep abreast of the views and opinions of their consumers and other interested parties.

Security

Viruses

One of the security problems that the internet has aggravated (though not created) is the threat from viruses. A virus is a rogue program that enters your computer without your knowledge, and carries out operations on it with more or less malicious intent. The mildest viruses display a friendly (and allegedly funny) message on your computer screen, and the most malicious may destroy the contents of your computer's hard drive.

You can protect yourself by installing virus software onto your computer. To do this properly you have to download software updates from the manufacturers at least monthly. The best known anti-virus packages come from Norton (**www.norton.com**) and McAfee (**www.mcafee.com**). It may be worth buying the software on a CD-Rom rather than downloading it from the web in case you need to re-install it on your computer at a later date.

Downloading software from mainstream sites is not normally a problem. Even so, there is no harm in virus-checking all programs, regardless of the source, before you run them.

The main source of viruses are attachments, files which accompany an email and are opened separately after you open the email. Never open an attachment from a source you do not know without virus-checking it: Save the attachment to your hard drive and then virus-check it. Some ISPs scan all email attachments for viruses.

Chain mail

Periodically you will receive an email forwarded by a friend or acquaintance telling you not to open any email named such-and-such. This is a hoax or an error, so don't do what they usually implore and pester all your friends and family with it. Simply opening and reading an email cannot infect your computer. But opening an attachment can, so beware attachments from unknown sources.

Protecting children from the web

The internet has fantastic potential to educate, entertain and inform children and adults alike, but there are also considerable dangers lurking online. Parents should use their common sense and exercise a degree of supervision and there are many tools available that filter out unsuitable material, such as sexual sites or those dealing with the occult.

Some filters work either by ruling in certain types of content, the so-called 'walled garden approach'. Others work by ruling certain types of content out, such as sites containing certain words, or pictures with a high percentage of bare skin. (In which case pictures of bald men wearing vests could well be blocked, which is possibly appropriate on aesthetic grounds, although the moral benefit is more dubious.) Inevitably, many of the filtering systems are American, and block access to information that would be standard reading for GCSE Biology. There are moves afoot to introduce film-style ratings for websites, but they have yet to be adopted widely enough to be effective.

Filtering programmes are rarely able to cover email, chat rooms and search engines properly. Moreover, children often have a more sophisticated knowledge of the internet than their parents, and can get round many policing techniques.

Special sites and services for children include the ISP **www.kzuk.net**, which offers monitored chat rooms (although it would be hard to prevent adults masquerading as children), Disney's kid's site **www.disneyblast.com** and a children's art site called **www.kinderart.com** (see Education). Search engines that show only material suitable for children include **www.yahooligans.com** and **www.ajkids.com**.

Many schools have addressed the problem of supervising internet usage by agreeing guidelines with students. Schools with websites usually publish their rules (for example, non-disclosure of personal details) on the site. The normal procedure is that internet access is withdrawn for those caught transgressing the rules. This may also be the best approach at home, although younger children clearly need closer supervision. A good code of internet conduct is available from the NCH Action For Children site on **www.nchafc.org.uk**.

As we go to press a new site called **www.chatdanger.com** is being launched to warn parents and children of the dangers of internet chat, and give some tips on how to avoid them. Inspired by the awful experience of one young girl, its tone is severe.

Breaking out of your employer's protective embrace

As well as being used by parents, some filtering software, such as SurfControl, is used by employers seeking to limit what their staff have access to from their work PCs. Employers not only want to prevent their employees wasting paid time, they also want to avoid their staff accessing and distributing material which could bring the company into disrepute.

If this is proving an annoyance to you, you may like to explore a type of website called an 'anonymiser'. These are websites which will get pages from other sites for you (in the jargon, they are 'CGI proxies', because they use a CGI program to act as your proxy). So, if **www.gamblersdelights.com** is blocked by your company's firewall, but **www.randomcgiproxy.org** is not, then you're in business – all you have to do is to bring up your favourite anonymiser page, type the address of your favourite online bookmaker into the appropriate box, and you can surf away. The fact that the anonymiser stands between you and the website you want to visit will slow you down a bit; every time you click on a link, the information has to go via your proxy, but if you are using a fast corporate connection, this should not make a very noticeable difference.

As the name suggests, anonymisers also have the effect of making it impossible for the site you are visiting to know your identity. This means that you won't be able to take advantage of the personalisation features of any site while you are using an anonymiser, so you'll have to keep typing in passwords. However, it can be useful for people who are particularly concerned about their privacy. Note, however, that the concealment is only one way; the fact that you have visited gamblersdelight.com will be evident from the cache on the hard disk of your computer, so if your employer is in the habit of closely monitoring and auditing your computer, it might be better to wait until you get home before visiting banned websites.

Also note that unless you're prepared to pay money for a proxying service (and you might not want to give your credit card number to an organisation whose business activity is helping you frustrate your employer's wishes), the proxy will serve only text to your computer, not pictures, chat or Java games. So, while CGI proxies are worth knowing about, and can be very useful ways around the more illogical actions of blocking software, they're not exactly a golden ticket to an uncensored web.

Selected sites

Getting online
www.freeserve.co.uk ○○○○
The pioneer of free internet access in the UK.

www.demon.net ○○○○
A reliable ISP if you are willing to pay for almost-but-not-quite guaranteed permanent access.

www.ntl.com ○○○○
Access via cable.

www.ondigital.com ○○○
Access via digital TV.

www.bt.com ○○
For Home Highway and other access services.

www.microsoft.com ○○○
For browser software, and much, much more.

www.netscape.com ○○○
The original contender in the browser wars, humbled by the mighty Microsoft.

www.sky.com ○○○
Offers a free SMS service.

Search engines

www.zdnet.com/searchiq ○○○
For up-to-date ratings of search engines.

Popular choices
www.google.com ○○○○○
Now powers Yahoo's searches. Not the largest search engine but certainly one of the fastest and the most specific. It also has a refreshingly clear screen.

www.inktomi.com ○○○○
Used to power Yahoo until Google bowled it a googly.

www.alltheweb.com ○○○
One of the fastest engines around, but overtaken in quality by Google.

www.yahoo.com ○○○○
The directory is categorised by human beings who actually visit each site, not robots who merely pick up words from sites.

www.AltaVista.com ○○○○
One of the first and also one of the largest – it claims to have indexed nearly every page on the web. Size has its disadvantages – any query on AltaVista is likely to yield hundreds of results. You generally need to use the Advanced Search facility to avoid this.

www.hotbot.com ○○○○
Another engine with admirable coverage.

www.askjeeves.com ○○
An attempt to provide a natural language search engine.

Meta search engines
www.copernic.com ○○○○
One of the first and best meta-search engines. A surprisingly powerful tool.

www.infospace.com/uk ○○○○
A thorough directory for finding people, places and things.

www.dogpile.com○○○○.
Quick and easy meta searcher.

Listings
http://www.sharpened.net/bestsites/index.php ○○
Listing of the best websites in categories such as office supplies and free stuff.

Electronic message forwarding services
www.efax.com ○○○○
Get a free virtual fax number. Create an account and enter your email address. You receive a fax number and the service forwards any faxes to your email. Senders pay more than normal to support the service.

www.fusionone.com ○○○
Enables you to synchronise your phone, your PC and your personal digital assistant.

Portals
www.yahoo.com ○○○○○
Named after a race of people in *Gulliver's Travels*, the great granddaddy of internet portals, still going strong, and personalised to many countries and regions in the world.

www.my.yahoo.com ○○○○○
A great portal to customise to display the content of your choice. A good site to set as your homepage.

www.mviva.com ○○○
A portal for WAP addicts.

Newsgroups
www.dejanews.com ○○○○
Your gateway to the wide and wacky world of newsgroups.

Email services
www.wellweb.com/WELLNESS/smiley.htm ○○○○
A host of fun things to spice up your emails.

www.iname.com ○○○○
Useful email forwarding service.

Filter programmes
www.chatnanny.com
www.netnanny.com
www.cybersitter.com
www.surfcontrol.com
The English one. The others are US-based.

Other services
www.worldlingo.com ○○
Free translation service of web pages or text. Mixed results.

www.yahooligans.com ○○○○
Search engine for kids.

www.nchafc.org.uk ○○○○
Code of conduct for kids online.

www.chatdanger.com
How to avoid trouble from chat.

2 Lifestages

Births and young children

Everything you ever wanted to know . . .

. . . about the consequences of sex but didn't want to buy a magazine to find out.

Babies. Most of us have them sooner or later, and now a lot of us are talking about them on the internet. There are thousands of personal testimonials and plenty of chat rooms, and there are also extremely good free online magazines with articles on a great variety of topics and links to useful organisations. Whatever your area of interest or concern, using the internet can make you very well informed and keep you that way. The internet can even help to get you pregnant: one site (**www.motherandbaby.co.uk**) sends out emails to alert you of the optimum moment in the month to achieve conception.

Deposits and withdrawals

If you need a sperm donor you can use the internet to search the records of sperm banks and select the donor you would like. Some sites, such as **www.fairfaxcyrobanks.com**, specialise in high-achieving donors, so you can search their site for a donor with a PhD in Space Physics who is of Anglo-Saxon heritage with curly auburn hair and blue eyes. (There weren't actually any of that exact choice when we tested the site, but being less fussy and not demanding blue eyes did indeed reveal a donor.) Unfortunately, at the moment it is mostly just American sperm banks who have gone online and they do not usually deliver to the UK.

"It's time to get into bed."

Message from Motherandbaby.co.uk

The culture of the internet is that you get stuff for free. Thus there is the generous philanthropic donor at **www.donor.com** who will send you his high-achieving sperm for free. Again, this only applies within the US.

28 THE INTERNET CONSUMER BIBLE

If you are on the other side of the fence and are contemplating being a sperm donor, **www.hellobaby.com** tells you all the things you should think about before making your deposit.

Find childcare

Some mothers complain that while the internet is great for helping you manage the nine months of pregnancy and decide your birthing options, once you have given birth it is far less useful as a resource. They say this is both because mothers are less of a community with shared interests than mothers-to-be, and also because it is more difficult to spend time on the internet, or even tap in a few emails, with a baby in your arms than it was when you were carrying it around inside you.

But one area where the internet is already useful for parents and will become increasingly so is in finding childcare. Whether you need a babysitter for the evening or an au pair for the year, it is easy to locate them on the internet. Obviously you will want to go through the same checks or references on a babysitter or potential au pair as you would with someone you found through an offline agency or advertisement in a newsagent window, but the reference process for most online babysitting agencies seems pretty rigorous.

Support, especially in times of trouble

There are a lot of chat rooms for parents and parents-to-be on the internet, such as at **www.motherandbaby.co.uk** ('we're awake whenever you are'), and they are very popular. The confidential nature of the internet, and the fact that you can use it from home, makes it especially useful for connecting with people and organisations to help you deal with sad events or difficult problems, such as miscarriage or autism. One site offering links to many such organisations is **www.cafamily.org**, and there are others listed below.

Shop for baby and for you

If you find it easier to shop from home than make a trip with a baby or a bump, then you have access to a huge range of toys, and a decent range of maternity clothes, baby clothes, and baby products from high street shops, as well as the chance to swap your children's clothes when they outgrow them.

Selected sites

Online magazines focusing on pregancy
Online magazines are free, informative, and offer a range of innovative features, such as pregnancy calendars and email birth announcement postcards. They also have a range of chat rooms.

www.webbaby.co.uk ✪✪✪✪
This fantastic site was set up in 1999, with articles about everything to do with babies, including tips for travelling when pregnant. There is also a comprehensive a web directory with contact details for a great range of organisations. A little slow to load.

www.motherandbaby.co.uk ✪✪✪✪✪
An excellent site with an easy layout, fast loading and very informative articles. The site has a number of chat rooms, a random name generator, and can send an email birth announcement card to all your interested (and uninterested) parties. It can also let you know via an SMS text message when is the optimal time in the month for conception.

www.women.com/pregnancy ✪✪✪✪
Good American magazine with information on the happy and sad events of pregancy. Takes you through a 'to do' list for the whole nine months of pregnancy and raises issues like whether it's possible to have too much folic acid.

www.babyworld.co.uk ✪✪✪✪
A good site for news and features as well as online shopping suggestions with notes of good offers. Start up your own pregnancy diary and read others'.

www.urbia.com ✪✪✪
A good magazine with a chat room.

Parenting advice
www.parentlineplus.org.uk ✪✪✪✪
A good site with a mass of information and articles on all aspects of parenting.

www.realparents.co.uk ✪✪✪✪
Unpatronising parenting magazine with a good layout and links to online and offline organisations.

Shopping for clothes
www.kidskiosk.com ✪✪✪✪✪
This excellent site lets you buy or swap nearly new clothes, nursery goods and toys. A brilliant resource for dealing with growing kids. Easy to navigate and quick to load.

www.mothercare.co.uk ✪✪✪✪
A well-designed site from which you can see the shop's full range of clothes, toys, baby products, etc, and it is now possible to shop without having the catalogue.

www.bloomingmarvellous.co.uk ✪✪✪✪
Cute site for maternity wear and baby wear, although the pics take a while to load. Easy to order with or without catalogue.

Shopping for toys
www.etoys.co.uk ○○○○○
This is the UK branch of the huge American online toy shop. It has a vast range, quick delivery and toy suggestions. Better keep it away from the kids.

www.toysrus.co.uk ○○○○
It is easy to search the site of this huge offline shop, but the site lacks recommended suggestions. Delivery in 72 hours costs £2.50.

www.babiesrus.co.uk ○○○○
A subsidiary of Toys'R'Us. It has a good range of products, and the advice section is useful.

www.hamleys.co.uk ○○○
This site shows you a lot of the stock of the world's most famous toy shop, with decent pictures. Delivery is very expensive – £8.95 for next day (if placed before 3 p.m. – or 4 p.m., depending on which bit of the site you believe), and the cheapest delivery is £3.95.

When you need support
You can find a great deal of information on a whole range of subjects and link to others in the same situation.

www.fertilityplus.org ○○○○
This is a very good American site, which can link you to information or chat-room sites to help you deal with sad issues such as miscarriage.

www.autism.clarityconnect.com ○○○○○
Excellent resource for all issues to do with autism. See especially the websites section (from the site index), which links you to websites for chat rooms and information on all kinds of autism.

www.altonweb.com/cs/downsyndrome ○○○○
Very good American site with a good amount of information and links.

www.gingerbread.org.uk ○○○○
This is a good site offering support for one-parent families in many languages. There is a freephone number and a discussion list online.

www.cafamily.org.uk ○○○○
This clear but minimal site offers support and advice for parents of children born with serious medical problems. The site offers limited advice, but on every condition you can think of, and a link to the relevant society for that illness.

www.actionforsickchildren.org ○○○
This is a highly informative site although with little interaction.

Advice about childcare
www.daycaretrust.co.uk ○○○
This is the site of the National Childcare Campaign, with information about childcare options on tax.

www.dfee.gov.uk/nanny ○○○
Government advice on issues surrounding hiring a nanny.

www.nannytax.co.uk ○○○
Does what it says on the tin: gives information on tax for nannies and their employers.

Find childcare
Find a babysitter for tonight, an au pair for the year, or look through childminders' websites.

www.sitters.co.uk ○○○
Here you can make bookings for babysitters for most parts of the country online. The site is minimal but the team are working on expanding the site and the service.

www.iapa.org (International Au-Pair Association) ○○○○
This clear site links you to all international agencies and organisations who are affiliated members, covering many sites.

www.childint.co.uk ○○○○
This website of the employment agency Childcare International Ltd tries to match parents and childcare. Au pairs and host families apply here, and the agency does the rest, contacting you by email if you like.

www.nannyjob.co.uk ○○○○
This is an excellent directory for childcare agencies or nurseries in the UK. It is free to post your vacancy for a childminder or to apply. Not to be confused with **www.nannyjob.com**, which is an American site doing much the same thing for the States, but advertising its services as 'where love is manufactured'.

www.kids.co.uk ○○○○
This site mostly has advice on choosing the right childcare, although it also has an excellent section of links, including to childminders' websites.

www.webnannies.com ○○○○
This is the clear site for Childcare Services Ltd. Search for an au pair or join the chat room.

www.childcarelink.gov.uk ○○○
Excellent clear site to find your local childminder, pre-school playgroups, out-of-school care, nursery schools, day nurseries.

www.kidsclubs.com ○○○
Finds kids' clubs near you, and has a section just for kids.

Specialist baby products or software

www.greenbaby.com ○○○
This site has a full catalogue of environmentally friendly baby gear, although you cannot yet order online.

www.babyserv.com ○○○
This American site offers you more free planning-for-baby software than you would have thought existed.

www.activebirthcentre.com ○○○
If you want to find out about active births and birthing pools, this basic site is a good place to start. You can research birth pools using the site, but can only hire them by phoning up.

Education

When you visit a school and see a couple of clunky old computers in the corner of a classroom, it is hard to believe the predictions that the internet will transform education. But polls suggest that more than half of school pupils are already using the internet in some form to help with schoolwork, helping themselves to the vast range of homework and revision aids available online. In the future, we can expect to see interactive and online education become increasingly important. Students will watch lectures online and write essays collaboratively over the internet. They may never get out of bed again!

For parents, students and everyone else, the internet is extremely useful for researching into schools, colleges, universities and adult education. With both exam results and government Ofsted reports available on the web, the task of initial research for a suitable school is greatly simplified. A lot of university information is posted on the internet, which is a great help when choosing a university course. Applying online also has several important advantages. Once you are at university, the task of researching academic work when at university is made easier by the availability online of plenty of research from universities around the world.

Schools

The place of computers in schools is changing fast. The old Information Technology (IT) approach of having computers bunched together in a separate room has been replaced (at least in theory) by the idea of spreading many more computers of various kinds around the school, and integrating them as far as possible into all subjects. The concept of IT was replaced in 1997 by that of ICT, Information and Communications Technology. In theory, this approach opens the door to greater use of internet and interactive software as teaching aids. In practice, the two challenges are to find enough money to purchase hardware and software, and to persuade Luddites that the internet is not a harmful replacement, but a useful addition to traditional educational methods.

'There will still be classrooms with teachers standing up and trying to calm everybody down.'
Bill Gates

The government says it is putting a high priority on introducing new technology in schools. The National Grid for Learning (**www.ngfl.org.uk**) has been set up as an electronic resource, linking schools and providing access to materials. The aim is to have all schools online by 2002. At the time of going to press 98 per cent of secondary schools and 86 per cent of primary schools were online. In a separate initiative, NTL has linked about 850 colleges with a broadband loop.

The government is also helping teachers buy laptops, and putting more money into training. Computer penetration in schools is rising fast; the ratio of computers to pupils is said to be 1:8 in secondary schools and 1:13 in primary schools. These efforts are being assisted by charities such as Anytime Anywhere Learning (set up by Microsoft and Arthur Andersen) to help provide laptops for poorer children in schools (using tax credits from richer parents).

However, these statistics say little about how computers are actually being used. One of the more progressive schools is Monkseaton Community High School, which produced the celebrated Oxford reject and Harvard undergraduate Laura Spence. At Monkseaton, interactive materials are being used alongside traditional techniques in many areas. In certain subjects, average exam results have risen by a full grade. But in many schools computers are still separated off from the rest of the curriculum. Some private schools have been particularly slow to take advantage of new technology, even though they have often greater resources. Moreover, the possession of an internet connection means little in practice: at one secondary school we contacted, the link could not support more than a handful of users at a time so the system kept going down. In addition, a computerised lesson is a non-starter if only a proportion of the children have computer skills.

> 'We have also been using video conferencing to let our students learn languages by speaking directly to people in France, Germany, and Spain, and this has proved very effective. So it's not just a question of the PC, but of other relevant technologies.'
>
> **Paul Kelley, Headmaster, Monkseaton Community High School**

Using the web to choose a school

It would be foolish to use the web as the only method to choose a school because it is no substitute for visiting and talking to staff. That said, parents can narrow down options by doing a good deal of preliminary online research. For a list of top local schools (both private and state) by performance, look at **www.upmystreet.com**. It also has a useful list of playgroups and schools by distance from your house, but this distance-based list is not comprehensive and the way the information is sorted is somewhat bizarre: in one area we examined, a school for butlers was listed alongside normal schools.

An increasing number of schools, particularly secondary schools, have websites. Because they are often partly run by pupils they can give more of the flavour of life at a school than the official prospectus. If internet access is an important criterion for you, the education section of the *Daily Telegraph* (**www.telegraph.co.uk**) has a special section on 'wired schools'. This is a list of schools with websites and links to them, from Arbroath High School to Ysgol Gyfun Gwyr in Swansea. The *Times Educational Supplement* (**www.tes.co.uk**) has a similar feature.

State schools

Choosing a state school used to be difficult because there was little if anything in the way of published analysis of performance. You had to rely on anecdotal evidence and personal impressions. But now both exam performance records and Ofsted (government inspection) reports are available on the web at the main Department of Education and Employment site (**www.dfee.gov.uk** – start at the Parents Centre). The DoEE site also includes a guide on how to interpret the tables. You can search both primary and secondary schools either by postcode or by school name. You can then proceed either to the performance tables or to Ofsted reports or to the school's website (if available). If you live on the edge of a postcode or an education authority, you should also look in the adjacent area.

One drawback of the DoEE's site is that manipulation of the tables is a little difficult for a novice browser. But with a little experimentation it is possible to track the performance of a school over several years compared to its local and national peers. Ofsted reports (also available via their own site, **www.ofsted.gov.uk**) used to be wordy and infested with jargon, but they are gradually becoming more succinct. Whatever their shortcomings, the Ofsted reports are important background reading when drawing up a shortlist or preparing to visit a school.

Private schools

The place to start research is at the website of the Independent Schools Information Service (ISIS), **www.isis.org.uk**. You can search 1,300 schools by various categories: facilities, subjects, scholarships and location – but not by fees. There are links to school sites for further investigation, some of which offer virtual tours, chat rooms and news. However, unlike the state sector, inspectors' reports on private schools are not available centrally and few schools make them available on their websites.

Online education

There is a wealth of resources online for children, teachers and adults. The BBC is recognised to be a leader in the provision of online materials and is putting a further £135m into developing internet learning aids for access on PCs and via digital TV. The promising Channel 4 site **www.homeworkhigh.com** also provides different material for different age groups.

For children tired of traditional learning techniques, the web can offer additional lessons, help with homework and revision aids.

There are some worries about children downloading material and passing it off as their own work, but good teachers are perfectly able to spot work that is suspiciously perfect and sentences and paragraphs that just do not fit. Moreover, software is being developed that will spot downloads. The internet is particularly good at encouraging inquisitive research. And those who are concerned that children may pinch essays from the net should reflect that it may be extremely educative to read essays by undergraduates from Harvard University on the influence of Anglo-Saxon values on the development of modern farming, or whatever. However, children do need protection from the less salubrious side of the net (see Getting Started for details of filter programmes).

Many educational web pages promise more than they deliver. For example, when we sampled the lessons on **www.telegraph.co.uk**, many were unavailable. The same was true on **www.schoolsnet.com** (which also had very unsatisfactory school searches). The interactive tuition on the Guardian's specialist education site **www.learn.co.uk** was much more satisfying. The British Educational Communications and Technology Agency (BECTA) has a searchable database of software on its site (**www.becta.org.uk**).

'Despite the huge commercial effort devoted to producing software for online teaching and learning, most of what is available is pretty primitive.'
Sir John Daniel, Vice-Chancellor, Open University

There is also a vast range of US websites aimed at educating and amusing children, although some of the sites push products for sale more than UK sites. In the US **www.superkids.com** provides detailed reviews of educational software.

For those studying foreign languages the internet is an invaluable resource. You can work up from simple tourism sites to those of foreign newspapers and magazines. Other sources of educational material include magazines such as *New Scientist* (**www.newscientist.com**) and museums. For example, the

Natural History Museum has virtual exhibitions on its site (**www.nhm.ac.uk**) including dinosaur datafiles.

Locating teachers

The internet is not particularly useful when it comes to finding language tutors or music teachers. For example, we attempted to locate music teachers in one particular part of London that we knew well. But none of the main directories, **www.yell.co.uk**, **www.fish4.co.uk**, **www.upmystreet.co.uk** or **www.scoot.co.uk**, produced a satisfactory result. Fish4 produced a list including a dyslexia centre and a business college. Upmystreet did produce a list of teachers, but it was far from comprehensive and did not specify which instruments were taught. It would be better to network in the playground.

Universities' use of the internet

Universities in America played a very important part in the development of the internet (see Preface), but those in this country have been a little slower in adopting the internet and spreading its use. All universities in the UK are now online, and indeed there is a web address ending (.ac.uk.) especially for universities – So, for example, the web address of Keele University is **www.keele.ac.uk**. Email addresses have the same formulation and all students at universities in the country are given an email address. Universities promote the use of the web by putting prospectuses, course requirements, and reading lists online; for contacting departments, lecturers and students, email is rife.

At an increasing number of universities, students are expected to file essays in printed form, rather than handwritten sheafs of paper, but the ratio of computers to students is generally good so students do not need to provide their own computer. Most universities also provide adequate printing resources and free paper for printing. Laptops are now commonly seen in lecture halls and are accepted even in the creaking wooden reading rooms of the Bodleian Library in Oxford.

Researching a course

UCAS (**www.ucas.ac.uk**) provides tools to search for courses and institutions. You can find out very easily which universities offer Arabic on its own or in conjunction with other languages. From the UCAS site you can also look at what individual universities have to offer, and there are links to their sites. Schoolsnet (**www.schoolsnet.co.uk**) offers a more detached view of different universities and their facilities (the content is taken from an offline guide book). Of course, after this initial research, the net cannot replace the need to visit the campus and talk to students and ex-students.

Applying for a course

In the last few years UCAS has been developing an electronic application system. It is easier to rectify mistakes on an electronic form, and UCAS can process the electronic forms much more quickly. In addition, students can keep track of their application through the process.

Electronic applications have to be sent from schools and colleges (rather than from individual students) because the forms also need a reference. UCAS can process electronic applications in three days compared with three weeks for paper forms. In 2000, UCAS extended the electronic system to the clearing process and for the first time 10,000 students used this process (roughly a quarter of those finding a place through clearing) and many more used it for checking information. There is a good guide to the clearing process on **www.educationunlimited.co.uk**.

Students contemplating study in Europe can find introductory material from Erasmus, which helps fund student exchange programmes (**www.erasmus.ac.uk**). There are links to participating universities and relevant parts of the European Commission website such as **http://europa.eu.int/comm/education/erascomp/index.html**. Links to worldwide universities can be found at **www.universities.com**.

Universities online

The limited resources available for teaching increasing numbers of students in the UK and in other countries mean that the nineteenth-century teaching techniques based around lectures are increasingly being questioned. While there will always be students who want a 'campus experience', some commentators point out that the quality of that experience is going down as successive governments have pushed more students through universities without lifting funding in parallel. This process has limited the resources available to students, and threatens to worsen the student–lecturer ratio. In addition, governments have increasingly pushed more of the cost of universities on to students and their families.

> 'The death of the campus is grossly exaggerated.'
>
> Sir John Daniel, Vice Chancellor, Open University.

According to Professor Scase of the Open University: 'Why bother to sit in a lecture theatre with 300 other students and spend three nights a week stacking shelves in a supermarket to pay for it, when you could download the same information on your computer at home?' But there is a lot of evidence that even if students use the web to kick-start a project, they still like book-based learning and value the social side of university courses. Even the Open University admits: 'the most powerful and popular use of the web is for communication between people about the course rather than for us to dump the content of the course on each student's computer'.

The internet is also likely to open up higher education and distance learning to many more people. Most of the Open University's 130,000 students already communicate via email rather than the post, and the OU now has about 15,000 students studying a small number of internet-only courses. It even held a virtual degree ceremony earlier this year. The economics of distance learning are also attractive to governments trying to broaden access to university education because it costs much less to educate students on a distance basis compared with a campus.

There are around 600 universities offering online courses of some sort worldwide. Some of the biggest online operations are in the US, such as Phoenix, Jones International and Capella Universities. In Canada there is Athabasca University, at **www.athabascau.ca**. Phoenix has 16,000 students studying full-time on its online courses (**www.phoenix.edu**) although only 5 per cent of these come from outside the US. Typical online courses cover management, marketing and computing, but the range is likely to expand into sciences, maths and languages.

Evening classes online

In the UK, the government-funded University for Industry (**www.ufiltd.co.uk**) is introducing major improvements in the options available for mature students in the areas of computing and technology. A nationwide network of 1,000 online study centres under the Learndirect brand (**www.learndirect.org**) is being established to help adults refresh or update their computer skills.

The aim is to put these centres in accessible places such as train stations and on the high street rather than in the gloomy buildings normally associated with adult education. So far, 250 of these centres have been set up – although there is not a single one in London, and the information on these centres on the learndirect website is far from complete. Learndirect retains its role as a central database of

'Learning is a fundamentally social process. The power of the internet is not just that it provides the content . . . it provides communities of specialist interest in which to facilitate learning.'

Dr John Seely Brown, chief scientist, Xerox

general adult education courses and can provide the answer to questions such as what Spanish courses are available in Bradford.

Advanced research

For more advanced research, the web cuts out the need to find a book with a good bibliography. Search engines can generate a huge amount of information on individual topics, and can help kick-start a project. If you are considering a subject for a PhD, you could see whether there was much secondary material already available. However, as one academic commented: 'the internet is pretty much useless for primary research'. For journals it is best to go to the site of a library like the Bodleian, a copyright library, which has a search machine set up specifically for academic research, **www.bodley.ox.ac.uk**. The Bodleian, and the University Library in Cambridge (**www.lib.cam.ac.uk**) are more welcoming than the British Library (**www.bl.uk**). Another source of journals is **www.ingenta.com**, where you can get access to some journals (such as those of the Institute of Fiscal Studies) on a pay-per-view basis. But its coverage is patchy.

Future

Nervous parents may want to use the internet to check that their children are at school and what they are doing. But the real impact of the internet should be to broaden access to education for mature students, and to help lift attainment in schools. Some of the trials with new technology at schools such as Monkseaton suggest that a judicious use of different teaching media does more to lift exam results than the efforts of even the best teachers. The internet is also likely to change the role of teachers. The vast amount of information available on the internet means that it is even more important for knowledge-based teaching to be supplemented by skills-based work, teaching students how to find and select the information they need and then to communicate it to others.

Selected sites

Government websites
www.ngfl.gov.uk ✪✪✪✪
National grid for learning. Government-funded network providing information about all aspects of education and providing interactive material. Reviews of educational software. Links to many other important sites, such as BECTA.

www.dfee.gov.uk ✪✪✪
Useful starting point for research about state schools and other educational matters.

www.becta.org.uk ✪✪✪
British Educational Communications and Technology Agency – database of educational software.

www.learndirect.org ✪✪
Search facilities for adult education. Incomplete databases. Telephone service is better.

www.lifelonglearning.co.uk ✪
Govt-funded magazine-style website. Weak content.

www.ucas.ac.uk ✪✪✪✪
Invaluable resource for university applicants.

www.prospects.csu.ac.uk ✪✪✪
Database of postgraduate courses.

www.fefc.ac.uk ✪✪✪
Further Education Funding Council – useful links page.

Other educational sites
www.bbc.co.uk ✪✪✪✪✪
Huge resource of learning and educational material.

www.schoolsnet.com ✪✪
Aspiring education portal but slow to load and content is very patchy.

www.topmarks.co.uk ✪✪✪✪
Provides access to hundreds of good educational websites. Provides teachers with internet material for teaching.

www.educationunlimited.co.uk ✪✪✪✪
Education site from the *Guardian*.

www.learn.co.uk ✪✪✪✪
Online lessons and revision materials, again from the *Guardian*.

www.telegraph.co.uk ✪✪✪
Particularly useful education section and includes a section on wired schools. But educational resources are thin. Click on "education" right at the bottom of the home page.

www.open.ac.uk ✪✪✪
Open University; information on distance and online learning.

www.familyelearning.org ☻☻☻
Educational resources for use at home.

www.ufiltd.co.uk ☻
University for Industry – computing courses for adults. Lacks content.

www.hungryminds.com ☻☻☻
Database of 37,000 online courses – links to major online US universities.

www.tes.co.uk ☻☻☻
Times Educational Supplement site: mostly aimed at teachers; includes reviews of educational software. Searchable archive (slow).

www.thesis.co.uk ☻☻
Times Higher Educational Supplement. Poor archive service.

www.newscientist.com ☻☻☻
Online version of magazine.

www.niss.ac.uk ☻☻☻
Links to UK universities and UK and world-wide libraries. Some links do not work.

www.eductionplanet.com ☻☻☻☻
Educational search engine.

www.zdnet.com/searchiq/hotlist/ ☻☻☻
List of education sites.

www.ilearn.com
Unlaunched educational portal.

www.universities.com ☻☻☻☻
World-wide university portal.

www.allacademic.com ☻☻☻
Search engine for free academic research.*

www.boxmind.com ☻☻☻☻
Superb resource for undergraduates set up by Oxford University Tap in 'The Reformation' and search engine provides useful sites.

www.gap-year.com ☻☻☻
Site offering information on gap years, including sources of funding and links to other organisations offering further information. However, main aim of site is to promote sales of an off-line guide book.

Childrens' sites and games

www.kzuk.net ☻☻☻
ISP for children up to 12; reasonable but slow to load.

www.kinderart.com ☻☻☻☻
US Art site for children; download projects and ideas.

www.gamekids.com ☻☻☻☻
US site specialising in games that can be played offline.

www.allmixedup.com ✿✿✿
US site with a range of online games. But some are not explained very well.

www.disneyblast.com ✿✿✿✿
Activities as well as Disney-style entertainment.

Libraries
www.bl.uk ✿✿✿
The British Library's much improved site, although searches are bizarrely not available on Sundays and bank holidays.

www.nls.ac.uk ✿✿✿✿
National Library of Scotland, easy navigation.

www.llgc.org.uk ✿✿✿
National Library of Wales, odd structure to site.

www.bodley.ox.ad.uk ✿✿✿✿
Bodleian Library's sleek site with a range of search options.

www.lib.cam.ac.uk ✿✿✿
Cambridge University Library.

www.lic.gov.uk ✿
Supposed to provide info on public libraries but it doesn't. Far better to use library page on the NFGL site (see above). Very few local libraries have catalogues online, so it's better to ring up if you want to hunt for a book.

www.lii.com ✿✿✿
Library of the internet. Leads you to other online resources.

Homework and revision
www.projectgcse.co.uk ✿✿✿
Revision tools for GCSE.

www.homeworkelephant.co.uk ✿✿✿✿
Wide-ranging resource for homework and reference.

www.howstuffworks.com ✿✿✿
Paradise for the inquisitive.

www.homecentral.com ✿✿✿✿
Huge US homework site.

www.homeworkhigh.com ✿✿✿
Channel 4 learning site for children.

www.talkfast.com ✿✿✿✿
Specialist language software seller.

www.anglia.co.uk ✿✿✿
Educational software (including mathsnet).

www.superkids.com ✿✿✿✿
US site that reviews educational software for kindergarten age and up.

http://encarta.msn.com ✪✪✪
Microsoft's Encarta encyclopedia.

www.britannica.com ✪✪✪
Not just an encyclopedia but also a guide to other websites (enhanced version **www.eb.com** available at £30 a year).

www.dictionary.com ✪✪✪✪
Also covers grammar and provides a thesaurus.

www.yourdictionary.com ✪✪✪✪
Useful language portal: translates texts into all western European languages (and vice versa).

Job hunting

Recruitment is in many ways an ideal activity to migrate to the internet, and the proof lies in the fact that recruitment sites are so common. A US recruitment portal, **www.jobfactory.com**, lists 23,000 and admits it is not exhaustive. Thousands of sites address the UK market; 100 new ones were launched here in January 2000 alone.

Recruitment benefits especially from the internet's speed of communication, its searchability, its ability to place enormous amounts of information at your fingertips, and the ability to switch at any moment between one-to-one communication and one-to-many. Human resource (HR) professionals and other employers are happy to experiment with recruitment sites because they are far cheaper than the traditional job ad media. Unlike newspapers, online recruitment sites do not have to cut down acres of trees and distribute them all over the country. And as they are generally stand-alone entities, they do not have to fund the activities of hundreds of journalists.

The UK Marketing Director of Monster says, 'It's so cheap to advertise online relative to hard copy. The *Sunday Times* charges £9,000 for an eighth of a page. The most expensive way you can put a job on our site for sixty days will cost you only £250 – and we are a premium service.'

Employers can also see that online recruitment sites work fast. They put an ad on a web site, and candidates can start responding by emailing their CVs immediately. According to a strategist at the French jobsite Cadres Online, 'Online recruiting is seven times faster than offline, and costs one-fifth as much.' Meanwhile, job hunters can access a huge number of adverts and CV databases, and use online agents to search for jobs which would suit them, all for free.

But does online recruitment work?

Managers in recruitment sites are naturally enthusiastic, but there are more cynical views as well. Specifically, sites are often accused of being dominated by technical and IT people, and of generating pointless applications from all over the world. The cynics go on to say that the only reason that employers still use the sites is that they are cheap, and that HR professionals are very rarely held accountable for results. This last point certainly seems to be true. HR professionals in most big companies cannot generally tell you where the candidates they offer jobs to have come from. A trainer who runs a wide range of seminars for HR people says, 'Seminars about how to track response to recruitment ads ought to be well attended, but in fact they do not do well.'

But does online recruitment work for you as a consumer? Can you get a job online? Can you find the *best* job online?

If you are in IT, you probably already know that the internet is a good place to find work, and has been for a few years. But the UK Marketing Director for Stepstone is adamant that the world has moved on since the time when jobsites were by and for the technical community alone: 'We place pizza delivery boys and chief accountants. We find social workers and geologists.'

Job hunting online does now seem to be working for more and more people in more and more types of careers. It is free, the searchability can save you time compared to scouring ads in a paper. In fact, looking for a job online takes as much or as little time as you want to give it. You can post your CV on a couple of sites and simply wait for enquiries to come to you. Or you can set up an intelligent agent to hunt down the right job for you. Or you can diligently scour a hundred job ad sites, if you feel like it. The main thing is to find out which are the best sites to use. We will explore this in the next section.

For employers, the problem remains of employers being deluged with CVs from India and America – places where technical skills are common, but access to work permits is not. Screening software mitigates but does not remove this problem. But that need not worry the job hunter.

Which are the best sites?

Obviously what you want as a jobseeker is to be using the site or sites with the best jobs for you. First some general tips, and then we shall explore the specific options.

If you know which company you want to work for, visit its site and research it thoroughly. You can then apply direct, either online or by post. But employers are busy people, and if a CV comes to them with a recommendation from someone they trust they may give it more time, which could easily make the difference between getting an interview and not getting one. So a good idea is to find out which recruitment consultancy they use, and see if they will present your CV to the company. This will work out more expensive for the company, but will cost you nothing – apart from the cost of visiting the recruitment consultancy.

If you do not know which firm you want to work for, the web is a great place to search for openings that suit your experience and talents. Where do you look? Start with the sites run by the people who have traditionally run ads for the sort of jobs you want. Thus the *Sunday Times* (owned by News International) is traditionally a good place to look for reasonably senior managerial jobs, so go to News International's Revolver site, **www.revolver.com**. *Computer Weekly* has long been the number one place for IT jobs, so visit **www.computerweekly.com**.

Then there are the new entrants to the job ad business, established by start-ups (like **www.stepstone.co.uk**) or by people who used to play a different role in the recruitment business, like recruitment ad agencies (for example, **www.monster.co.uk**, which was launched by job ad agency TMP). There are companies in this category that advertise jobs across all sectors, and others that specialise in a particular sector (such as **www.jobserve.co.uk**).

What you should look for as you evaluate these companies is whether they have lots of jobs that interest you, are they trustworthy, and do they offer the bells and whistles you like (such as intelligent agents, and career advice). You can find the answers to these questions by browsing the sites, and there are tips below as to how to tell the good sites from the bad. You should also ask your friends, colleagues, and other people in the industry you want to work in.

Recruitment ad agencies

TMP is probably the world's biggest job ad agency. Its jobsite, Monster, is probably the biggest jobsite in the world, and for most people it will be worth a visit.

Publishers

Publishers of hard-copy titles are concerned about the impact of the internet on their business. According to the marketing director for one of the jobsites, 'Print media get maybe 60 per cent of their revenue from job ads. It is no coincidence that they tend to charge twice as much for them as for their non-job ads. The *Sunday Times*, for instance, makes £70 million a year from job ads.'

Since publishers make lots of money from hard copy ads they are reluctant to allow employers to advertise on their web sites if that means they will not buy the expensive hard-copy ads. Traditionally they have 'bundled' the online ads: an employer could only get an ad

'www.monster.com was only the 450th URL ever to be registered. We have gone on to be the 60th most-visited site in the world.'

UK Marketing Director, Monster

on the *Sunday Times* web site by buying an ad in the offline paper. As more and more people use the web to find jobs, this bundling policy is becoming untenable, and publishers are starting to abandon it. In any case, although bundling is bad news from the employer's point of view, it is pretty much neutral from the point of view of a jobseeker.

Newspapers

As well as trying to counter the threat of lost revenues, newspaper publishers are using their web sites to try to broaden their audiences. Offline, each of them reaches only a particular kind of person. Online, they hope, they can jettison this restriction. Thus the *Guardian* is building its Unlimited brand with **www.searchunlimited.co.uk,** News International has **www.revolver.com**, and Associated News has **www.Bigbluedog.com**. From the point of view of a jobseeker, this is fairly irrelevant – as long as they keep their old 'franchise' while going after new ones.

Trade magazines

The major trade publishers publish a bewildering array of titles, as viewers of *Have I Got News For You* will testify with a smirk. Many of these titles carry job ads for their specific trade or industry, and some (for instance, *New Scientist*) are the leading job ad media for their sector. Check out the online jobsites of your industry's trade magazines. For instance, **www.totaljobs.co.uk** is the aggregated job site of Reed Business Information (part of publishing giant Reed Elsevier and no relation to Reed the employment agency). At the time of writing it lists twenty-nine sectors and is substantial, listing 41,000 jobs.

Local newspapers

The local press is usually the best place to find blue-collar jobs and jobs for people who are not particularly career-minded. Fish4 is a classified ad consortium of the biggest local press publishers. If you are looking for a bookkeeper's job in Wigan or a job as a plumber in Abergavenny, then the regional press is probably your best bet at the moment, and **www.fish4jobs.co.uk** a good place to start.

Internet-only jobsites

Numerous recruitment sites have been set up from scratch. The earliest were, naturally enough, focused on the IT sector. One of the best is **www.jobserve.co.uk,** established in May 1994, and now boasting 65,000 jobs. This and other purely internet companies in the technical sector are locked in a fierce battle with the online versions of established trade magazines, such as **www.computerweekly.com**.

Probably the biggest of the internet recruitment sites is a relatively recent arrival from Scandinavia. (Our Nordic neighbours are enthusiastic users of the internet, and Sweden experienced a national scandal recently when a journalist discovered that some schoolchildren there did not have email addresses.) Stepstone (**www.stepstone.co.uk**) was launched in the UK in mid-1999, but has spent lavishly on marketing to build its brand and to attract a critical mass of advertisers and jobseekers.

Aggregators

Sites such as **www.jobfactory.com** in the US, and Keljob and Tchoo in France use 'robots' or 'spiders' (automated search agents) to 'collect' jobs from existing sites – without permission, and often against the wishes of the other sites. These sites often have huge numbers of jobs listed, but their audience of candidates may not be so large.

> 'We have achieved 25 per cent brand awareness among UK consumers, not far behind Freeserve on 45 per cent and Amazon on 35 per cent. We get 57 per cent of all job searches conducted at home.'
>
> **UK Marketing Director, Stepstone**

Does all this mean I should not use recruitment consultants?

In a word, no. In the early days of the web, internet consultants and business people talked a lot about 'disintermediation', the idea that the improved information flow created by the internet heralded the destruction of intermediaries such as estate agents, insurance brokers, and recruitment consultants. So far, things have turned out otherwise.

In the jargon, intermediaries have become 'infomediaries', helping us all navigate across endless seas of disorganised information. Recruitment consultants now routinely find candidates on web sites, and use web sites to advertise the jobs they are looking to fill for their clients. The UK Marketing Director for Stepstone is clear about the continuing importance of recruitment consultancies: 'There are 6,000 in the UK, and 50 per cent of our ad revenue comes from them. We have no intention of competing with such a large section of our revenue base. However, the arrival of the internet and of job boards means that recruitment consultancies have to become more professional.

Those who do not will disappear. Everybody has to add more value than they did, to go further up the value chain.'

The French site **www.cadremploi.fr**, which may well be the oldest online jobsite in the world (it was established on France's Minitel system way back in 1990), takes the idea of partnering to its extreme. It is owned by fifty recruitment consultancies and twenty-three job ad agencies, and has partnerships with almost all the 500 serious recruitment consultancies in the country.

The services on offer

> 'Candidates cannot simply paste in their pre-written CV, although they can paste in entries to individual fields. Obviously this means it takes longer for candidates to register with Monster than with rival sites. CVs are removed from Monster if they are not reviewed by their owners for a year. Interestingly, most candidates put their names and contact details on the visible part of their CVs, despite plentiful notices from Monster that they can leave them hidden.'
>
> **Marketing Director, Monster**

Job ads

Job ads are the basic constituent of a recruitment web site. The first questions you will want to ask about a site are, 'How many jobs does this site have?' and 'Does it have the kind of jobs I might apply for?

The number of jobs on a site can be misleading because some sites have certain jobs listed several times over. Sometimes a number of different recruitment consultancies will advertise jobs on a site at the same time as the client, and some of them may advertise the same job several times (perhaps entering it under different towns) in order to make themselves look bigger. The better jobsites take steps to minimise this problem, but the lesson is that while job numbers are important, they are not the whole story.

Stepstone argues the best way to rate a jobsite is by how much revenue it makes. Naturally it also claims that its own revenue is higher than any other UK site.

CV database

Some sites encourage you to enter your CV into a database which can be searched by employers – the converse of you searching through their jobs. The better sites allow you to hide your contact details if you want to, and even to block your CV altogether from certain companies or types of company. Reassurance about confidentiality is as important in recruitment as reassurance about credit card fraud is in retail. The way in which CVs are submitted can have a big impact on how useful they are to employers, and hence on how likely they are to lead to an offer of employment. Monster argues that its CV database is more useful to employers because candidates have to fill in a bespoke CV that is searchable in every field.

Jobsearch agents

Many sites allow you to set up standing queries or instruct job 'agents', which will report back to you when a job is advertised that meets the criteria you stipulate. There are downsides to these sophisticated services. First, there is the danger that people will be unsettled and made unhappy in perfectly good jobs if they spend too much time looking over the fence at what alternatives are on offer. Secondly, research commissioned by one jobsite found that many people find the additional services too complicated. The marketing director says he took the time-honoured approach to market research that produces unpalatable results: 'We are ignoring that and going ahead with our plans anyway. We want to give the users tools. Adding value is the way to differentiate our service. You can't expect people to say they want a new product or service until they have experienced it and understood its benefits. Market research of the Sony Walkman before it was first launched would probably have killed the project.'

CV screening software

Online recruiters are competing with each other to offer screening and analysis software to employers. For instance, Stepstone offers a bespoke service where candidates are asked to fill out an online form, from which their background and their approach to work are assessed. The questions are framed by psychologists and are designed to be hard to cheat. The output is a database of profiles, and the employer can carry out data mining in that database, asking different questions until he or she has compiled the best possible shortlist of candidates to invite for final interviews. These tools are at an early stage in their development, however. Humans are not going to be removed from the recruitment process any time soon!

Content

The larger jobsites carry advice for both employers and jobseekers on how to find the best candidates and jobs respectively. Mostly these amount to little more than brief articles setting out the common-sense basics, but some are more ambitious. Stepstone, for instance, is building a directory of professional training courses on its site. Sites linked to hard-copy publishers are in an advantageous position with regard to content, as they can simply download (perhaps with some editing) material created for their offline publications. For information about employment law, many of the legal websites (see The Law) have pages that look at the main issues and problems from both the employee's and employer's points of view.

Working abroad

If you have itchy feet and fancy taking a job in Paris, for instance, where should you start looking? Many of the bigger sites are expanding their coverage across Europe, but it is early days and for the moment at least, your best bet is probably to use the French sites (providing you can read the language!). See below for a list.

The future

According to one estimate, 95 per cent of job advertising spend goes on hard copy and 5 per cent online, although probably more than 5 per cent of vacancies are filled from online adverts. Online recruiters hope and expect these spend figures to reverse in a few years. An interesting question is whether that will increase the prices the jobsites can charge to nearer the rates achieved by the hard-copy media. That depends partly on whether one or two sites emerge as dominant in each national market. Monster has some grounds to claim it has achieved that status in the US, and prices have not risen there. But perhaps Monster is simply playing a long game, trying to consolidate its dominance.

In any case, almost everyone in the industry is adamant that jobseekers will not pay fees to use the basic online services for the foreseeable future.

Selected sites

Generalist sites
www.monster.com ❶❷❸❹
The site others need to beat. Clearly laid out, tons of jobs, fun design (although some prefer a more serious approach).

www.stepstone.co.uk ❶❷❸❹
A relative newcomer, but benefiting from very deep pockets. Clean, crisp design, and determined to be one of the leading career management sites.

www.totaljobs.co.uk ❶❷❸❹
Reed Business Information is the country's leading trade publisher, and it owns a huge number of titles.

www.fish4jobs.co.uk ❶❷❸❹
Brings together over 600 local newspapers, so there are one or two jobs for builders in here!

www.searchunlimited.co.uk ❶❷❸
The *Guardian*'s site is best in its traditional sectors of media, education and public services.

www.revolver.com ❶❷❸
News International has had a patchy track record on the internet, but with the power of the *Sunday Times* appointment section behind it, it cannot be ignored. Its 6,800 jobs were dominated by technical positions, with a fair representation in new media and the law.

www.bigbluedog.com ❶❷❸
Associated News owns the *Evening Standard* and the *Daily Mail*, so this site is good for secretarial and fairly junior positions.

www.ft.com
Amazing but true – there are no UK jobs here! Monster provides a clutch of US positions, and Hay Group chips in with career advice pages, but the 'pink' un' (utterly obsessed with the internet in other ways) is not providing an online counterpart to all those Financial Director ads.

Sector specialists

Every kind of career niche imaginable is catered for on the net. By way of illustration, and since it has typically been at the cutting edge, here are some sites dedicated to IT.

www.jobserve.co.uk ❶❷❸❹
The doyen of IT recruitment start-ups.

www.computerweekly.com ❶❷❸❹
The market leader in IT publishing.

www.jobworld.co.uk ❶❷❸
Publishing giant VNU's job site is being re-branded **www.newmonday.com**, but buried in there somewhere is *Computing* magazine, the number two in the market.

French sites

www.cadresonline.com ❶❷❸❹
France's 13th most-visited website. It receives over 770,000 visitors per month, has 8,000 jobs, and 100,000 CVs. Its contributing press partners include the national daily *Le Monde*; business magazines *L'Usine Nouvel*, *Expansion*, *L'Express* and *Strategies*; major regional papers *Sud Ouest*, *Le Parisien* and *Ouest France* (whose 1m circulation is the biggest of any daily paper in France), and the sports journal *L'Equipe*.

www.cadremploi.fr ❶❷❸❹
Has jobs from fewer press partners than its rival cadresonline, but it has *Le Figaro*, France's main job ad medium for managers as well as the great majority of recruitment consultancies and recruitment ad agencies.

www.emailjob.fr ❶❷❸❹
Originally a specialist site for technical staff, now France's biggest independent player.

Dating, marriage and divorce

The popularity of internet sex sites is notorious, but the web also provides useful resources (and plenty of pitfalls) for those embarking on relationships – or seeking to dissolve them. Low-cost internet dating agencies are booming, but there are concerns about the lack of regulation in a sector that handles sensitive personal information. Wedding sites in the UK are a mixed bag. They can be a useful source of information about venues or service providers, but the information provided is rarely comprehensive.

It may be tactless to consider divorce in the same area as marriage, but with many marriages lasting only a few years, the topics are clearly linked. It's now possible and fairly straightforward to use online resources to arrange a simple divorce, and this route could save a substantial amount of money. But if the situation were complex, you would need to consult a solicitor in the traditional way.

Dating

> *'The traditional agencies are really good at spotting the married guys. [They check marital status and that the address tallies.] They don't just accept a mobile phone number.'*
> **Lyn Davies, Association of British Introduction Agencies**

Internet-based chat rooms are becoming the adult education classes of the 21st century, allowing people to start friendships and even relationships without having to go through the motions of pretending to want to learn Russian or pottery, let alone the cost and hassle of dating agencies. Nevertheless there are also a huge number of companies specifically offering dating services either free or at low cost. Some are related to existing offline agencies with good reputations, but many others are internet-only businesses where you cannot be sure that your personal details will be seen only by those you have chosen. They are cheap, cheerful – and possibly risky.

Venus.com

Most internet dating agencies give you a free trial period in which you can post your details and picture (although many choose not to) and see initial details of other members. The usual system is that you can contact other members indirectly, so both parties' surnames and email addresses are kept confidential. You disclose personal details only when you want to. Some sites allow free access until you actually want to contact someone, other sites charge between £10–15 a month or about £60 a year to gain access to substantial databases of other people. For example, Match (**www.match.com**), a Texas-based site, claims more than 3m members worldwide, with more than 10,000 in the UK (when counted with its sister site **www.oneandonly.com**). Match.com promises that 'Venus will deliver profiles direct to your email' and that the service costs 'less than dinner and a movie'.

Home-grown rivals include **www.datingdirect.co.uk**, **www.loveandfriends.com** and **www.onesaturday.com** (a joint venture between three traditional offline dating agencies: Dateline, Sirius and Elite). Apart from competitive pricing and some level of discretion, internet agencies also offer members the option of choosing any member whose details are posted online, whereas traditional low-cost dating agencies such as Dateline (**www.dateline.co.uk**) selects potential partners for members by postcode or area. However, unlike internet-only dating agencies, Dateline does check the addresses of its members (and has recently cut the cost of joining by a third to £99 for those who sign-up online).

Some people running internet dating sites, such as Mary Balfour (who runs the upmarket agency Drawing Down the Moon, **www.drawingdownthemoon.co.uk** as well as **loveandfriends.co.uk**) thinks they are good because 'they're cheap and they allow people to dip their toes into the dating market. I'd say that 90 per cent of people on internet sites are kosher.' Unfortunately that leaves 10 per cent to wonder about. 'You do get the odd weirdo,' she admits.

Other observers feel that internet dating is just as risky as using classified ads in newspapers – although it may be perceived to be safer. According to Kate Corbett of Sirius, a mid-market agency: 'I wouldn't give my details to an internet dating site. I'd be afraid about who would be on the other end.' Observers are concerned because internet dating is:

- Completely unregulated. The more reputable offline dating agencies (see below) are members of industry associations such as the Association of British Introduction Agencies (ABIA), which has a code of conduct

- Many internet dating sites do not list their contact details or even a phone number. Some do not respond to emails

- Data entered by individuals may not be secure. The ABIA has heard that hackers have lifted personal information off one site for transfer onto another

- Internet agencies can disappear with customers' money just as quickly as they appear – just like offline agencies that are not members of the ABIA

- Like classified ads in newspapers, internet dating agencies rarely vet people who upload their details, and members can describe themselves as Prince or Princess Charming. Internet sites certainly do not weed out married men looking for affairs.

- Internet sites are more likely to attract time-wasters than newspapers. You often have to pay to place and pay for an advert in a paper, whereas registration online is often free.

People using internet dating agencies certainly should be wary about handing out any kind of personal details at an early stage. For example, you should particularly avoid giving out a land-line telephone number to another member because they could use a reverse telephone directory to trace your address.

Information about offline agencies

What goes on at internet dating agencies bears little relation to the matchmaking and selection that takes place at companies such as Sara Eden and Executive Club. More details on these types of agencies (and their substantial fees) can be found from the Association of British Introduction Agencies (**www.abia.org.uk**) or from their own web sites. Most long-established agencies are making more use of the web for communication. For example, if you are a member of Sirius you can receive pictures of other members by email. But the agencies that offer the highest service, such as Drawing Down the Moon are sticking to one-to-one interviews and handwritten profiles. According to Mary Balfour: 'Handwritten profiles tell you almost everything about someone – you can tell if someone is anally retentive, for instance.'

'The problem with many of the internet sites is that they do not provide a contact number or an address. If something goes wrong, no one can hear you scream in cyberspace.'

Lyn Davies, Association of British Introduction Agencies

Marriage sites

In the US there are so many sites relating to marriage that there's a site that provides links to the hundred best options (**www.top100weddingsites.com**). Some wedding sites are generalist – a mixture of magazine and information directory; others cater for particular aspects of marriage, such as dressmaking or flowers. The leading UK marriage website is **www.confetti.co.uk**, which has attracted a stream of management refugees from Marks & Spencer. Confetti has recently taken control of two other rivals in this market (**www.weddingguideuk.co.uk** and **www.webwedding.co.uk**) and now claims the largest database of impending marriages in Europe. At the time of writing the sister sites do not appear to have been reorganised, although they now share a database. WeddingguideUK provides some bizarre links to **www.USbridalguide.com**, which might come as a surprise for someone expecting to consult material geared to a UK audience.

Find the venue, order the cake

For those getting married, the most useful features offered by wedding sites are databases of suppliers enabling you to search for venues or different types of service providers in different parts of the country. You can look for marquees on Merseyside or cakes in Cornwall – particularly useful if you are holding a wedding in an area where you don't live. Confetti has the most comprehensive information on venues because it has a licensing deal with Noble's Wedding Venue Guide, a directory that covers the 2,000 venues that have recently been licensed to hold civil marriages. There are detailed descriptions and information about the facilities available at each site (although only a few pictures). Inevitably, this list excludes many good reception-only venues.

The venue searches on other sites are much less satisfactory. For example, on WeddingguideUK, if you search for venues near Chesterfield, the system pushes advertisements for venues in Herefordshire and Birmingham before providing a list of places near Chesterfield. Other sites have very restricted lists of venues.

The listings for associated services also tend to be patchy. For example, **www.wedding-day.co.uk** appears to have listings mostly in the Oxford area. **Coolwhite.com** concentrates on some of the most expensive service providers (and venues) in London. Other sites such as Webweddding appear to have geographical coverage, but strangely omit Cornwall – so it would be hard to find a cake-maker there after all. Some sites also treat London as one area, with the result that you get a cascade of listings, with little idea of how to choose between the different suppliers. Some regional directory sites, such as **www.gmini.co.uk**, which provides a huge amount of information about weddings in Northern Ireland (including where to obtain ice sculptures), may be worth a look.

That best man's speech in full . . .

Most marriage websites provide magazine-style background articles about weddings. For example, there are tips about speeches, coping with divorced parents and honeymoon destinations. Probably the most useful advice concerns how to choose caterers (checking what is included and what might be charged as extras). But the usefulness of many of the tips is questionable. WeddingguideUK, for example, notes that some ministers object to the playing of the Bridal March from Wagner's *Lohengrin* because the marriage in the opera only lasts twenty minutes.

Once you have chosen the venue, many websites offer tools to help you prepare for the big day. There are online budgeting tools – worth considering given the average wedding is said to cost about £14,000. You can announce the details of your impending union on the internet, and leave an email address for friends and relatives. Some sites also offer an updated wedding list service. Putting the information about your wedding party online could be useful for guests who lose invitations. Most sites protect wedding lists and venue details with a password to ward off gatecrashers (or worse), but some allow general browsers to see the details.

Divorce

Several web sites have been set up to help couples cope with the process of divorce. One of the best sites is **www.divorce-online.co.uk**, which looks at the divorce process and the various financial and custodial issues that are raised. There are also details of other agencies (such as Citizens Advice Bureau and Law Centres) that may be able to help.

Another reasonable site is **www.divorce.co.uk** (established by the Cambridge solicitors Mills & Reeve). Again, there are links to other useful service providers such as mediation and counselling, but background information is scantier than on Divorceonline.

Another Scottish solicitor, Donald Wright, has put up **www.divorceuk.com** which – unusually – provides information on Scottish law as well as case studies. There is a useful flow chart of the divorce process as well as advice about embarking on a DIY divorce (see next paragraph). Both Divorceuk and **www.family-solicitors.co.uk** (which covers all aspects of family law) have a searchable database of solicitors, but the selection of lawyers in both cases is fairly modest.

A straightforward divorce costs on average £350 before court fees, and with the use of internet sites, you may be able to obtain your divorce yourself and save most of that money. For example, Divorce-online offers a DIY divorce kit for £55 for a basic package and £80 for a premium service (with email support for free). In theory it would be possible to buy the basic legal stationery from Oyez for a fraction of this figure – but then you would have no help filling in the (relatively simple) forms. For uncontested divorces, an online divorce is certainly an option, but if there are children or complex financial issues, then you should take legal advice.

Selected sites

Dating
www.abia.org.uk ✿✿✿
Association of British Introduction Agencies. List of member agencies, their methods and fees. Relatively unsophisticated site, but good advice.

www.i-s-f.co.uk ✿✿
Introduction Services Federation. Newish rival to ABIA with more flexible approach to regulation. Smooth presentation but short on content.

www.thematchmaker.co.uk ✿✿
Executive Club of St James, one of the most expensive agencies.

www.sara-eden.co.uk ✿✿✿
Slow to load; upmarket agency.

www.drawingdownthemoon.co.uk ✿✿✿
Upmarket agency with 1,400 members. Useful guide to dating agencies on site.

www.onlylunch.co.uk ✿✿✿
Slick site.

www.canapecrowd.com ✿✿
Slow to load, membership £175 a year; organises introduction parties.

www.clubsirius.co.uk ✿✿✿
Sirius website.

www.significantothers.co.uk ✿✿
Basic site for agency for gay men. Access to 500 members.

Online dating agencies
www.datingdirect.com ✿✿
Claims 85,000 members, contact details obscure.

www.dateline.co.uk ✿✿✿
Online arm of Dateline. Joining online is much cheaper at £99 compared with £150 offline.

www.loveandfriends.com ✪✪✪
Internet site from Mary Balfour of Drawing Down the Moon. Slick, upbeat site, free basic membership but contact details obscure.

www.oneandonly.com ✪✪✪
Soon to merge with match.com.

www.match.com ✪✪✪
Texas-based site claiming 3.1m members (around 10,000 in the UK when combined with oneandonly.com).

www.onesaturday.com ✪✪✪
New site from Dateline, Sirius and Elite.

www.introsearch.com ✪
Very basic site, no phone numbers or contact address. Offers free trial period, but the password provided did not work.

Weddings

www.confetti.co.uk ✪✪✪
Leading UK wedding site.

www.weddingguide.co.uk ✪✪
Smaller supplier database than confetti but may include some different suppliers, depending on the area.

www.webweddinguk.com ✪✪
Magazine-style, but supplier database is same as weddingguide.

www.touring-classics.co.uk ✪✪
Wedding car hire; very expensive unless you live in Devon.

www.farrer.co.uk ✪✪
Legal site with a briefing note about pre-nuptial agreements.

www.tophundredweddingsites.com ✪✪
Directory of US wedding sites.

www.coolwhite.com ✪✪
Links to expensive venues and suppliers, mostly in London.

www.wedding.co.uk ✪✪
Patchy coverage of venues, no descriptive details.

www.directwedding.co.uk ✪✪✪
Stationery specialist.

www.wedding-day.co.uk ✪✪
Restricted supplier lists, mostly in Oxford area.

www.wedding-and-brides.co.uk ✪✪
Links to some very expensive dress designers and other suppliers.

www.gmini.co.uk ✪✪✪
Extensive database relating to wedding suppliers in Northern Ireland.

www.trading-direct.co.uk ❍❍❍
Upmarket wedding list service.

www.wedding-pages.co.uk ❍❍
Restricted supplier list, concentrating on northern England.

www.hindunet.org ❍❍
Incredibly cluttered site. But it includes Hindu men and women seeking arranged marriages.

Divorce
www.divorce-online.co.uk ❍❍❍
Most comprehensive divorce site.

www.divorce.co.uk ❍❍
Site from Cambridge solicitors Mills & Reeve.

www.lawrights.co.uk ❍❍❍
Consumers Association site offering free divorce pack.

www.divorceuk.com ❍❍❍
Useful advice from solicitor Donald Wright.

www.familyadvice.co.uk ❍❍❍
Site aimed at solicitors, but useful for general public as well. Provides a sketchy list of solicitors in different towns. Useful links page.

www.family-solicitors.co.uk ❍❍❍
Covers all aspects of family law, not just divorce and separation.

www.legalservices.gov.uk ❍❍
Advice about government-assisted legal support.

www.dss.gov.uk/csa ❍❍❍
Information about Child Support Agency

www.gingerbread.org.uk ❍❍❍
Support group for single parents; advice in many languages.

Silver surfing

The internet is not only for the young, as many older people have already found out and many more are finding all the time. Calling this chapter Silver Surfing could be taken to imply that older people only use the net for 'old people' stuff. This is clearly not true, but there are sites which cater specifically to the older surfer. However, the main reason that we chose to dedicate a chapter to silver surfing was to try to convince those not yet using it that the internet can be a great way to find out about a hobby or interest, to link up with other people, or simply to play bridge, scrabble or backgammon online when you don't want to leave your house. You can even find archives of crosswords.

Research a hobby or interest

If you are interested in the American Civil War, particular makes of old Russian tanks, the history of Singer sewing machines or just about anything else, the internet is a fantastic resource for finding things out, or for finding other people who are interested in the same thing. For example, if you like 1950s memorabilia, **www.lileks.com** has an excellent take on the era. Note the recipe book for 'Cooking with 7up' which is at **www.lileks.com/institute/gallery/7up/index.html**.

As Matthew Darroch-Thompson, internet columnist for *The Oldie* magazine, and editor of *Mole Magazine* says, 'I have found that most people don't want to look at retirement sites, but are using the internet to explore something they are really interested in. Once they get started they cannot believe just how fantastic the web is for this.' For example, the site **www.bibliomania.com** displays the full text of hundreds of works of literature – from Shakespeare to Brontë to Brooke. Plus it is easy to track down a poem from a half-remembered line: simply type the phrase you know into a good search engine, such as **www.google.com**. If you were trying to do the same task with a book you would need to know the first line or the name of the poet. For clues about how to use search engines, see Getting Started.

Online magazines

We don't mean to disparage retirement sites, and there are a great number of them, ranging from online magazines to sites that publicise the activities of offline organisations. Although many of the sites are American, they have an international reach and welcome seniors the world over.

One of the largest magazines now online is **www.saga.co.uk**, which allows access to its current issue for free, and a provides a notice board where you can post a message to old friends or old flames. However, don't expect too much success from this – because the site does not do anything with your message other than literally post it up there, which means that the person you are trying to contact (or one of his or her friends) has to see the message. The magazine *The Oldie* (which of course is not focused on oldies despite its name, but is just focused away from 'youf culture') has a good site at **www.theoldie.co.uk**, on which you can find many of the magazine's excellent articles for free.

Link up with others

For sites that help you connect with others, there is a range of options. The Association of the Retired and Persons over 50 (**www.arp.co.uk**) has news on a great number of topics, an excellent directory of health issues, an active forum and an excellent page of links to organisations and charities. Another good UK site is **www.onseniors.com**, or you can try the American **www.seniornet.org**. If you want a pep talk about how you don't need to feel old try **www.idf50.co.uk** (I don't feel 50) or **www.2young2retire.com**.

Play bridge, scrabble or backgammon from home

You can obtain the software for playing games against other people online for free, or you can buy the software, (for around £50), to let you play games such as bridge or chess against your computer. The place to start for all such gaming interests is **www.thinks.com** which is an excellent site, and links you to a great number of sites for every type of game. If it is bridge you are interested in, you will find a lot of clubs on the net, although at present these are mostly American. You can download the software you need for free from **www.e-bridgemaster.com**, for instance, and then play online at the same site, or at another club. The largest American club is at **www.okbridge.com**, whose home page tells you how many people are playing online at the time you log on – often around 500. Of course there are certain conventions for playing online; to find them out go to **www.annam.com**.

For other games, such as scrabble or backgammon, you may find the official site (for example **www.scrabble.com**) useful. You can learn how to play backgammon online at the website for the British Isles Backgammon Association, **www.cottagewebs.co.uk/biba**.

You could astonish your friends by improving your bridge by practising against your computer. You can buy the software from a number of sites including **www.gibware.com**, which many people think is the best. If you want to look around for alternatives, try the comprehensive but not very user-friendly Jim's Software Review at **www.mcn.net/~jimloy/review.html**.

Crosswords in Greek

If you would like to try your hand at crosswords in foreign languages, or a vast range of other games, begin at **www.thinks.com/crosswords**. Note that you have to print off the crossword and fill it in. But beware the pressing temptation to cheat. It is very easy to do so – just click on the reveal button and all is, as it were, revealed.

Selected sites

Magazines online
www.theoldie.co.uk✪✪✪✪✪
Clear, straightforward site with a great number of free articles and features from *The Oldie*.

www.saga.co.uk/publishing✪✪✪✪
Good, easy-to-navigate site of the popular magazine *Saga*, with the current issue online, and a noticeboard for contacting old friends or family members.

Retirement organisations online
www.arp.org.uk ✪✪✪
The website of the Association of Retired and Persons Over 50. Notice board, links, an active forum, and an excellent directory of health issues.

www.seniornet.org ✪✪✪
American site, but a good information resource and with a free and easy-to-follow course on how to use the internet. The seniornet round table links to 'seniors across the world'.

www.the-retirement-site.co.uk✪✪✪
Website of the retirement counselling service. Information on pensions, social security and tax for people who are about to retire. Excellent links section briefly guiding you around the whole of the net at **www.the-retirement-site.co.uk/weblinks/webfr.html**.

www.2young2retire.com ✪✪✪
If you want a pep talk about not feeling old.

www.idf50.co.uk ✪✪✪
UK version of the American site I don't feel 50. Good site, but still with a distinctly American flavour.

Games

www.thinks.com ✪✪✪✪✪

Superb site with a host of puzzles and games to play online or download. Vast number of links to sites with advice about, or where you can play, almost every game you can think of.

www.acbl.org ✪✪✪

Find out the options for software to play bridge with others across the internet you can also use.

www.e-bridgemaster.com ✪✪✪✪

Provides free, downloadable bridge software enabling you to play online, at this American site.

www.okbridge.com ✪✪✪✪

Bold site for America's largest online bridge club, boasting a great number of people playing online at any one time.

www.annam.co.uk ✪✪✪

Explains the conventions for bidding online.

www.scrabble.com ✪✪✪

Find out about all those things about scrabble you never knew from this professional-looking site.

www.cottagewebs.co.uk/biba ✪✪

Play backgammon online from the British Isles Backgammon Association and obtain tournament information.

Death

The UK funeral industry has not been quick to adopt internet technology: no one yet offers anything like a one-stop online service for making funeral arrangements. This is partly because the industry is relatively conservative and localised, partly because the process of arranging a funeral is seen as too personal and too emotional to be handled remotely through the web. It is also partly because some of the legal arrangements still have to be made offline.

Nevertheless there are resources on the web that will help you arrange a funeral, and make the experience less stressful. You can find certain suppliers, research the legal issues, discover alternative ceremonies and procedures, and find people to share your experiences and grief.

You can also find sites that cross over into the lighter side of death, if that is your bent.

If you are arranging a funeral, you are likely to be feeling delicate. It could be unwise to punch a broad request for information into a search engine, as they cannot discriminate between helpful funeral sites and creepy, scary or black humour sites.

Finding out about funerals and related services

The Office of Fair Trading at **www.oft.gov.uk/html/funerals** explains the procedures that have to be followed after a death in England, Scotland, Wales and Northern Ireland, as well as covering what to do if somebody close to you dies while abroad.

A search on **www.scoot.co.uk**, **www.yell.co.uk** or **www.countyweb.co.uk** will identify your local providers of funeral services, and there is also an excellent directory site at **www.funeralsuk.com** which provides a description of what each firm listed does. The biggest funeral director in the country is the Co-Op, and **www.funerals.co-op.co.uk** gives basic information about its services.

You cannot actually arrange much online apart from flowers because florists were early adopters of the internet (like **www.florist-uk.co.uk/shop** and **www.interflora.co.uk**).

66 THE INTERNET CONSUMER BIBLE

Alternative funerals

If you want to know about alternatives to religious or cemetery burials, start with the Cremation Society of Great Britain at **www.members.aol.com/cremsoc/**. Woodland burials are becoming increasingly popular, and can be both financially and environmentally friendly; try **www.greenburials.co.uk** for more details.

For an established non-religious option start with **www.hkara.freeserve.co.uk/funeral.htm**, which neatly describes humanist funerals. The British Humanist Association site at **www.humanism.org.uk** provides more background to humanist thinking. Even more alternatively, you could organise to send your ashes into space at **www.celestis.com**.

More an addition to a funeral than an alternative, a funeral director in North Syracuse, New York has become the first undertaker in the US – probably the world – to offer to broadcast funerals over the internet. 'This service is geared toward someone who is stuck in a hospital, or snowed in at the airport, and simply not able to attend,' said Fredrick Fergerson. 'It's a basic human need to be part of the grieving process. Without the closure of the funeral, many people have problems coming to terms with the loss of their loved ones.' Kelly Smith of the National Funeral Directors Association is sceptical: 'The majority of people organizing funerals are from the WWII generation, and they are not as attuned to computers as the younger generations.'

Counselling

There are sites offering counselling services and general advice about bereavement by email, but the quality of help provided is variable. Watch out for cowboy operators preying on vulnerable visitors: and think twice before paying in advance to people with no recognisable qualifications and no offline contact details.

The London Bereavement Network at **www.bereavement.org.uk** has information on how to seek advice and help. A fully online counsellor can be found at **www.onlinecounselling.co.uk** where you can request email, phone or face-to-face counselling for a fee, and you can also browse a wealth of bereavement-related counselling links and advice. Chat groups might also be worth considering: although not as personal, they are a helpful form of communication if you feel isolated, or if you are dealing with a death in unusual circumstances. Go to **www.egroups.com** and look for topics that have had recent postings and discussions, since some topics may be out of date, or simply unpopular with other users.

Legal issues

For an overview of inheritance tax, try **www.friendsprovident.co.uk/services/inheritance.cfm**, which has a handy inheritance tax calculator. Advice on wills is hard to find using search engines, because 'will' is such a common and ambiguous word. At **www.60-plus.co.uk/legal.html** you can find plenty of tips and some helpful links to get you started, also otherwise look at general legal sites (see The Law).

For transplant and organ donation information, The British Organ Donor Society at **www.argonet.co.uk/body** covers UK and worldwide topics. The Voluntary Euthanasia Society, at **www.ves.org.uk** has essential content on related law, news and activities.

And now for something completely different . . .

For an opinionated and cynical/humorous take on all aspects of death and funerals try **members.tripod.co.uk/funeral**. For a friendly reminder of how many seconds you have to live, check out **www.deathclock.com**. For grave hunters, **www.findagrave.com** allows you to search for famous and non-famous US graves. Finally, there are sites for famous last words, for instance **www.geocities.com/thens/acropolis/6537.realidx.htm**, which has epitaphs, obituaries and some good links.

Selected sites

Funeral planning and services
www.funeralsuk.co.uk/ ○○○○○
Comprehensive, directory-style UK site for funeral information. Neat and easy to navigate, with links to a wide range of death-related subjects via the topics and index pages.

www.oft.gov.uk/html/funerals ○○○
Practical consumer site. Although easy to navigate, it is slow to load and could benefit from greater use of menus and drop-down lists.

www.bbc.co.uk/eduction/archive/grave/index.shtml ○○○
General information site which accompanied a BBC Radio 2 programme.

www.funerals.co-op.co.uk/funerals.htm ○○
Co-op funerals, the country's biggest funeral director.

www.greenburials.co.uk ○○○○
Pleasant site with a good introduction to woodland burials.

www.funeralnet.com ○○
US site with a useful information centre.

Particular services
www.florist-uk.co.uk/shop ○○○
Helpful site.

www.interflora.co.uk ○○○
The site of the market-leading franchise. Expensive-looking website.

www.namm.org.uk ○○
National Association of Monumental Masons.

Counselling and community
www.onlinecounselling.co.uk ○○○○
Ignore the site's design and focus on the vast amount of supportive content. Counselling services by email, phone or face-to-face

www.bereavement.org.uk ○○○
Information about the London bereavement network.

www.egroups.com ○○○
Exchange views and experiences with people in similar situations.

www.pbs.org/weblab/living ○○○○○
Discussion forums, directories and articles relating to suicide. Offers support to those affected and seeks to de-stigmatise suicide.

www.fortnet.org/widownet ○○○
Written by and for widows and widowers. Online discussions and other bereavement resources.

www.tcf.org.uk ○○○
Support for families after the death of a child.

Miscellaneouse
www.inlandrevenue.gov.uk/stats/inheritance.html ○○
Dry but comprehensive account of tax issues.

www.docasap.com ○○
Copies of death certificates can be requested online.

www.60-plus.co.uk/legal.html ○○○
Helpful site to get you started on how to make a will.

www.argonet.co.uk/body ○○○
Essential information from The British Organ Donor Society; covers UK and world-wide topics.

www.ves.org.uk ○○○○
The Voluntary Euthanasia Society site; news and debates on a difficult topic.

Alternative death sites
www.celestis.com ○○○
Amusing and surprising (American) site will send your ashes into space or transmit a high-energy digital message to the stars.

www.deathclock.com ✪✪✪
A macabre reminder that your time is running out.

www.findagrave.com ✪✪
Genealogy enthusiasts and obsessive fans can search for famous or non-famous graves here, although the graves are US-only and the layout is dull.

3 Shopping

Buying online

The internet contains a wealth of useful and entertaining content, and a lot of money has been spent on its provision in the hope and expectation that web users will become web consumers. So when it comes to shopping, is the web a revolution, or just a useful tool?

Shopping online allows you to browse reactively or search purposefully – just like you can on the high street. But there's a major plus: it saves you pounding the streets, and jostling people in crowded stores.

There are bargains to be had on the web. For instance, we shopped for a top-of-the-range Sony Vaio laptop computer. It was selling on Tottenham Court Road (London's centre for electronic bargain hunters) for around £1,600. We bought it from Sony's own site, **www.sony.co.uk**, with exactly the same warranty and with VAT included, for £400 less.

With certain kinds of goods (books, CDs, computer equipment, and non-tangible goods such as software, information, entertainment, financial services) it can make the process of comparing prices and specifications more effective. With other kinds of goods and services (furniture, haircuts) it can provide some useful input but cannot usually take you all the way to a purchase decision.

Few people have internet connections that are as fast and as reliable as they would like. The situation is improving fast, but remains a major impediment to fully-fledged e-commerce.

And then there is the vexed issue of delivery. Any experienced online shopper will have stories from the front line about a basket of goods arriving with some essential items missing or replaced with hilariously ill-judged alternatives. Van drivers can't find your house or turn up at the wrong time; sometimes it seems as though they wait round the corner until you pop out for a pint of milk and then rush to your door to leave a note saying that you were out when they called.

Again, things are improving. E-tailers are working hard to offer more helpful delivery slots (evenings and weekends) and experimenting with various drop-off points like newsagents, petrol stations and train stations. Home delivery will be a growth industry in the coming years, and companies with logistical skills (for instance, milk delivery firms) and the Royal Mail are moving to exploit it.

Payment

Most online consumer purchases are paid for with credit cards, with debit or charge cards as also-rans. This has some disadvantages: it tends to cut the under-eighteens out of online commerce, and if you are careless you can end up with surprisingly large bills. But these problems are far outweighed by the advantages. Credit card transactions can be executed immediately, and the fact that a vendor has an agreement with one of the big credit card companies gives you a degree of confidence in its integrity.

Numerous digital cash schemes (**www.digicash.com**, **www.beenz.org, www.cybergold.com**) have been launched and if they ever get off the ground, we may all be paying for online purchases with online currency, but for the time being a credit card is a necessity.

A fair amount of nonsense has been written about security on the web. Journalists need exciting, headline-grabbing stories, and 'Internet fraud threatens civilisation' is far more likely to attract the casual reader's attention than 'Internet fraud has so far caused no serious problems to any consumer'. Despite assiduous sleuthing by Fleet Street's finest, this second headline essentially tells the story. Yes, the computers of the US Defense Department are hacked into on an almost daily basis, and yes, some big companies who really ought to know better have allowed customer details to be temporarily accessible to public view. These stories sound frightening until you dig behind them and find that no one has actually been harmed in the least.

It does not help when the big companies concerned react defensively or aggressively, and either deny what has happened or threaten the very people who discover the problem and try to help rectify it (Powergen). It is true that there are important issues about internet security that need to be addressed. But in terms of buying goods and services online, the security issue is like the Sherlock Holmes story about the dog that didn't bark.

If you use a credit card, it is entirely sensible to consider whether there is any danger that the online recipient of your card number might misuse it. (It is ironic that this worries people who would not hesitate to hand their card over to a waiter earning a minimum wage and who has had no background checks carried out on him/her.)

But as far as you the customer are concerned, one fact stands out above all else: *if you use a credit card, you are protected by the consumer credit laws*. This means that your financial relationship is not with the company you bought from, but with the credit card company. They are liable for any amount falsely spent on your card – so long as they cannot prove you were involved in a fraud. This is true regardless of whether the internet business is UK-based or abroad.

The same is not true of debit cards, so think twice and three times before using a Switch or Delta card for a transaction with any firm smaller and less financially secure than Amazon.

The internet industry's response to consumer fears about credit card security was to introduce Secure Socket Layer (SSL) technology (**www.verisign.com**). SSL is a standard of encryption and certification that ensures that the connection over which your credit card number travels has the vendor's computer at the other end, and that your details are encrypted with industrial-strength scrambling to ensure that they can't be stolen in transit over the internet. Unfortunately it can also make it difficult to buy things over the internet from machines behind corporate firewalls.

Taxes

The take-off of online commerce has been helped by the fact that you can end up paying less purchase tax than with the equivalent purchase in the real world. It's a grey area where observance of the law is often left up to consumers. The growth of e-commerce would be severely hindered if the authorities applied the law diligently: an online merchant in San Antonio may not be willing or even able to sort matters out with HM Customs and Excise for you.

In the US consumers are supposed to pay the rate of sales tax in the state that they live in (rather than the state where the e-commerce business is sited) but this law is rarely enforced. In the UK you can buy anything from an EU-based website without incurring duty or VAT (although this does not include buying cigarettes or alcohol from, say, Belgium, where normal UK duties would apply). You can buy books from anywhere without paying any duties or tax (which is great for Amazon).

In theory, if you buy goods from outside the EU, you will be liable to import duties and then VAT on top if the invoice total (including the postage) comes to £18 or more. The rates of duty vary from 3 per cent for CDs up to 50 per cent for some goods. There is a higher allowance of £136 available for 'gifts' but this is supposed to be used for goods bought by someone abroad and then sent separately. The theory is that it prevents people in the UK sending 'gifts' to their neighbours, although it doesn't stop you cultivating your friends in Alabama. There is a Customs & Excise leaflet on this complex subject at **www.hmce.gov.uk**.

Customs & Excise inspectors claim to be good at spotting e-commerce parcels at sorting offices, but in practice customs simply don't have the resources to intercept and bill for every package ordered online by UK citizens. Obviously, if you're spending five-figure sums on jewellery and watches from www.swisswatches.ch, then you're taking more of a risk not notifying customs. It may be worth considering what duty would be payable before you order an electronic item from Hong Kong, and if you order a big box of CDs it might be worth splitting the order. But it's largely up to your own conscience and level of paranoia.

However, in certain areas you can pay less tax by doing business online entirely legally. Online betting owes some of its popularity to the convenience of being able to see the odds updated in real time at your desk (provided your corporate firewall doesn't prohibit the sites). But it also helps that online betting avoids the 9 per cent tax to which all offline betting in this country is subject. For betting sites and issues, see the Sport section.

Data protection

You may wonder what e-commerce operators do with the personal data they seem to be keen on collecting about you. The answer often seems to be, anything they like. Most sites have a privacy policy that promises they will not sell your details to any other company, but these policies are typically 'subject to change without notice', in other words, potentially useless.

The EU is bringing in a law that makes it illegal to pass on information on a customer or potential customer to another business unless he or she has agreed (opted in); however, it is not in place yet, and in any event it will not apply to non-EU sites. Unfortunately, accepting that companies are going to leverage your personal data to the hilt is part and parcel of buying things on the web; the value of your customer data to them is one of the things that funds the discounts available to you.

One thing you can do to minimise any resulting annoyance is to use 'junk email accounts'. Typically, whenever you sign up to create an account with an online shop, you will have to provide an email address. You can get a free email account from **www.hotmail.com** or **www.yahoo.com**, and use that for your commercial dealings. Your main email inbox remains free of the 'special offers' and 'preferred customer announcements', although you do have to remember to check more than one email account; it depends which inconvenience bothers you more.

Bargain hunting

One of the main attractions of buying things over the net is that it is often possible to get things cheaper online than off, even when the cost of postage and packaging is taken into account (which, in web advertising, it often is not). There is a huge amount of variation in the pricing of identical goods on the web, so a bit of diligence can end up saving you a large percentage of the cost of your purchase.

There are pieces of software – called 'shopbots' – which allow you to compare prices across a wide range of online retailers, so that you can see at a glance where the best deals are. The sites **www.shopsmart.com**, **www.kelkoo.com** and **www.valuedirect.co.uk** are three of the best for a great range of white goods, for instance, and Shopsmart will compare book prices for you and tell you not only which site sells the book for least, but also which is cheapest when you include delivery charges, and which can get the book to you fastest. It is the kind of development that makes observers concerned about the business models of online book retailers.

However, shopbots are not always the silver bullet solution to bargain hunting online. They work best for things like books, CDs or other goods where it is possible to be sure that like is being compared with like. If you are trying to buy a computer, however, you may find that the shopbot quotes do not take into account the fact that one retailer is selling the machine with Microsoft Office installed, another is throwing in a higher-quality modem, and so on.

Don't assume, however, that every shopbot visits every shop. Some experienced online shoppers claim that they can often beat a shopbot's best price by looking for themselves. Nevertheless, the bots are a good place to start.

Electronics

There are a huge number of sites selling electronic goods on the web; the difficulty is finding a way to sift through them to find the products which are right for you. As with many items you can begin with the shopbots (see above) for new goods, or use a free ad site, such as **www.preloved.com**, to register your request to buy or sell computers, laptops and so on. However, you can also use the internet in the same way as an offline warehouse shop (such as Argos) to find cheaper goods than those sold on the high street. Look in the high street shops and decide exactly which model you want and then check whether you can buy it directly from the manufacturer's website, at a lower cost.

Last Minute Buying

It is interesting to see how the internet is enabling consumers and vendors to benefit more often from different ways of pricing goods and services than the standard 'fixed price' approach.

For instance, the imbalances between supply and demand sometimes leave vendors willing to sell off valuable goods and services for much less than their list price, and the web makes it practical for the average retail customer to take advantage of this fact. The most famous provider in this category is **www.lastminute.com**, which specialises in selling off travel, accommodation and similar goods that would otherwise go unsold.

Collective buying

Buying groups have been around in commercial environments for donkey's years. The web has introduced them to consumers. The best-known in this country is probably **www.letsbuyit.com**, which allows individuals around the country to club together in bulk orders, splitting the savings between them. You may of course be kept waiting quite a while for a suitable buyer group to form on letsbuyit; a few people were disappointed last year by trying to buy Christmas trees in this way. The site describes the kind of purchases that is best suited to: it's probably best to take their advice. Letsbuyit.com is now in financial difficulties, but the basic idea will probably survive.

Auctions

Most online auctions are timed to last a week, with a reserve price set by the vendor and with the highest bid outstanding at the close of the auction taking the item. Auction site veterans will be aware of the numerous ways in which sites can be customised; it's possible to set up automatic bidding to rise intelligently up to the maximum bid you're prepared to make, or to get email notification when your leading bid has been trumped, or even in some cases to be notified over a mobile phone.

It is tempting to believe that many purchases on auction sites are made for the fun of the process rather than the utility of the item purchased — and what's wrong with that? Auction veterans will also tend to own quite a lot of junk that they've bought with speculative bids, often with the intention of reselling on the same site.

The main auction sites in the UK are **www.ebay.co.uk** and **www.qxl.com**. Unfortunately, these are pretty pale shadows of **www.ebay.com**, the originator of web auctions in the US, or of the auction areas of **amazon.com** or the big portals. However, most US vendors aren't really interested in dealing with the complications of shipping goods outside the USA, so it is probably best to stick to the UK sites.

If you use an auction site you will be buying something from a private vendor (or indeed, selling something yourself), which is more of a risk than dealing with a big company. Typically, it's not possible to use credit cards in these transactions, so you're left with payment against delivery, and all the potential trouble which that entails (another good reason for only dealing with UK sites). Most of the auction sites try to solve this problem by encouraging users to report on their experiences, so that bad apples can't carry on dealing for long, but this is definitely a risk reduction exercise rather than risk elimination. There are many more good vendors than bad out there, but for any really significant expense, like a second-hand car, it's probably best to check the physical object yourself before handing over payment.

A variant on the traditional auction is the 'reverse' or 'Dutch' auction. On **www.priceline.com**, for instance, you state what you're willing to pay for a flight, say, and Priceline looks for a supplier who's prepared to supply you. QXL also offers auctions of goods supplied new by the manufacturers as well as second-hand items.

Delivery

If you buy something online that is too large to fit through a standard letterbox, then you may face difficulties in getting it delivered. Veterans of catalogue shopping will be familiar with the problem of valuable goods left lying around on their doorstep. Most online retailers are still only able to deliver during working hours and are not able to specify a delivery time.

In the US, companies like **www.kozmo.com**, and **www.urbanfetch.com** are trying to solve this problem by offering within-one-hour delivery round the clock. They have started to extend their service to the UK, along with home-grown replicas like **www.koobuycity.com**. These firms charge a surprisingly small premium (often less than £5) for the service, but their business is based on the hope that large numbers of people will take them up. The service has only been available in big cities, and Urbanfetch has recently decided that it is losing too much money and has scrapped its London service.

A promising solution to these delivery headaches is the idea of drop-off points. Streets with houses rather than flats may begin to be peppered with 'bear boxes' in front gardens. These are large, lockable boxes into which your shopping can be put. For flats and apartment blocks the solution may come in a revival of concierges or a new use for your local newsagent. Petrol stations and rail stations, which people pass routinely on their way home from work, are also vying for the business.

Hello . . . is anybody there?

Things go wrong with the best-laid plans of mice and men, and when they do, you want to be able to contact someone and get a response. Many US e-tailers will promise to respond within 24 hours to any customer enquiry and in usually respond much more quickly quicker. Sadly, a lot of UK e-tailers do not achieve this.

The best retail sites have people in call centres as a backup to the automated web-based service, and they often have a 'call-me-back button' on their sites. You click the button and someone at the call centre phones you: your enquiry is dealt with and you don't even pay for the call.

Even when a transaction is running smoothly, the best sites communicate with you frequently by email to let you know how your order is doing: you get an email to confirm receipt of your order, another when it has been sent, and so on.

What you see may not be what you get

Another practical problem which online shopping has in common with catalogue shopping is that the article delivered to you may not match its description or photo. It's worth remembering that only 256 colours out of the whole spectrum are typically considered 'web-safe', and that only the most expensive, professional quality monitors are typically balanced to provide true colour. So it's quite likely that your purchase will look a bit different from the image on the monitor.

If this proves to be a real problem, you will end up investigating the retailer's returns policy. Most of these are actually pretty good; they tend to be modelled on Amazon's, which is summarised by Amazon's CEO Jeff Bezos as 'essentially, we'll take your word for it'. But it's best to check the policy ahead of time. Remember that the mere fact that you're on the web doesn't deprive you of any of your normal statutory rights when dealing with a UK-based retailer (**www.which.net** is the Consumers' Association site). However, if you're buying from overseas, you are basically at their mercy.

Regulation of the net

Regulation of sites on the web is in its infancy. As a consumer it is difficult to know which sites you can trust and which you need to be wary of. But various bodies, official and otherwise, are trying to find solutions to this to enable you, the consumer, to have confidence when you enter your details or trade online.

There are several different codes of conduct that businesses can sign up to and then show the code's logo on their site. The codes are similar to each other and are primarily concerned with security and privacy. The Office of Fair Trading (**www.oft.gov.uk**), has a list of the codes of practice that it has endorsed. It has also established a standard that sites can comply with, and a Trust UK logo for display by those that comply.

The code of practice that covers the greatest range of UK sites is the Which Webtrader code from the Consumers Association (**www.which.net**). To qualify as a Which Webtrader, the business has to satisfy the Association that it meets its criteria for security, privacy, quality, standards of delivery and so on. Unfortunately, doubts have been raised as to the checks that Which performs to ensure that the business is actually complying with the standards. Furthermore, it appears that there is little opportunity for redress if a site advertising the Webtrader marque fails to live up to the standards. The OFT states that if a consumer has a complaint with the site and the code of practice organisation fails to deal with it, the consumer can take the complaint directly to the OFT. But trying to get redress in this way is rarely a joyous experience, and threatening to take your case to BBC1's *Watchdog* or Radio 4's *You and Yours* may get you better results.

Enter Clicksure, **www.clicksure.com**. This UK company is aiming to regulate companies on the web in a proactive way by charging them around £5,000 to be a Clicksure member – provided they reach the required standards, again primarily in security and privacy, and provided they keep to those standards. The principle is that there is a high hurdle to become a Clicksure member, both in terms of the price and in terms of the standards, and so it will become known as a marque consumers can trust, which will keep sites wanting to stay members. The problem is that many online businesses are struggling to keep up with increasing orders or battle against technological difficulties and don't always find time to dot the 'i's and cross the 't's of security. As a result there are not a great many companies yet able to display the Clicksure marque; seven to be precise. You can therefore have great confidence in these exalted companies, whose ranks include **www.blackwells.com** (the bookshop) and **www.qxl.com**, the auction company. You can find the others listed on Clicksure's website.

Does this mean that you can't have confidence in any of the other millions of websites out there? Not necessarily. Firstly there is a US regulatory organisation, E-trust, which many US and some UK sites subscribe to; you can see details at the site **www.etrust.com**. Secondly, although only a very few sites meet the high standards of Clicksure, this does not mean that you should conclude that all other sites are there to rip you off or to give away, intentionally or unintentionally, your personal details. Nevertheless, if dealing with a site from an unfamiliar company it is wise to do some basic checks yourself before you order what may turn out to be non-existent goods, such as checking that the address of the physical company is listed. If there is a phone number you could try phoning it up to check it is real. If a site is the online branch of an offline organisation, these should be the first people you hassle if something goes wrong. Do not take excuses like 'the website is an entirely different branch of the organisation': somebody in the offline company will have responsibility. And above all remember that the old saying *caveat emptor*, buyer beware, applies in the online world just as much as it does in the offline.

Selected sites

Shopbots
www.shopsmart.com ❶❷❸❹
Quick and easy way to find the cheapest supplier on the web for a particular product, including the cost of delivery.

www.kelkoo.com ❶❷❸
A similar shopping bot.

Quick delivery sites
www.koobuycity.com ❶❷❸❹
Anything you like, delivered within two hours in London.

www.leapingsalmon.com ❶❷❸❹
Gorgeous meals ready for you to make up in an instant delivered the same day in London and overnight elsewhere.

Auction sites
www.ebay.co.uk ❶❷❸
Well-established American auction site. You are likely to encounter delivery problems if you buy from an international seller.

www.qxl.com ❶
Probably someone in Britan has managed to buy something from this site, but we haven't met them.

www.priceline.com ❶❷
Pioneer of reverse autions for consumers.

Homes

The internet is ideally suited to shaking up the UK property market because of the ability of search engines to sort housing information by price and area. But there are too many property listing sites in the UK, and none have enough accurate information for them to be a reliable search tool for housebuyers. The online property market is almost as fragmented as the offline one. The most positive development is that the internet is easing the process of private property sales, and this route can save individuals thousands of pounds in commission.

Online property services

On the perfect property site you could search for different kinds of property by area and price. You could specify details such as the number of bathrooms. Moreover you could ask the site to email you when something comes in that matches your requirements. In the US the industry association for estate agencies has set up **www.realtor.com**, which lists well over one million properties and claims to have on its site 95 per cent of properties that are for sale. Therefore buyers go straight to Realtor for research.

But in the UK the web is doing nothing about the fragmentation of the offline estate agency business (there are about 12,000 agencies nationwide), which means that it is still very hard to track down comprehensive and accurate information about properties in a particular area. With about 1.1m houses changing hands each year, there are some 250,000 properties on the market each quarter. Although there are dozens of property sites, none of them list enough properties to eliminate the tedious process of identifying and dealing with all the agents in the area where you are searching. (You can find them at **www.scoot.co.uk** and **www.upmystreet.co.uk**). You would not expect the websites of a chain such as Haart (**www.haart.co.uk**) to carry more than its own properties, but even the sites claiming to carry well over 100,000 properties from many agencies, such as **www.homemovers.co.uk**, **www.assertahome.com**, **www.080004homes.com**, **www.fish4homes.co.uk** and

'I don't see how all these sites can survive. We need two or three really comprehensive sites and the possibility of sharing data between sites.'

Hugh Dunsmore-Hardy, National Association of Estate Agents

82 THE INTERNET CONSUMER BIBLE

www.rightmove.co.uk, are patchy in their coverage. Before you use a site on an area you want to research, try it out where you live and see how good the results are.

Although some of the newer sites such as **www.assertahomes.com** and **www.080004homes.com** have good pictures and descriptions, others such as those on **www.Fish4homes.co.uk** are poor. The other problem is that estate agents appear to be even slacker about updating websites than they are about their own shop windows. In theory agents are able to upload fresh data on to sites on a daily basis. But several sites we examined had inaccurate information: prices had been reduced or the properties were under offer. On Fish4homes, for example, two properties we had identified as being for sale were actually under offer and the estate agent in question expected to use our enquiry to direct us to a completely different property. One south London agency said it was not bothering to update Homemovers because it was not producing many referrals. That may be due to the fact that Homemovers fails to offer a postcode search option in London.

'We tried hunting on the web, but it was hopeless.'

London property buyer

The top end of the market has been quite well served by **www.propertyfinder.co.uk** which had the most extensive listings of houses costing more than £100,000 – inevitably with a focus on London. However, this site was sold in the summer of 2000 to a consortium of estate agents who are planning to launch an as yet unnamed new site in early 2001, which will focus on expensive properties in central London.

There is general recognition that the current situation is serving neither agencies nor customers particularly well. Many of the current property sites are likely to disappear in a consolidation process that is already under way. Some chains of agents are linking up with financial services companies such as CGNU to form sites like **www.assertahome.com**, hoping to mop up much of the information from smaller agencies. This may put pressure on some of the weaker multiple listing sites. Meanwhile there are moves to set up a big UK property website called **www.askdaisy.com** modelled on Realtor in the US.

'Most agents only really have between ten and fifteen properties on their books. All the rest of the information is rubbish'.

Onepercent.co.uk

Private sales and low-cost agencies

On a more positive note, the net is helping people to sell their properties privately, thereby avoiding traditional estate agencies altogether. In the past, advertising a private sale was difficult because newspaper advertisements are expensive and ephemeral. But

> 'How do you finance not charging a fee for property services but also having enough money to build a national presence?'
>
> **Matthew Jackson, Homefreehome**

www.houseweb.co.uk offers a service where you can advertise your home on its site for £47 for a year. You post a picture of your house and describe the property yourself. If you manage to sell through this route (and thousands have) the savings are substantial compared with the 1.5 – 2 per cent commission charged by high street estate agencies. The number of private house sales, which currently account for about 5 per cent of the market, is growing rapidly.

Houseweb has various imitators such as **www.easier.co.uk** and **www.homefreehome.co.uk**. Easier makes no charge to vendors and makes its money through advertising on its site and by sending information about a wide variety of 'carefully selected' products to vendors. Traditional estate agents are not happy at this approach. According to Richard Crosthwaite at Knight Frank: 'When you put your property on the Easier site, they take a lot of personal details that they hand over to Scottish Widows – but they don't tell you that at the time.'

Another innovative site is **www.onepercent.co.uk**, which is a low-commission online agent. Onepercent is making full use of the web by providing several big pictures of its properties and detailed floor plans. However, a year after launch it has only fifty-five properties on its books. A company called **www.propwatch.com** has started an online property auction service. An auction also cuts out the agent entirely, but the usefulness of the service depends on attracting a good number of bidders.

To DIY or not to DIY

Once you have bought your property, the web offers a useful range of information about DIY and property maintenance. Most of the sites are linked to suppliers of tools, materials or DIY chains. On sites such as **www.diyfixit.co.uk** you choose which room you want to work on, and then you pick from detailed indexes of tasks. This works well if you want to remind yourself how to renew the sealing around your bath. Checking this online will be cheaper than buying a DIY manual – and you can choose to ignore the product promotion.

If you don't feel up to the more advanced tasks explained online, some sites are addressing the old problem of trying to find a reliable (and available) tradesman to unblock your toilet or rewire your kitchen. For example, **www.improveline.com** is a Kingfisher-backed site that attempts to match your requirements (you provide details of the job) with three suitable contractors who are available and who then provide quotes. Improveline claims it has vetted all the 90,000 tradesmen on its books – but it is not nearly as rigorous in its use of references as a smaller company, **www.homepro.com**. Homepro offers a free insurance scheme to protect you if the tradesman goes out of business during the job, and will provide a conciliation service if you are not happy with the work. But Homepro is currently restricted to the south-east of the UK.

There are also some practical tools available online. Many of the DIY sites offer calculators that work out how much paper or paint you need to decorate a room.

Some sites also offer design facilities. For example, on **www.dulux.co.uk** you can try out various colours schemes in different model rooms, although the extent to which this will be helpful will depend on the quality of the colours on your computer screen.

In terms of furnishing, there are almost as many websites as there are shops. And in many areas there are significant disadvantages to shopping online. Even if your sofa is cheaper, it may not be comfy. A good place to start to hunt for specialist websites is **www.shopsmart.co.uk**. For products that are more exactly specifiable, such as white goods, the price comparison features of the net come into their own. You can check out which kind of fridge you like in a traditional store, and then hunt for the best price on the net using a price comparison tool or shopbot (see page 76) The three best sites for price comparison software are **www.shopsmart.com**, **www.kelkoo.com** and **www.value-dirrect.co.uk**.

Utilities online

If you're tired of well-dressed gentlemen interrupting your supper trying to convince you to move one or more of your utilities services to a cheaper supplier, you can trump them all by arranging this on the internet. There are a variety of sites such as **www.buy.co.uk** that will analyse your utility bills and tell you whether you could save money by switching to another supplier or by bundling the utilities up in a package. The advantages of this approach are that you could have one account covering several utilities, and save money. One of the best sites offering this service is **www.servista.com**, which explains its package clearly. Servista offers an electricity, gas and telecoms deal and will shortly add mobiles, ADSL and internet access. Other sites offering a similar approach include **www.kura.co.uk**, **www.ukenergy.co.uk** and **www.power-brokers.com**. However, there may be disadvantages to combining your telephone account with other utilities; and you should also check the small print covering maintenance arrangements and check to see if there any penalties if you move suppliers.

One website claims to offer a solution to the problem of comparing all the different packages of phone services now on the market. **www.phonebills.org.uk** holds the prices of nine big telephone companies, and you can see whether you could save money by switching. To be really useful, the information on a site like this ought to be up to date. But when we examined the information on offer, it was four months old.

Finally, for those who like art but haven't got time to get out to galleries, there are several online galleries such as **www.artrepublic.com/search.asp**. Depending on the kind of art you like, you can get a good idea of what is showing in a gallery before you go to the trouble of visiting. The net also enables artists to set up their own sites and sell direct (thereby avoiding the huge commissions charged by commercial galleries). You may or may not be confident enough about your artistic judgement to buy a painting without having seen it in person.

Selected Sites

Online Property Listings
www.houseweb.co.uk ❂❂❂❂
Innovator in private sales market.

www.easier.co.uk ❂❂
Free for advertisers, but controversial use of data according to competitors.

www.homefreehome. ❂❂❂
Free for advertisers.

www.ukpropertysales.com ❂❂❂
More expensive private sales site.

www.assertahome.com ❂❂❂
CGNU-funded site, good design with 200,000 properties.

www.080004homes.com ❂❂❂
Claims 170,000 properties; rated highly by some, but search engines did not always work.

www.homepages.co.uk ❂❂
Claims 62,000 properties, but patchy coverage. From Moneyextra stable.

www.homes-on-line.co.uk ❂❂❂
Portal-style site that also offers a selection of houses, but it is hard to see how deep the pool of properties is.

www.rightmove.co.uk ❂❂❂
Halifax-sponsored site; good navigation and easy search.

www.smartestates.com ❂❂
Claims 50,000 houses in UK, also has foreign properties.

www.findaproperty.com ✿✿✿
Bias towards London; good search facilities.

www.propertyfinder.co.uk ✿✿✿
Lists 43,000 properties but concentrates on more expensive properties in UK and abroad. Is likely to be superseded by new site in 2001, concentrating on top range houses in London.

www.onepercent.co.uk ✿✿✿
Online agency (as opposed to listings site). Specialises in London and commission is limited to 1 per cent. Great pictures and floor plans. But very few properties. Site to watch.

www.home.co.uk ✿✿✿
Claims almost 200,000 listings.

www.ukpg.co.uk ✿✿✿
Claims 40,000 listings; close links with housebuilders.

www.homemovers.co.uk ✿✿
200,000 properties but poor search facilities and out-of-date information.

www.fish4homes.co.uk ✿✿
180,000 properties, but coverage patchy; poor pictures or no pictures; information out-of-date. Lacks detailed search in urban areas.

www.linkprop.co.uk ✿✿
Site of Link-up Properties: semi-online agency with low commission, but few properties.

www.completehousebuyer.co.uk ✿✿
Another property search engine.

www.askdaisy.co.uk
Ambitious new site due for imminent launch.

www.home-repo.org ✿✿✿
Covers issues related to repossession.

www.homecheck.co.uk ✿✿✿
New site that provides useful information to house buyers. For example, whether a house might be at risk from flooding.

Rental/ International property

www.globalresident.com
Central London flats to rent, but thin on detail.

www.gonative.co.uk ✿✿✿
Upmarket houses and flats to rent in London for visitors.

www.letonthenet.com ✿✿
Claims 3,000 properties to let in UK, but coverage thin.

www.loot.co.uk ✿✿✿
Online listings of rental options.

www.ired.com ✿✿✿
Huge directory of online property companies around the world; but not all links are up to date.

www.hagglepages.com ✪✪✪
Site claims Figet commission on house sales down to 1.5 per cent by putting out the sale to tender to several agents offering similar service for convergancing and surveys. But the cheapest provider may not necessarily be the best.

DIY

www.homebase.co.uk ✪✪✪
Clear site. Delivery takes up to three days and costs £5 during the day and £6.50 in the evenings or Saturday morning i.e. when most people want it.

www.diy.com ✪✪
B&Q site. Navigation rather strange; we could not find the checkout. Not even sure there was one. Site designed to provide information rather than e-commerce. Delivery from stores costs £10 up to five miles. More for heavy goods or greater distance.

www.homecentral.com ✪✪✪
US DIY site; advice on a huge range of jobs.

www.diyfixit.co.uk ✪✪✪
Useful source of DIY tips; site supported by heavy product advertising.

www.homepro.com ✪✪✪
Source of vetted contractors.

www.improveline.com ✪✪✪
Kingfisher-backed site that vets contractors. Claims to have vetted 90,000.

www.Learn2.com ✪
US site that covers everything from writing a CV to planting a tree; but when we tested the site it was not working.

Gardening

Even if you don't have room for the Hanging Gardens of Babylon on your patio, you can find pretty much all you need to know about gardening on the internet. Such is the wealth of gardening websites that there's even a book dedicated to the subject – as if there weren't enough books on gardening already.

The internet is particularly well suited to sorting through the reams of information about plants and the rich loam of comment from celebrity gardeners on everything from black spot to bumpy lawns. You can also tinker with garden designs online and exchange ideas with other greenfingered types. These features may be particularly useful for those without a friendly garden centre. Virtually all gardening-related products are available online, although the net really comes into its own for large orders, rare plants or humble seeds. For more basic plants, you may get better value from a local garden centre.

The global garden

A big gardening website is a cross between a magazine, an encyclopaedia and a radio programme such as *Gardeners' Question Time*. For example, if you are unsure what kind of clematis you should buy you can examine the available varieties and compare pictures and climatic/soil requirements. Alternatively, you can check how to care for an existing plant. The most ambitious sites such as **www.garden.com** and **www.vg.com** are US-based, but there is still plenty of useful information for UK gardeners (just ignore the advice about the climate in Arizona); and UK sites such as **www.greenfingers.com** and **www.e-garden.co.uk** are starting to rival their US peers in content.

The UK sites are more likely to contain seasonal tips relevant to a UK browser, and most have a line-up of expert gardeners to answer typical problems. So you might find a range of suggestions about what to do about moles under your lawn. The BBC gardening site **www.bbc.co.uk/gardening** (which is distinct from the *Gardeners' Question Time* site **www.gardenersworld.beeb.com**) has a good section on pests that covers everything from cuckoo spit and frog hoppers to nuisance cats (they suggest using curry powder as a deterrent). Choosing between celebrity gardeners is a matter of personal taste: for example, **www.expertgardener.com** has Charlie Dimmock.

Gardening websites offer two ways of solving individual problems not covered by the general advice published on their sites. Some (such as Greenfingers) offer the possibility of emailing questions to an expert for reply within 48 hours (at no charge). But others (such as the BBC) just select the most interesting questions for inclusion on the website – so you might not get any kind of reply. The other option is to post your problem on a message board or join a forum and wait for other gardeners to comment. Most gardeners are fairly generous with their expertise, and answers seem to pop up quickly on sites such as the BBC's. Another site with good forums is **www.gardenweb.com**. Although this started out as a US site, there are now forums for most European countries covering a huge range of topics. It also has a service that links gardeners wanting to exchange seeds or plants.

Some of the garden sites have particularly useful features. For example, **www.vg.com** has its own search engine ('dig the net'), which comes up with links with other sites that cover specific gardening topics. A common feature is a Latin translator (see for instance, **www.e-garden.com**), which renders the common name of a plant into Latin (or vice versa).

If browsing on the web leads you to rare or exotic plants that you cannot buy from your garden centre, the Royal Horticultural Society (**www.rhs.org.uk**) provides a facility for you to find the nearest supplier for any one of the 70,000 plants on its database. The BBC's *Gardeners' Question Time* site offers a plant search engine that is supposed to match plants to the soil and light conditions of your garden. But this option is either underpowered or unreliable or both. Oxalis (**www.oxalis.co.uk**) posts a chart illustrating the conditions needed by each plant. However, it's worth remembering that you may find better advice about specific plants more easily from an online nursery or a specialist retailer than from a generalist site.

Traditional gardeners might scoff, but several sites offer rudimentary screen-based 'design' facilities, usually in the form of a range of prepared garden plans. The biggest range is at **www.garden.com**, which covers options from a 'deer-resistant' garden through to a 'humming bird' garden; the site also offers free garden design software for downloading. UK sites like the BBC's tend to have fewer of these sorts of options, although some of the specialist nurseries such as **www.classicroses.co.uk** let you order a rose garden design online. Some sites are specifically focused on design. For example, **www.dreamgardens.co.uk** sells detailed plans for garden beds for £25.

Garden visits

If you are more interested in visiting other people's gardens than doing the work yourself, several websites pull together information about gardens that are open to the public. For example, the Royal Horticultural Society (**www.rhs.org.uk**) has a listing, and details of 3,000 annual events, shows, walks and talks. You can search by geographical area or garden name, which may be useful if you have a trip coming up and you want to know what might be open in the area or *en route*. Other good sources of gardens to visit include the National Gardens Scheme (**www.ngs.org.uk** – with particularly good search software) and the National Trust (**www.nationaltrust.org.uk**).

Some of the most famous gardens such as Kew have their own websites. Kew's site includes visitor information and detailed information about the collection and also access to botanical research (**www.rbgkew.org**). You can also check what is coming up on radio and TV both on the BBC's site and on sites such as **www.greenfingers.com**. However, you may need to check several sites to get a complete picture of forthcoming events. For example, we found details of a potato extravaganza at an organic garden on Greenfingers that was not included on the RHS site.

Online purchasing

You can buy virtually anything for the garden online: from sheds and barbeques down to seeds. The net allows more imaginative presentation of plants and seeds than traditional mail order catalogues. Generalist sites have a wide range of goods but for depth in a particular area – say, irises – you might have to go to a specialist nursery. However, some nurseries have under-powered websites and you may have to be patient for the beautiful pictures to load.

It's worth checking delivery charges carefully when placing an order because some sites have a unit-based approach and others make it much cheaper to buy in quantity. Typical charges range from £3 for a rose bush to £10 for a tree. Whether this represents value would depend on the plant and individual circumstances. Postage for seeds is generally free with orders over about £3. While the net is particularly good for tracking down rarer plants (from the RHS site), hunting for value is more time-consuming. The *Gardeners' Question Time* site has comparison software which supposedly allows you to compare nurseries for unit/total price or delivery time, but unfortunately it is unreliable. For common plants, your local garden centre is probably a better bet.

In case you are worried that a plant might arrive in poor condition, some sites offer plant 'guarantees' – for example, **www.classicroses.co.uk** replaces roses up to a year after sale if they fail to flourish. The RHS says it does random tests of suppliers on its e-commerce site **www.grogro.com** (which specialises in rarer plants) and it only uses nurseries that come up to scratch. Like any other area of e-commerce, you have to consider whether a company with a long track record in mail order (such as Thompson & Morgan) is likely to provide a more reliable service than a web start-up.

Selected sites

General UK sites
www.greenfingers.co.uk ✪✪✪✪
The most ambitious UK gardening site.

www.gardenersworld.beeb.com ✪✪✪
Some good content but plant selector and value search engines are unreliable.

www.e-garden.co.uk ✪✪✪
Generalist site with some useful links.

www.expertgardener.com ✪✪✪
Magazine site featuring Charlie Dimmock.

www.oxalis.co.uk ✪✪✪
Good links to specialist nurseries and garden centres.

www.gardenworld.co.uk ✪✪✪✪
Very useful site that finds your nearest local garden centre and what you can buy there.

www.which.net
Access to *Which?* gardening articles – but for subscribers only.

US sites
www.garden.com ✪✪✪✪✪
Huge US site, although not all information relevant to UK.

www.vg.com ✪✪✪✪✪
Useful US-based gardening search engine.

www.gardentown.com ✪✪✪
Some useful plant information and access to forums.

www.gardenweb.com ✪✪✪✪
Best source of gardening forums.

Visiting gardens
www.rhs.org.uk ✪✪✪✪✪
Royal Horticultural Society: searchable information on gardens, events and the annual shows; also invaluable plant finder service.

www.rbgkew.org.uk ✪✪✪
Visitor information as well as research facilities for botanists.

www.ngs.org.uk ○○○○
'Yellow book' of gardens online. Good search facilities.

www.nationaltrust.org.uk ○○○
Information about National Trust properties.

Specialist sites and e-commerce
www.thompson-morgan.com ○○○○
Vast range of seeds and information. Navigation is sometimes odd. Links to other suppliers and specialist gardening websites.

www.suttons.co.uk ○○
Long-established seed company.

www.unwins-seeds.co.uk ○○○
(Not to be confused with the off-licence chain at **www.unwins.co.uk**.) Site is as cheerful as the company's packets of seeds.

www.flowers.org.uk ○○
Cut flowers and florist information, but patchy coverage.

www.firstflowers.com ○○○
Bouquets from £14.99.

www.shrubsdirect.com ○○○
Shrubs from Grasslands Nursery in Cheshire.

www.nickys-nursery.co.uk ○○○
Seeds and plants. Brash approach.

www.chilternseeds.co.uk ○○○
Postage is 60p up to £15, free thereafter.

www.classicroses.co.uk ○○○
Some of the beautiful pictures take ages to load.

www.roses.co.uk ○○○
Harkness Roses site.

www.grogro.com ○○○
New site from RHS and EMAP. Good for books and some rare plants but selection is currently restricted. Site to watch.

Cars

It might seem perverse to buy something over the internet which you want to test-drive, and since a car is such a major purchase, people are understandably nervous about transacting online with a dealer they haven't met. On the other hand, if you have already chosen your perfect car, there is no reason not to buy it online. New cars are generally ordered from the manufacturer, so even if you buy from a traditional dealer, you do not see the actual car that you are buying before it is delivered to your door. And you may well find that you can buy a new car for the best price from an online site. Only a few websites enable you to buy the car online: on many sites you still need to telephone the company or visit it in person. But you can use the internet to organise the purchase of an imported car, although now that manufacturers have reduced their prices in the UK, this will not save you as much as it used to.

You are far more likely to consider buying a new car without seeing it than a second-hand car. Until we follow the US and introduce a system whereby an organisation like the AA vets a used car and promises a money-back guarantee in the event of problems, this is unlikely to change. As people in the industry say, the internet is unlikely to be used for buying second-hand cars because you want to 'kick the tyres'.

The internet is very useful for researching both new and second-hand cars. Not only can you read a range of reviews on a make and model you are interested in, but you can also find out the different prices and stock levels at dealers around the country. You can search for private sales and find out the prices you should be paying. That's the good news. The bad news is that as yet you are unlikely to find comprehensive listings for either new or used cars on any single site. Moreover, sites which that connect you to dealers by sending them emails are not as useful now as they might become, because often the dealers do not respond.

A great advantage of using the internet to research or buy a car is that you avoid meeting car dealers, with their well-known hard-selling tactics. And **www.virgincars.com** offers a price guarantee – that everyone pays the same price for exactly the same model of a new car thereby trying to dispel some of the industry's reputation for sharp practice.

But beware – although you will be covered by a manufacturer's warranty in just the same way as if you bought the car from an offline dealer, the fact that you did not buy the car from a dealer or manufactuer in person may mean that they feel less obliged to you and so are less helpful if something goes wrong.

Import a car using the internet, if you think it is worth it

Before the turn of the century it seemed that the internet was going to be a fantastic resource to enable you to buy an imported car easily, and so avoid the UK's high prices and save thousands of pounds. But then the car manufacturers started dropping their prices – partly in response to competition from the internet, partly because of government pressure, and partly because consumers stopped buying cars in the expectation that prices would fall. It is still cheaper to buy an imported new car than a UK-supplied new car, but the gap has shrunk. In order for the process to be worth the trouble, your chosen car would probably have to be an expensive one. The savings on a £10,000 car might amount to about £700, whereas the figure will climb to about £1,500–£2,000 on a car costing £20,000, according to a salesman from D. C. Cook. In the past it could have been double this.

There are four key disadvantages in buying an imported car:

- Delivery usually takes significantly longer – sometimes twice as long (five months)

- Most cars from the Continent come with only a one-year warranty rather than the three-year package now common in the UK

- An imported car may have fewer features fitted as standard. This means that when you are comparing prices you need to be very careful that you are comparing like with like. For example, the 8 per cent difference on Oneswoop, **www.oneswoop.com** between the EU and UK price list of a Mercedes CL 500 was reduced to only 3 per cent after on-the-road charges were included. There are many variable features on cars, and the search mechanisms on car sites do not all go into the same level of detail. So it can be difficult to ensure that you are looking at the prices for exactly the same Renault Mégane coupé

'If you buy a car via an online agent and there is a problem, you may find that everyone tries to blame everyone else. With cars bought direct from a dealer there are fewer companies involved so it is either the dealer's or the manufacturer's fault if there is a problem. Also whilst a car bought from the likes of Oneswoop is covered by a manufacturer's warranty and in theory you can take it to any dealer for after-sales care, in reality your local dealer may not be as helpful if you didn't buy the car from him. Virgin seems to be trying to get round this by putting people who have bought imported cars in touch with designated local dealers for after-sales care.'

Liat Joshi, Consultant

CARS **95**

- UK dealers often offer cashback, 0 per cent finance, 'final payment financing' or free insurance, which foreign dealers tend not to do. Haggling with UK dealers can often get the effective price down to near-Continental levels.

If you are still interested in importing, there are hundreds of sites to help you. Two of the most high-profile are **www.virgincars.com** and **www.oneswoop.com**. But some observers question how long these companies will continue specialising in importing now that UK prices have come down so much.

Compare prices quickly

The internet enables you to compare prices for cars from a range of car sellers and find the nearest dealer to you who stocks the car you are interested in. But remember, as we said above, that although you can compare prices quickly, they are not always accurate, because different features may be fitted as standard. Try to be sure that you are comparing like with like. First stop is **www.autobytel.co.uk**. Although this is not the easiest site to navigate around, we have found it the most comprehensive. However, you can't buy a car on the autobytel site: you still need to telephone, and probably visit, a dealer. Some manufacturers (such as **www.renault.co.uk** and **www.ford.co.uk**) are also getting into the matchmaking game – matching you with your dream car. But of course they will only offer you their own brands and their tied dealers to sell it to you.

You will want to cover the full range of options so you should probably visit the websites of the huge out-of-town sites known as car supermarkets, such as the Slough-based car supermarket Trade Sales, at **www.trade-sales.co.uk**, and the Derby-based Motorpoint, at **www.motorpoint.co.uk**. You should also look at the offerings of internet-only businesses such as Direct Line's **www.jamjar.com**, or **www.virgincars.com**. Then you can compare these with the offerings from car manufacturers, such as **www.toyota.co.uk**, **www.vauxhall.co.uk** and with dealers' prices, such as **www.dccook.co.uk**, and **www.network-q.co.uk**.

Even after all this research, you are still unlikely to have comprehensively covered all the possible places to buy your new car. The information about tied dealers on the internet is far more sophisticated than that from independent dealers, many of whom are still struggling to put up sites. At the time of writing there is no single site that pulls together all the information covering both the tied and independent dealers. Moreover, we found that dealers frequently did not respond to emails. Many independent dealers do not even have email facilities.

Break dealers' ties

Currently, dealers in new cars are tied to a single brand or a small number of brands, whereas car supermarkets and websites such as **www.jamjar.com** offer the full range of brands by having links with multiple dealerships, giving you more choice from a single port of call. This situation could change even more dramatically if the government enforces a waiving of 'block exemption' (expected in 2002) which ties dealers, because this could enable somebody such as Tesco or a new dot.com company to enter the market and sell a complete range of brands cheaply.

Finance

Almost all the major car sites on the internet offer financing, as do all the major offline companies. There is no evidence that you can get a better deal on the internet than you can off it, but there is the advantage that dealers are tied to certain finance providers whereas most websites have a number of partners, making them more impartial. For an explanation of the range of financing options, see the website **www.fffdirect.co.uk**. Remember that whether you are buying the car online or offline, from a dealer or manufacturer, companies do not tend to offer you something for nothing – 0 per cent finance usually just means the company is clawing the money back from you on something else.

The internet is not yet proving very helpful with regard to insurance. For this, see Money.

Second-hand and classic cars

You would have to be extremely trusting (or indeed mad), to buy a second-hand car without having seen it, and with no money-back guarantee from a reputable organisation. But although this would stop you buying a second-hand car over the internet, the net is a great research tool for working out the best options and searching for cars that are for sale.

The sites for car magazines such as **www.whatcar.com** and **www.topgear.com** have an archive of reviews of cars to help you work out the best car for you. And you can peruse the online versions of Parker's price guide at **www.classiccarsworld.co.uk**, without being under the baleful eye of your newsagent if you should find yourself looking at the magazine quickly in the shop without actually purchasing it, as we have heard has happened very occasionally.

Not only can you search for second-hand or classic cars through online magazines such as **www.autotrader.co.uk**, **www.loot.co.uk** and **www.classicmotor.co.uk**, but you can also link up with other people who own the same type of car, see the photographs of their restoration projects, find out about the problems associated with particular models and even find a wealth of advice taking you through the process of how to fix your classic car. The magazine site **www.classicmotor.co.uk** has a huge number of links and is a good place to start or try the direct approach at, for example, **www.triumphspitfire.com** or **www.mgcars.org.uk/midgetspriteclub/** for events, news and features on Midgets or Sprites.

Selected sites

Online magazines
www.whatcar.com ✪✪✪✪
Excellent coverage of a huge range of subjects about cars. Substantial archive of car reviews in this busy site.

www.topgear.com ✪✪✪✪
Car reviews, price guides, news and views about cars.

Price guide
www.classiccarsworld.co.uk ✪✪✪✪✪
Clear and simple site giving instant price information from Parker's price guide. Produces mileage-adjusted prices and a price-range showing whether the deal is good, fair, or extremely good.

www.parkers.co.uk ✪
A minimal site with no information from the magazine, only a plea to subscribe.

Dealers
www.network-q.co.uk ✪✪✪✪
Good simple site showing stock and prices for all Netwok Q dealers.

www.lancasterplc.com ✪✪
Flashy, fussy site which is slow to load. Details of new car prices and contact details for dealers.

Intermediaries
www.jamjar.com ✪✪✪✪✪
Highly professional site offering all car services. Very easy to navigate and very specific search facility.

www.virgincars.com ✪✪✪✪
Usual Virgin-style with good search facility for a range of cars. Price promise guarantee that the same specification car is always sold at the same price.

www.oneswoop.com ✪✪✪
Clear site specialising in imported cars. Limited brands of cars.

Matchmakers

www.autobytel.co.uk ❂❂❂

Good clear site which finds the car you are searching for near you, and then acts as your intermediary.

www.autolocate.co.uk ❂❂

This site only lists the dealers near you; no stock or price information.

Manufacturers' sites

www.ford.co.uk ❂❂❂

Professional site letting you search the Ford range of new and used cars in national stock (with price on request only) and connecting you to the minimal sites of Ford dealers.

www.toyota.co.uk ❂❂

Pictures and details of the Toyota range with contact details of your local dealer.

www.vauxhall.co.uk ❂❂

Pictures of Vauxhall's new cars. Connects to Network Q's website for used cars.

www.peugeot.co.uk ❂❂❂❂

Good listing of used cars near you ranked by price. Contact details for dealers.

www.peugeot.com ❂❂

Nice for reading about Peugeot's cars, if you like to read about French car chic in French.

www.renault.co.uk ❂

Further propaganda that with the Clio less is more, and with the Mégane you stay beautiful. Telephone number and address of your nearest dealer.

www.vw.co.uk ❂❂❂

Lets you search for used cars in any of VW's dealers local to you. **www.vw.com**, the US site, has some spiffy animations, but they require patience.

www.rover.co.uk ❂❂

Classy site, but requires patience because weighed down by clever software. If you can be bothered to download extra software you can take a virtual tour.

Classic cars

www.classic-car-directory.com ❂❂❂❂

Sales, parts, price guide on this very easily searchable and comprehensive site.

www.classicmotor.co.uk ❂❂❂❂

News, events, articles, classified ads and a fantastic number of links to classic car sites all over the world.

www.triumphspitfire.com ❂❂❂❂

Great American site, celebrating this 'under-appreciated' little British sports car. Recent classified ads from all over the world.

www.mgcars.org.uk ❂❂❂❂

Can be difficult to find your way around and slow to load, but rewarding site with a great deal of information, links and events.

Clothes

The internet provides a hassle-free way of buying clothes that you already know will fit you such as repeat purchases of shirts for men and women. There are many good and reliable sites to choose from. Some of them have even been known to deliver to your office within two hours, although sites like that (**www.dressmart.com**) tend to go bust at an alarming rate!

The only high-street shops that have moved on to the internet effectively are those that previously had a mail-order catalogue business, because buying on the internet is very similar – it is convenient, but you don't know exactly what you are getting until it arrives. For real adventures in not having a clue what you are going to get, the internet enables you to look at the clothes in shops on the other side of the world. Either way, you should not generally expect clothes to be cheaper on the net – the online providers are too concerned to keep their offline shops in business to do that – unless you look at aggregators or online-only catalogues.

There is technology that allows internet sites to give you a virtual view of yourself wearing clothes you are considering buying, but it is too slow on most machines to be acceptable. Until it is much faster, it will be tricky to sell non-repeat clothing purchases on the internet because, fundamentally, you can't be sure they will fit.

Portals

There are lots of American portals on the net, such as **www.fashionmall.com**, **www.fashion.net** and the site with a huge number of listings, **www.dmoz.org**. These are less relevant to the UK consumer than our home-bred portals, such as the *Guardian*'s at **www.shoppingunlimited.co.uk** or **www.topoftheshops.co.uk** or **www.thebestofbritish.com/shops/fashion** or UK Yahoo's shopping section, **www.uk.shopping.yahoo.com/clothing**. The problem with all of these portals is that they recommend very few shops, particularly surprising in Yahoo's case since it normally lists enormous amounts of everything. So you may be better off looking directly at shops' sites.

High-street shops

Next, at **www.next.co.uk**, claims to have been the biggest UK high-street clothing retailer on the net for the year 1999 in terms of sales. This business is run on the back of Next Directory, a long-running catalogue business. It has a good clear site with next-day delivery for £2.50, and free returns by post or to any Next shop. It has all the Next stock on the site (with some items previewed before they arrive in shops) for exactly the same price as you can buy them in the shops.

The equivalent of a bricks and mortar shopping centre is **www.zoom.co.uk**, the online arm of Arcadia, the shopping giant which owns Burton (**www.burtonmenswear.co.uk**), Topshop (**www.tops.co.uk**), Topman (**www.topman.co.uk**) Dorothy Perkins (**www.dorothyperkins.co.uk**), Evans (**www.evans.ltd.uk**), Principles (**www.principles.co.uk**), and catalogue retailers **www.landsend.co.uk**, **www.hawkshead.co.uk** and **www.racinggreen.co.uk**.

All of these are very good sites (although it is difficult to order from Dorothy Perkins without having its catalogue) and all use Arcadia's central delivery system. This means that next-day delivery is standard, although prices do vary (Evans is the cheapest at £1.95) and unfortunately they have not linked up the shops, so you cannot combine a shirt from Topman and a shirt from Burton in the same delivery.

Other major high-street shops have either only just launched websites or are just about to. Marks & Spencer is just getting going online at **www.marks-and-spencer.co.uk**. It is a reasonable site, and if items do not fit they can be returned to a store. Marks believes its site could be very successful because customers know what they are getting with their clothes, although their recent fall from grace may undermine this.

Laura Ashley is supposed to be launching **www.lauraashley.com** at the end of 2000, and Gap UK hopes to get its act together sometime in 2001 to enable you to buy their clothes from this country rather than just from the States.

Beware Gap's website, **www.gap.com**, however. While you can browse through the selection in order to see what is in the shops at the moment, you will be very disappointed if you try to buy. The site lets you go through the whole process and only then informs you that you can buy only if you are in America. The shops in the UK are very apologetic about this and explain that they do offer a service where you can order clothes over the telephone from a shop and they will deliver it to you for a mere £4.50 – hardly the height of efficient e-commerce.

Can I get top designer brands at low prices?

The short answer is yes, sometimes. In the offline real world there are things called factory outlet shops. These are often in fact a set of shops in a kind of mall, such as at Bicester Village, **www.bicestervillage.com**, in which last season's clothes from a range of designer brands are sold at half price. There are a few of these aggregators on the internet, but they do not stock all the brands you might want. Probably the best is **www.haburi.com**, launched in mid 2000, where you can find a range of brands at good prices. Also good is **www.designerdiscount.co.uk**, which has good offers on a small range of brands. The good site of **www.ready2shop.com** does not offer you brands at cheap prices but does take you through a range of different brands and tries to mix and match to suit the style you specify.

Don't be fooled by the brilliant-looking **www.fashionbrokers.com** – it is an American site and does no international orders.

Otherwise you can also try **www.bestofbritish.com**, and the catalogue sites **www.freemans.co.uk** and **www.kaysnet.com**, where you can find everything from Levi's jeans, Boxfresh underwear and many more. But you are very unlikely to find brands that have their own shops, such as Next, Laura Ashley or Karen Millen (due to set up a site in 2001), taking part in these arrangements. So your best chance of finding these clothes online at good prices is through special offers on their sites, when they have them.

Suits you, Sir

Do you want to buy your work or casual shirts over the internet? Do you know your neck size? Then it's easy. There are a bunch of sites that are easy to use and reliable. Choose from brands like **www.thomaspink.com**, and Charles Tyrwhitt at **www.ctshirts.co.uk**, **www.coles-shirtmakers.com**, or **www.shirt-press.co.uk** for the miracle of shirts that don't need to be ironed. The site **www.cafecoton.co.uk** provides French-style cotton shirts, and you can visit the shops on **www.jermynstreet.com**. But don't expect prices to be cheaper than in the shops.

Some well-established shops selling tailor-made suits are getting online too. James & James of Savile Row have launched their online operation, **www.jamesjames.co.uk**, and while the site is primarily intended to bring customers into the shop, it is perfectly equipped to make a suit for you solely on the basis of the measurements you type in. Such tailors have a tradition of using a self-assessment form to make up suits in the absence of the customer, meaning that they know what they are doing by using the internet in this way, so you can be confident of a good result. The shop is well-placed to make up suits for men in New York or in Newmarket.

Underwear

The privacy of the internet suits underwear sales, whether sexy or sleepy, provided you feel confident that the item will fit, or that you can return it. Perhaps the best UK underwear site on the web is **www.easyshop.com**, a very well laid-out site with a great range and an excellent returns policy. This business has established a good reputation as an internet-only underwear shop and sports an increasing number of brands. Others to try are **www.mapledrive.com**, which has a substantial range of underwear for women and offers with special tips for 'our gentlemen customers' and **www.ishop.co.uk**, which sells a curious range of lingerie, not quite all of which is male rubber playsuits.

Alternatively, if you know and like a particular underwear brand, you can try going direct to the company's site. More of these are putting some of their business on the web every month – they are happy to do so because most of them do not have their own offline shops. So, for example, the Gossard site (**www.gossard.co.uk**) is very good in terms of special offers, although it is hard to tell what the fabric of the underwear is like.

Design your own clothes

There are as yet only a few sites offering to let you design your own clothes, partly because the sophisticated technology needed slows down sites so much that customers get too bored to carry on, and partly because in general you and I do not design clothes very well. If we did, we would probably be clothes designers. So it is not a great business idea to have a site that lets you create your designs and then finds them all returned for refunds because when the clothes arrive they look like a ghastly mistake.

However, some people are trying it. Perhaps the best site is **www.ic3d.com** (get it?) which has you model the shape of an item of clothing you want and choose from a choice of over a hundred fabrics. So if you really want a purple suede bustier you can have one. But don't blame us if you don't like it when it arrives.

'We recently had a wine-maker from Waga Waga in Australia log on to the site, put in his measurements and we had the suit ready for him, in case he needed final fittings, when he dropped into London for a two-day conference. The system we have is very high-tech. The measurements the customer puts in are sent automatically to the factory in France, where a machine cuts the fabric with laser beams according to the exact measurements required.'

Eric James of James & James.

Or you could try **www.hatsrus.com** which is a specialised hat shop coming soon, from New York.

Shops around the world

You can easily access hundreds of American shops from the American portals listed above, but you can end up paying a lot for delivery, and sometimes the site will not even tell you how much until you receive an invoice. You can also look at shops in more exotic places – such as silk shops in China or cotton from India. It is possible to see some fantastic fabrics and designs, but the prices are often high and you cannot be sure that you will get what you ordered. Whatever your query is, **www.yahoo.com** is a good starting place.

For exotic silks, a couple of good places to start are **www.chinasilk-info.com** and **www.thailanddutyfreeshop.com**. The latter offers free shipping to anywhere in the world, but are quite high prices.

The future is bright – the future is body-mapping

There is potentially a great future for internet clothing shopping when body-mapping or an equivalent technology takes off. This will enable a scanner to make a virtual model of your body. This will not just measure your arm length, waist, etc., but will also take note of the configuration of your body – the slope of your shoulders, the curve of your back, and so on. With this information a 'virtual you' can be created, and virtual clothes put on to see which ones will suit the real you. This could revolutionise shopping; but it is still a few years off.

We can expect broadband (see Getting Started) to arrive before body-mapping does. This will enable huge volumes of data to be transmitted very fast, and enable the use of clever 3D graphics, thereby making the experience of buying clothes on the internet more interactive and interesting.

Selected Sites

Underwear
www.easyshop ○○○○○
Great site with lots of ranges and lots of tips.

www.joeboxer.co.uk ○○○○
Great, clear site, although with a smaller range than you might expect.

www.gossard.co.uk ○○○○
Re-modelling itself as the 'brand with attitude', Gossard brings you a good range on its site and easy navigation through it.

High Street
www.next.co.uk ○○○○
A good site with more clothes put up every month.

www.marks-and-spencer.co.uk ○○○
Well laid-out site with a big range of clothes as well as foodstuffs and home furnishings.

www.dorothyperkins.co.uk ○○
Unclear site. Easy to shop here if you have the Dorthy Perkins catalogue, difficult if not.

www.principles.co.uk ○○○
Easy to navigate site, with decent photos of the clothes. Searchable by type of clothes.

www.tops.co.uk ○○○ (Topshop)
Good-looking site at first, then becomes rather less chic as it uses the same design as the Evans site.

www.evans.ltd.uk ○○○
Good clear site, although with cranky design further in. Cheap postage and packing at £1.95.

www.lauraashley.com
Due to launch an online shopping site at end 2000.

www.topman.co.uk ○○○
Fine if you want to look at clothes modelled by something out of Thunderbirds.

www.burtonmenswear.co.uk ○○○
Decent site with good pictures.

Catalogue
www.hawkshead.com ○○○○
Very clear and easy to navigate site with good pics, recommendations and special offers.

www.landsend.co.uk ○○○○
Easy to search site with good close-ups of fabrics and the hallmark Landsend slushy language.

www.racinggreen.co.uk ○○○
Decent site with somewhat inadequate pictures.

www.boden.co.uk ○○○
Not as easy to search as the other catalogue sites, but good enough.

www.indexextra.com *and* **indexshop.com** ○○○
Littlewoods online.

www.kaysnet.com ✪✪✪
Busy online version of the huge Kays catalogue.

www.freemans.co.uk ✪✪✪
It is pretty easy to navigate this huge site boasting many brands.

www.tie-store.com ✪✪✪✪
This site has a huge range of ties at good prices – silk for £6. Delivery in 2–3 days is free.

Designer

www.designerdiscount.co.uk ✪✪✪✪
A very easy-to-use site with good discounts on a few brands.

www.haburi.com ✪✪✪✪
Good searchable site with a range of designer brands at good prices.

www.ready2shop.com ✪✪✪
Attractive site with good facilities on matching clothes, but often freezes mid-page during transmission.

www.pink-soda.co.uk ✪✪✪
Fun, bright-pink site that is easy to search.

www.wadesmith.co.uk ✪✪✪
Can be very slow to load and wants you to use Flash 4 or 5 because the site is very flashy. Nice clothes, though.

www.ozwald-boateng.co.uk ✪✪✪
Smart couture menswear site, although with cranky ordering graphics. Limited range of clothes.

ellecreation.co.uk ✪✪
Well-designed site but poor pictorial presentation of the clothes.

www.skinzwear.com ✪✪✪
Exotic clothes for the body-confident.

Groceries

Grocery shopping on the internet is a trade-off. It has advantages over visiting the supermarket and it has disadvantages. Whether you choose to do it depends on the value you place on each factor.

What you gain is avoiding the drudgery of visiting the supermarket, and for some people that is worth a great deal. Supermarkets are superb examples of logistical and marketing expertise in action, but few people would consider them a joy to spend time in. Navigating through the busy aisles, where inconsiderate fellow shoppers have abandoned their trolleys everywhere you turn; corralling your bored and unhappy kids, then queuing up for what seems like ages in a tedious, plastic environment; struggling back to the car in the rain, and the repetitive packing, loading, unloading and unpacking of fragile plastic bags – all this is some people's idea of hell. Selecting your weekly or fortnightly Big Shop from the comfort of your own home is an improvement worth significant sacrifice.

And sacrifice there is. First it costs money – usually £5 per delivery. Second, the online experience is far from perfect. The pages with information take a while to load, and the pictures are never quite big enough, or the information complete enough. For many products you know exactly what you want to buy, so it doesn't matter, but sometimes you feel you are entering a lucky dip. Your computer crashes halfway through your selection, or gremlins sabotage the checkout process. And of course you can't grope the avocados to see if they're ripe.

The third and most serious problem is with delivery. Even the most avid fan of online grocery shopping will tell you they rarely get a delivery with everything as they ordered it. Items are out of stock, and the alternatives chosen by the supermarket can sometimes seem bizarre. Deliveries are also often late ('stuck in traffic', 'the van broke down') and occasionally do not show up at all. Whatever you do, do not rely on a supermarket delivery to provide the ingredients for dinner the same evening.

So the main question is, how much do you hate visiting supermarkets? If it is the low point of your week, you could find it liberating. You may even come to regard a delivery that was ninety minutes late and contained bananas instead of cauliflower as an amusing quirk rather than an annoying inconvenience.

No longer like peas in a pod

In the real world, most consumers probably regard the major supermarkets as pretty much alike. One may be cheaper for bread this week, and the other cheaper for milk, but in a basket of up to £100 or more, those details get lost. Their product ranges, car parks, shop layout, employees are all pretty similar. Surprisingly, that is not true offline; faced with the challenge of making huge investments to provide internet shopping services, the companies have adopted varying strategies, and there are real differences between the services provided.

Traditionally seen as a cheap-and-cheerful vendor of frozen foods, Iceland was first off the internet blocks, embracing the new economy wholeheartedly, and even rebranding its physical shops as Iceland.co.uk. The website (**www.iceland.co.uk**, of course) is quick and easy to use, offering phone and internet shopping and free delivery. However, the product range is relatively narrow.

The clear e-commerce leader at the moment is Tesco (**www.tesco.com**), which already covers 90 per cent of the UK. With deliveries now topping the million mark, it claims to be the biggest e-commerce grocer in the world, including the USA. Tesco made such rapid progress by getting individual stores to do the picking and delivery, rather than setting up dedicated warehouses and delivery fleets. They gained in speed, but the strategy may backfire in the longer run. Local store-based staff will vary in their expertise and dedication, and in our experience Tesco's delivery performance has been extremely patchy. Another drawback is that the database that powers the website cannot know what is out of stock in all Tesco's local branches, so product substitutions and omissions are rife.

Sainsbury's (**www.sainsburystoyou.co.uk**) took the opposite route and is setting up dedicated warehouses around the country. This left them looking sluggish, but the service is starting to look impressive as its major teething problems are being sorted out. The pages on Sainsbury's website seem to load much faster, too.

All this matters enormously to these firms. A recent report forecast that Tesco and Sainsbury's could not expect profits from their internet supermarkets until 2005 – and only after spending £400m and £160m respectively.

> 'Apparently the software in the warehouses keeps crashing. We got a call on Friday evening just when we were expecting delivery of our shopping for the weekend. Sainsbury's said that they might possibly be able to deliver on Sunday. We just cancelled the order.'
>
> **Sainsbury's customer, London**

> 'Tesco seems to have tried pretty hard to get our deliveries right, but the website has been very buggy, and the staff we have dealt with have been rather variable.'
>
> **Tesco customer, London**

Part of the John Lewis partnership, Waitrose (**www.waitrose.co.uk**) took the interesting approach of offering deliveries to workplaces rather than homes. Visitors to **www.waitrose.com/atwork/index.htm** will find it is aimed at businesses who want to save their employees the time and effort of having to visit the supermarket during the lunch hour or after work. Your company must be registered to use the service, but delivery is free for orders above £5. For home-based consumers, Waitrose also has a home delivery service for drinks, flowers and gifts.

It will be interesting to see what approach is taken by Asda (**www.asda.co.uk**), which is now part of the US giant Wal-Mart. At present you have to register and be sent a CD-Rom or a catalogue before you can start shopping. The arrival in the UK of Wal-Mart was supposed to unleash a tidal wave of change in the industry, but the Americans seem to be finding the UK market harder going than they expected.

Smaller players like Budgen and Somerfield have dabbled with the online market but withdrawn and the future of Safeway's e-commerce service (**www.safeway.co.uk**) is in doubt. Finally, the troubled Marks & Spencer (**www.marksandspencer.co.uk**) has begun internet shopping trials in the south of England and intends to expand its operations.

It would be grossly unfair to review grocery shopping without giving an honourable mention to one of its pioneers: Food Ferry, based in London's New Covent Garden. Providers of excellent quality food with exemplary service from an attractive and user-friendly website (**www.foodferry.co.uk**), the only problem is that prices are steep. It seems that outstanding quality in food products and delivery just doesn't come cheap.

The online shopping experience

A useful feature is a running total of your bill as you shop. You can still collect points on loyalty cards although you may need to shop in person to redeem the vouchers or points you collect. With the biggest shops, you will be provided with a virtual supermarket (either by downloading it from the site or using a free CD-ROM). This means that you don't have to be connected to the internet while you fill your shopping basket, saving on your phone bills. You then re-connect to send your order through.

In addition, the supermarket sites have interesting content and handy features like recipe selectors and automatic ingredient selection direct to your shopping trolley, general healthy eating tips, ask an expert reasons to buy vegetarian and organic food, and a wine selector to choose wine to suit your meal.

Organic and 'fresh from the farm' food

The major supermarkets are staking claims to be environmentally friendly: Iceland mounted a high-profile move towards GM-free, organic food, with reduced additives and artificial ingredients. Sainsbury's seems to be the supermarket with the largest range of organic foods.

Keen consumers of organic food reckon that shopping on the internet can work out cheaper than at a supermarket. Two highly-rated sites are **www.simplyorganic.net** and **www.organicsdirect.co.uk**. The first is run from London's New Covent Garden Market and offers a slick shopping experience, a large range of organic foods and non-food items, with free delivery within 36 hours for regular shoppers. Organics Direct was awarded Box Scheme Of The Year in the 1999 Organic Food Awards, and has a nicely presented range of products at low prices.

For farm-fresh meat, eggs and cheese try **www.farmersmarketdirect.co.uk**, run by a group of UK farmers who will deliver anywhere in the UK. The meat is guaranteed British and is reared in accordance with the RSPCA's Freedom Food Welfare Scheme. At present, however, the site is poorly designed, and carries little information about what is on offer.

Ethnic groceries

Offline, the supply of sensibly priced, good quality ethnic ingredients in the UK is pretty limited unless you live in a big city. In the US the ethnic food industry has embraced the internet: **www.ethnicgrocer.com** is great for recipes, but is unable to send orders abroad. The best site for the UK is probably **www.fifthsense.com**, based in Ireland but delivering throughout the UK within a week. You can search a huge variety of ingredients for all sorts of national cuisines, delivery is £4.50 and free for orders over £65.

For Chinese cooking, **www.qinglung.co.uk** has a limited range of oriental foods, but the site is easy to use and good for basics. Bristol Sweet Mart, at **www.sweetmart.co.uk**, is a family-run business specialising in ethnic foods and spices as well as Indian sweets. Standard delivery in the UK is £3.50 per order for the general public and restaurants. For fine European fare try **www.porcini.co.uk** for regional specialities, hampers and gifts.

Drink

The internet has a vast wealth of information on vintage wines, how to select a wine, special offers and recommendations. And of course you can order your favourites by the case.

The site **www.enjoyment.co.uk** has been launched by a group of high-street drinks retailers, including Bottoms Up and Threshers. The site is attractive and easy to navigate, and offers reasonable prices with £5 p&p. Enjoyment is thin on descriptions, though, so you could visit a specialist site like Berry Bros and Rudd at **www.bbr.com**. Other sites worth a look are **www.finestwine.com** for rare French wines and hard-to-find champagnes; you can celebrate with a bottle of something from the year of your birth or your marriage.

For lovers of the malt, **www.whiskyshop.com** has a big selection of single malts, blends, and liqueurs on an elegant, efficient site.

Gift and speciality foods

The internet is great for hampers and food gift packs. However, there are plenty of small, regional suppliers finding their way online: everything from specialist cheese shops to Scottish smoke houses, many with excellent websites.

Start with a good portal site like Yahoo! in the regional UK sub-directory of businesses, shopping or food and drink. Alternatively, **www.foodconnect.co.uk** has a selection of traditional food producers from around the UK described online along with news and events. The sensibly named **www.hamper.com** has a big selection of hampers and other gifts.

Caffeine connoisseurs should check out tea and coffee merchant **www.whittard.com**. The site has around 600 products and is quick and easy to use. Whittard did an interesting deal in June 2000, buying the *Daily Telegraph's* luxury goods e-commerce portal, **www.bestofbritish.com**, for £1.2m. Hollinger (owners of the *Telegraph*) also took a 7 per cent stake in Whittards.

Selected sites

Supermarkets
www.tesco.com ○○○○
Best coverage for delivery but a slow site which could be more user-friendly.

www.sainsburystoyou.co.uk ○○○○
Poor geographic coverage but shaping up to provide a better service. Good for organic foods.
www.sainsburys.co.uk is an online magazine site.

www.iceland.co.uk ○○○
News, home delivery and appliances. Narrow product range

www.marks-and-spencer.co.uk ○○
Nice design but slow.

www.waitrose.co.uk ○○○
A wine, flowers and gift direct service, with deliveries to businesses offered at www.waitrose.com/atwork/index.htm.

www.safeway.co.uk ○
Site unavailable during the writing of this book.

www.foodferry.co.uk ○○○○
Excellent site, excellent service, excellent produce, high prices. Mainly London-based, but with plans to expand.

Organic
www.organicsdirect.co.uk ○○○○○
Excellent site, loads of choice, good prices and more.

www.simplyorganic.net ○○○○
Good range covering wine and non-food items too.

www.farmersmarketdirect.co.uk ○○○
Covers fruit, veg, meat, dairy and ready meals. Thin site.

www.freshfood.co.uk ○○○
UK delivery of organics and lots more.

www.iorganic.com ○○
Limited delivery times, covers fine food, vitamins and health products.

www.meatdirect.co.uk ○○○○
Organic and free-range meat, buy in bulk for best value.

Ethnic
www.fifthsense.com ○○○○

www.qinglung.co.uk ○○○

www.sweetmart.co.uk ○○○

www.porcini.co.uk ○○○○

www.hoohing.demon.co.uk ○○

www.ethnicgrocer.com ○○
US site, so don't order from here, but good for new food ideas and recipes.

Drinks
www.whittard.com ○○○○
Over 600 products on offer from the tea and coffee merchants.

www.matthew-algie.co.uk ○○○
If you are a coffee anorak you'll love the coffee police on this site. No online ordering facility.

www.teacouncil.co.uk ○○○○
An information site for tea drinkers and caterers, health benefits of tea, links to the best tea sites, statistics and top tea tips.

www.enjoyment.co.uk ○○○
High-street online off-license, lacks detailed descriptions.

www.finestwine.com ○○○
US site shipping abroad. Good if you know what you want.

www.bbr.com ○○○○○
Berry Bros and Rudd's site is great if you are looking for more detail about the wine you drink and should be drinking.

www.winecellar.co.uk ○○○
Limited detail on individual wines and a tricky to navigate.

www.lastorders.com ○○○○
Next-day delivery to home or office, easy selection.

www.amivin.com ○○○○○
Catering to all tastes, loaded with everything from special offers through to wine clubs and 'ask the expert'.

www.whiskyshop.com ○○○○
Scotland-based whisky seller.

www.whisky-world.com ○○○○
Slick site to search and buy your favourites and swap information with other drinkers.

Speciality
www.foodconnect.co.uk ○○○
Online magazine site with a limited directory of online sellers.

www.hamper.com ○○○○
Big hamper selection to suit all tastes and budgets.

www.culinary.com ✪✪
US site with recipes, links, newsletter and food news.

www.fromages.com ✪✪✪✪
Based in France and dedicated to cheese; prices include shipping and tax.

www.lobster.co.uk ✪✪✪✪✪
Claiming to be the Harrods Food Hall of cyberspace, the site sells fine foods and wines, including caviar, pasta, and of course lobster.

www.stgeorgessquare.com ✪✪✪
Yummy indulgent sweet stuff, organic food, hampers. Delivery is free but site is rather drab.

chocolate.scream.org ✪✪✪✪
Mouthwatering US site with a comprehensive directory of suppliers, sites and recipes.

4 Entertainment and leisure

Travel and holidays

There is a huge amount of travel information on the net to help you plan trips and to navigate your way around the world when you are away. For many kinds of trips you can save yourself a great deal of time and money by using the internet well. For travel within the UK see 'Getting Around' on pp. 201–7.

Timetables and basic fare information for flights, trains, and ferries all around the world are instantly available. Tourist boards across the world have set up substantial sites to guide you through the sights, facilities and entertainments of their area. And you can access for free the entire text of most of the Rough Guide books, **www.roughguides.com**, and updates of Lonely Planet, **www.lonelyplanet.com**, and Trailblazer, **www.trailblazer.com**, guidebooks. These are in addition to what most people know about the internet for travel – that you can get very cheap tickets on a great range of airlines. Indeed, you can even register to receive emails about courier flights which has to be the very cheapest way to travel.

Travel agents

It is possible to book an entire holiday online, through a portal or an online travel agent. There are a great many sites which can book for you a flight, a hotel, a car, insurance and basically everything you need for your holiday, such as **www.yahoo.com**, **www.thefirstresort.com**, the absolutely excellent **www.a2btravel.com**, or **www.lastminute.com**. The difference is that portals such as Yahoo connect you with a set of different holiday, or flight or car reservation providers, whereas the last three all act as travel agents, finding you deals according to your specifications. In many of these and other sites you have access to almost the same level of sophistication in the database of options as travel agents themselves have. This has led many people to see the internet as boosting consumer power.

The difficulty is that although you can see the same information as a travel agent, your search facility is nothing like as good as theirs, and at first you will not be as expert at using it. The result is that you are best off searching for a holiday only if you either know precisely what you want or are prepared to take up deals put in front of you. If neither of these applies to you, you may find that you are best off booking at least some of your travel components from a travel agent who you speak to personally. This can be a much more efficient way of communicating a great deal of variable information. For example, it is easier to say: 'Well, I'll go on Sunday, I suppose, if it will be cheaper' than to try to manipulate the blunt search tool yourself.

Package holidays

Package holidays would seem like the perfect thing to sell online. You can see the whole brochure, which is all the information you get offline, and there are few variations in terms of add-on extras to ask for or avoid. But unfortunately, with the exception of Kuoni, the package holiday companies have not advanced far with the internet. Although they have websites, they are often very minimal and usually ask browsers to phone their local office. None has yet replicated their brochure online. Thomas Cook (**www.thomascook.co.uk**) has the most information on the resorts, but it still is not substantial. Airtours links you to all of its branded holiday companies, such as Tradewinds, **www.tradewinds.co.uk**, Going Places, **www.goingplaces.co.uk**, Cresta, **www.crestaholidays.co.uk**, Direct Holidays, **www.direct-holidays.co.uk**, or you can see the Airtours deals offered in the UK at **www.airtours.co.uk**. However, **www.kuoni.co.uk** is an excellent site which enables you to search for a holiday by destination, price or date – and you can book it online.

Out of the ordinary

Finally, the internet is a superb way of linking you with a huge range of holiday destinations. If you want to find a farmhouse in Estonia to stay in with three kids, or swap your home with a family from Hawaii for the summer holidays, you can locate them much more easily than if you were having to rely only on expensive long-distance telephone calls to make contact, sort out arrangements and make a booking. See the section on obscure holidays on page 122 for more on this.

Booking a flight online can save money

America has taken to booking flights online with abandon. This led the big American sites such as **www.travelocity.com** and **www.expedia.com** to expand operations to the UK, where they expected to repeat their success. But it has not worked quite so well, not because of our internet backwardness, but because the UK travel industry has a tradition of deep discounting. This means that travel agents often get you the best deal because they sell you a ticket at a significant discount to the published airline price. In America published airline prices are far lower – they are realistic prices the public would expect to pay. This has meant that putting these prices and the booking of them online has been a relatively simple task. But not so here. This means that rather than searching for price deals on a range of airline websites or Travelocity or Expedia, you need to look for low-cost airlines and price comparison sites; and these are where you can get some seriously good deals.

Low-cost airlines: Easyjet (www.easyjet.com) has the best internet deal of the low-cost airlines because all internet prices are £5 less than if you book by telephone. Meanwhile, the British Airways low-cost airline Go has an excellent site at **www.gofly.com** where you can easily book flights from Stanstead to a number of European destinations. Other useful sites include Buzz (**www.buzzaway.com**) which is the internet child of KLM, British Midland (**www.iflybritishmidland.com**), Ryanair (**www.ryanair.com**), and Virgin (**www.fly-virgin.com**).

Price comparison sites: Probably the best price comparison site for flights from the UK is **www.cheapflights.com**, which lists all the flight offerings for a certain destination and time including low-cost ones, such as those mentioned above, and travel agents' fares. The site sadly does not list the flights in ascending order of price but they are all there somewhere if you scroll down. You cannot book online, but the site provides links to travel agents with internet facilities and the telephone number for those without. Bob Geldof's holiday business **www.deckchair.com** is a good site which shows available flights ordered by price, but as with many sites it requires you to search for a specific date and time. Another site worth a look is **www.airnet.co.uk**.

'Cheapflights.com is a cheap and nasty looking site, but it does give you a list of different prices for a flight and gives you access to lots of bucket shops, which is what Teletext used to do for people, and can be just what you want. It's not the perfect web experience, but it's a fantastic resource.'

Richard Lord, editor, Revolution *magazine*

Auction sites can get you a good price, at the cost of your time

If you really want to, you can bid for your airline seat. This means that you can set the price you are prepared to pay for flying from A to B, and/or back again. It sounds like a fine idea, but the problem is that airlines are not actually keen on selling you seats way below the full price because they are concerned about losing control of ticket prices. So, unless you put in a bid at the kind of price you would actually expect to pay, the sites will tell you that you have very little chance of buying a ticket at your price. And to get your price up to this level requires you to spend ages adjusting and re-adjusting your price. And then you have to put in your credit card details when you have decided on your final bid – i.e. before you are told whether you can have a ticket at that price. You can find such mouse-clicking fun at **www.priceline.com**, or **www.e-bookers.com**.

Use a travel agent when you are not sure of your options

If you are travelling to a destination where you are not sure which are the cheapest airlines that fly there, you may save yourself a lot of time by contacting a travel agent rather than by inputting a variety of different dates or airports in searchers. There are travel agents on the internet but when we tested the US ones such as **www.tripquote.com** they never returned our e-mails, while an STA consultant responded thus to our query about their website: 'The site has not been a great success. To be honest I wouldn't trust it as far as I could throw it.'

Telephoning a travel agent is very likely to be your best option if you are planning a complicated long-haul flight. For example, not all searches on the internet would find the cheapest way to fly to Hanoi – which is often to buy tickets to Bangkok and then separate tickets from Bangkok to Hanoi – but any decent travel agent would. And no sites yet allow you to pre-select to avoid changing at Kuala Lumpur, for example (which you might want to do to avoid docking in a country which imposes the death penalty for bringing in drugs).

Hence many UK travel agents, such as **www.trailfinders.com**, have decided just to post information on their site, albeit quite extensive information, and leave booking to the telephone.

Travel guide information

If you are prepared to put up with carrying sheafs of paper around with you rather than a book, or a selection of books, you can jet off to anywhere in the world, or even visit the wilds of Wales, with all the guide information you might want for free printed from the internet. The main guidebook companies – Lonely Planet, Rough Guide, Fodor's Trailblazer, and Moon – all have excellent sites with a significant amount of content for free.

'The internet doesn't really work for booking complicated travel arrangements. Anything flexible or open-ended has so many permutations that it is far easier to communicate what you want to a human being to than by typing in data to a processor.'
Richard Lord, editor, Revolution *magazine.*

'A lot of people are setting up travel websites with no real knowledge of the travel industry. They just put a site up without having the facility to get the best deals behind it. There is a lot of rubbish out there. These sites focus on design – the polish is there but behind the scenes it's chaos.'
Alison More, editor, Trailfinders *magazine, from* **Trailfinders**

> 'The only way customers in the UK would be able to search online with the same confidence and knowledge as a travel agent would be if all the airlines got together and agreed to simplify the system whereby they charge different fares for different seats at different times. This won't be happening soon.'
>
> **Alison More, editor, Trailfinders *magazine*.**

Rough Guides, **www.roughguides.com**, is the most comprehensive site, putting online the entirety of most of its books, closely followed by Fodor's, **www.fodors.com**, which makes available all of its mini guides and most of its country guides. The Lonely Planet site, **www.lonelyplanet.com** has updates of its books for free, as does Trailblazer, **www.trailblazer.com**, and Moon, **www.moon.com**. If you want a personal view to augment what is posted on the site you can also email the authors directly and ask them to do your research legwork for you. And if this isn't enough information, you can go to a site specialising in city guides around the world, such as the excellent **www.sidewalk.com**, which focuses on the USA and Canada although it covers Europe too. And if you still want more, tourist offices around the world are increasingly producing fantastic sites enabling booking of hotels or theatre tickets online, and with very well-produced information on the sights, sounds and activities of the city and country, such as **www.londontown.com**, **www.paris.org**, **www.nycvisit.com** and **www.visitbritain.com**.

Can you fly as a courier?

Yes, you can. Courier flights have been around for decades, but the migration of information on flights to the net makes the process much simpler. Courier flights are very rarely free but they are nearly always significantly cheaper than any standard flight. If you act as a courier on a flight you will be responsible only for carrying papers which vouch for a cargo in the hold. You will also have the standard baggage allowance for your luggage. Courier flights often come up at very short notice (like the next day) and these are when the very best deals are to be had, but they can also be booked up to three months in advance. The two drawbacks are that there can only be one courier per flight, if you are travelling with someone they will have to buy a different ticket, or you could buy a courier ticket each on adjacent flights. And the destinations for courier tickets are limited to the US, South America and the Far East, including Japan.

By far the best way to find out about courier flights is to join the UK branch of the International Association of Air Travel Couriers, **www.aircourier.co.uk**. You can join association from the site for £32 a year. This does not guarantee you any flights but it gives you access to the only comprehensive source for information on forthcoming courier flights by a monthly newsletter. Recently the association has begun sending out emails to members of immediate courier opportunities. The only other way to find out about courier flights coming up is to telephone all the courier companies every day, and not surprisingly, they are not keen on this. They greatly prefer to deal with an intermediary, one Dave Sands who runs the association.

Health and safety advice

Before you travel anywhere exotic you should check that the region is considered safe and what health precautions you need to take. Several sites on the net have helpful updated information on these issues.

Perhaps the best place to start for safety advice is at the website of the Foreign Office, **www.fco.gov.uk**. This clear site is constantly reviewed by Foreign Office staff who provide the official line on which areas of the world are considered safe to travel in, set out the risks associated with some others, and when necessary say which areas should be avoided by British citizens. The guidebook sites, such as **www.lonelyplanet.com**, etc (see above) are then good places to turn if you are trying to weigh up whether to go somewhere or not. These have bulletin boards with messages from travellers who are travelling through, or have just returned from, potentially dangerous areas.

'Whenever we know we will need a courier I send the details over to Dave and he sends them out. Then we have someone phoning up and because they are a member of the assocation we can feel confident that they understand the issues. But still we need to speak to them on the telephone to be sure they will do the job, which is why we haven't tried to put our requests for couriers on the internet.'

Sheena from ACP Travel

The Foreign Office website **www.fco.gov.uk** has links to all the British embassies abroad – in case you are the sort of VIP they would actually help. Contacts for Consulates and English-speaking or English company lawyers can be found at: **http://uk-vietnam.org/consular** (substitute the country you are interested in for Vietnam).

For health advice world-wide we found that the best advice was to be had at the site of the Centre for Disease Control and Prevention, **www.cdc.gov/travel**. This has easily understandable information on which immunisations are considered necessary for which countries and regions, and what protective measures should be taken once you are there. The site is kept up to date with the latest news of outbreaks and how serious they are. The sites of the guidebooks also have good coverage of health issues. The most user-friendly is that of the Lonely Planet, **www.lonelyplanet.com**, which has a separate health section. The other sites cover health within the information on that country. The Lonely Planet site also has an excellent set of links for special needs travellers.

Obscure holidays

If you are planning a holiday to Estonia and want to stay in a country farmhouse but not too far from a town, the internet can be invaluable connector. Rather than having to make long-distance phone calls in shouty English to the plumber who happens to be working on the house you are trying to stay in, you can find local agents, see pictures of it and email the proprietors to find out more.

There are two good options for starting your research. The first is the guide book sites. They list hotels, tourist boards, letting agents, etc. and you can contact them directly to see what they have to offer. An alternative starting-point is the excellent **www.virgin.net**. This is a good resource for finding, for example, a whole range of accommodation in Latin America, or anything too difficult for most of the other search engines.

A way of finding a great deal of potentially unfocused information and then narrowing it down to country-specific information is to use **www.yahoo.com**. The way to do this is to go to **www.yahoo.com**, then choose the region you are interested in, then travel, and accommodation. Then click on the links, and you're away.

Swap your house

People have been exchanging their semis in Ealing for a sumptuous villa in Hawaii for the summer holiday for decades. Surprising but true. Apparently Americans will do almost anything to stay in London, and indeed England in general. Of course it is not only Americans, and you may not wish to go to America; in many ways the world is your oyster if you have a house that other people might reasonably want to stay in and you want to stay in someone else's.

Previously such swaps happened by phoning up the person listed in a guide you had to pay around £20 for. Today, many of the sites offer postings of your house for free and it is free to view other people's, although some charge. Some people are concerned that putting such details on the net is almost asking for trouble, but many are not: some major sites boast very grand properties in London, New York and elsewhere. The two most reliable sites that we have found are **www.holi-swaps.com** and **www.home-swap.com**.

Future

One innovative development being worked upon by, amongst others, **www.biztravel.com**, is the fare guard. If you purchased this facility with your flight ticket you would be informed if anyone bought a ticket on the same flight as you for less, and given the option to exchange and lose nothing. Sounds great, but even if it actually happens it is hard to see how it could apply to the UK, rather than the US, given our practice of discounting. A more realistic target is that with the advent of broadband and with airline cooperation we, the consumers, may be able to enjoy the same level of sophistication of searching techniques which travel agents have access to. Then it really may be possible to book an airline flight to anywhere in the world at any time for the best price, quickly and easily online.

Selected sites

Guidebook sites
www.lonelyplanet.com ୦୦୦୦
Excellent site with updates for free. Printed, they fit within a Lonely Planet guidebook.

www.roughguides.com ୦୦୦୦୦
Find all of the contents of most of the Rough Guides for free.

www.trailblazer.com ୦୦୦୦
Updates and features on new and old Trailblazer books and you may even be able to catch up with the author from, for example, *Vietnam by Rail*.

www.sidewalk.com ୦୦୦୦୦
Key resource for city guides for many US cities, and an increasing number of Canadian and European cities.

Airline information
www.oneworldalliance.com ୦୦୦୦୦
In theory the only site you need for real-time aeroplane information. A joint venture between several airline companies.

www.baa.co.uk ୦୦୦
Lists all flights scheduled to land in BAA airports (ie excluding Luton, Manchester, etc.) with real-time information on delays posted.

Good tourist board sites
www.nycvisit.com ୦୦୦୦୦
Great site, New York style, showing you round the city. Through the site you can book at an excellent selection of hotels and restaurants. Superb maps. Good itinerary ideas.

www.officialtravelinfo.com ❂❂❂
From this site you can be connected to some good foreign tourist board sites.

Health and safety advice
www.cdc.gov/travel ❂❂❂❂
Excellent comprehensive coverage from the centre for disease prevention and control.

www.doh.gov.uk/traveladvice ❂❂
Broad coverage of health issues when abroad.

Travel agents
www.asiasafari.com ❂❂❂
Good online brochure for this offline travel agent. Look especially at the motorbike tours which seem tremendous fun.

www.thefirstresort.com ❂❂❂❂
Attractive and well laid-out site which really does make it as easy for you as they can to select a holiday. Photos, guides, articles and good quick descriptions of possible holidays, but not equivalent to an online brochure.

www.deckchair.com ❂❂❂❂
Highly informative site with full information on flight restrictions and conditions. It remembers your searches. But the flight comparison page is sometimes slow to load.

www.sta-travel.co.uk ❂❂❂
Reasonable site for searches, but booking online is time-consuming.

www.trailfinders.com ❂❂
Minimal site, advises visitors to telephone an agent.

Adventure trips
www.spaceadventures.com ❂❂❂❂
Did you know that you can do an Antarctic expedition with NASA for $30,000? Or you could fly on a MiG fighter plane for $6,000 or take a sub-orbital flight for $100,000.

www.adventurequest.com ❂❂❂❂
Excellent site for all the holidays you always wanted to have, or never thought you could. Everything from learning to cook in France to animal treks. This company is about to merge with **www.greentravel.com** to form the integrated company, **www.away.com**.

Specialist holidays
www.virgin.net/travel/guides ❂❂❂❂❂
A key resource for researching anything obscure. The only letdown of the site is that we have found that not all web addresses are linked even though that exact address exists.

www.gitesdirect.com ❂❂❂❂
Slightly erratic English-language site with a substantial listing of gites in France with pictures as well as prices and available dates.

www.cheznous.com ❂❂❂❂
A great range of places to stay in France, from modest cottages to chateaux.

www.narrow-boat-holidays.com ❂❂❂
Site for narrow-boat holidays, not surprisingly.

www.iski.com ❂❂❂
Packed with information and news on skiiing holidays, plus silly animations of skiers.

www.naturenet.net/orgs ❂❂❂
News of nature-loving activities to get involved in, in the UK.

www.holi-swap.com ❂❂❂
Full details, often including pictures, of a great range of properties for free.

www.home-swap.com ❂❂❂
Easily navigable site showing a substantial number of properties around the world.

Business travellers
www.frequentflier.com ❂❂❂
This site really tells you how to choose between different plans, but it is aimed at Americans.

www.biztravel.com ❂❂❂
All manner of news for business travellers. Members will be offered fare guard for free, if it comes into operation.

Package holidays
www.kuoni.com ❂❂❂❂❂
Great, easy-to-use site which enables you to choose a holiday by destination, price or date. Gives you the full itinerary with good description of facilities and shows several pictures of each resort. You can book online.

www.thomascook.co.uk ❂❂
Maps, advice, last-minute deals but no brochure, so you have to input travelling details before you can see where you could go. No pictures.

www.lunn-poly.co.uk ❂❂
Fast, inviting site, but only descriptions of resorts and destinations and no pictures. This is not an online brochure.

www.thomsom-holidays.com ❂❂❂
Good search mechanism with some information on resorts and destinations, but you need to contact Thomson's direct or a local agent for a brochure or bookings.

www.airtours.com ❂
Links you with all the Airtours brands available in your country including Tradewinds, Cresta, Going Places, Direct holidays, and Panorama. All have minimal sites with no detailed information about holidays and no online booking. Airtours puts up just a few of its own last-minute deals on its site with no pictures and no online booking.

Accommodation
www.placestostay.com ❂❂❂❂
A great list of great hotels around the world, but they are not cheap.

www.budgettravel.com ❂❂❂
This is where to look for cheap travel, including hotels.

www.hoteldiscounts.com ✪✪✪
Good site, but the hotels pay to be on it, so you never quite know . . .

www.hostels.com ✪✪✪✪
Good list of hostels in obvious tourist districts. No links to the hostel, contact details only.

www.all-hotels.com ✪✪✪
60,000 hotels worldwide

www.hotelworld.co.uk ✪✪✪
Search facilities covering 2700 UK hotels some special offers available.

www.8lh.com ✪✪✪
Site covering 250 small luxury hotels worldwide. You can search by geographical area or by type of hotel such as safari or island.

www.holidayzone.co.uk ✪✪✪✪
Good database of hotels and it is easy to search for accommodation across the world, although not in difficult countries such as Syria or Cambodia.

www.hotelnet.co.uk ✪✪✪
Reasonable database of hotels in the civilised world.

Miscellaneous

www.deutschebahn.de ✪✪✪✪
Invaluable site for booking complex European rail journeys.

www.holidayextras.co.uk ✪✪
Good idea, to enable you to book parking and lounges at UK airports but irritating site which requires you to fill in every detail. For London airports, the combined hotel and parking deals are good value.

www.egypttour.com ✪✪✪✪✪
Fantastic official site for visual history and information on Egypt including the whole of *The Book of the Dead* online. Also good links on activities in Egypt such as diving.

www.abtanet.com ✪✪✪✪
The official site of ABTA, the Association of British Travel Agents, lists all agents that are ABTA-recognised, online and offline. It is a little slow to load.

Radio, TV and films

Hundreds of radio stations from around the world have put their output online, so by connecting to the internet you can listen to French radio, American radio and even Indian radio. You can also of course listen to a great number of British radio stations at the same time as you surf – from amateur sites to Radio Four. Plus there are an increasing number of short films available for free on the internet which you can watch online; there are no long films yet, because they take up such a huge amount of bandwidth. And as those who were caught up in the *Big Brother* mania will already know, you can watch people's lives as if they were on your TV, brought to you through 'webcams' – web cameras.

What's on?

The internet also enables you to find out what is on your television or at a cinema near you in an instant. At present you can only rarely book tickets online, but this situation will undoubtedly improve. Film-lovers have taken to the internet with great enthusiasm: you can find whole screenplays, connect with other film-buffs, or find the most obscure role ever played by the star you are most interested in. In addition there are sites that will recommend films based on those that you have already seen and liked.

Radio

It is easy to enable your computer to play the conversations or music put out on radio stations. (If your computer does not have a sound card you will have to buy one and fit it into the sound card slot). Some radio stations (usually amateur ones) are broadcast only on the internet. You also need certain software for your computer to be able to relay the output to you. The software can be downloaded for free.

Some radio stations use Windows Media Player, which your computer may already have installed. The rest use Real Player, but you can download this for free, so long as you only download Real Player basic 8. (There is another version called Gold Pass, which you have to pay for.) You can download Real Player basic 8 from a huge number of sites, including the very user-friendly **www.download.com**. Make sure you scroll to the bottom of the home page and select Basic 8. Alternatively you can load it from the CDs that come with a number of computer magazines.

With the software installed, you are ready to play. It is as simple as that. If you know the particular radio station you wish to listen to you can go direct to their website, for example, **www.bbc.co.uk/radio4**. Alternatively you can choose a radio station from the list of hundreds at the very user-friendly site **www.webradios.com,** or the comprehensive **www.internetradio.about.com**.

Most radio sites have pages devoted to particularly popular programmes or DJs. For example, *The Archers* is at **www.bbc.co.uk/radio4/archers/index.shtml**

Listings

It is very easy to find complete listings for TV and radio, terrestrial channels and satellite. For radio as well as TV, and for regional variations in television viewing look at the BBC site, **www.bbc.co.uk/whatson** – although the need to choose 'BBC TV' or 'TV and radio' in order to find radio listings is somewhat counter-intuitive. For all channels of TV the easiest and fullest listings are at **www.unmissabletv.com** and **www.radiotimes.beeb.com**. You can also check out the listings section on **www.bbc.co.uk**, but the two commercial offerings are better – beeb.com is a commercial arm of the BBC.

TV

The amount of bandwidth available on the web at the moment isn't really enough to support broadcasting of live TV pictures in any reliable manner – most attempts at webcasting of big events have fallen over as too many people tried to access the 'streams' of pictures and sound at once and immediately consumed all the available bandwidth. However, for more specialist programming, where the demand is more manageable and for events which don't go out live (so that demand can be spread out over time), webcasting is reaching the point where it is viable for people with high-speed connections. Channel 4's *Big Brother* coverage managed to stand up to huge demand for live feeds from the house. In order to view webcasting, you will need either Windows Media Player or RealVideo, available from **www.windowsmedia.com/download/** and **www.real.com** respectively.

A lower-bandwidth way of getting live pictures over the net is the webcam. Rather like some security cameras, these are static cameras (cams) set up to take a snapshot of whatever is in front of them and post a new picture to the Web every fifteen seconds or so. Most cams available on the web are pointing at people's desks, but some are a bit more interesting – live feeds from town centre surveillance cameras, or behind the scenes at television stations. A directory of webcams is available at **www.camville.com**, though be warned: many of them are run by people who are keen on exhibiting themselves to the whole world . . .

Future

With the advent of broadband it will become possible to view full-length films over the computer, but another development may make this unnecessary. Many people think that in the future we will be accessing the internet over our television rather than from computers. For more on this, see Getting Started.

Fan sites

All the main channels, terrestrial and satellite, have websites where you can find extra news, gossip, features, chats and sometimes extra material from the programmes aired by that channel. The coverage varies according to the popularity of the programme, but they are often very good indeed. Battles are currently raging between certain independent production companies and the channels their programmes are aired on because the channels are claiming the exclusive right to the official programme website. The BBC in particular has maintained that it would not be proper for it to link to a commercial site. However, at time of writing the BBC had just agreed to allow the independent production company Hat Trick to operate websites for its programmes and to provide a link to them from its website. So, you can look at **www.bbc.co.uk** for gossip and caption competitions from *Have I Got News For You*, or you can go direct to the programme's excellent website at **www.hignfy.com**. Other independent production companies have not yet followed suit, but you can expect them to do so, meaning that more sites are likely to be set up for changingrooms.com, groundforce.com, etc.

In addition to finding out the latest developments in a soap or its history and gossip, you can link up with, for example, people in the Deep South who you had no idea cared about Dot Cotton from *Eastenders* – **www.pagesz.net/~eastend**.

Perhaps the best of all TV fan sites is the one devoted to *The Simpsons* at **www.snpp.com**. This fantastic site keeps on going despite Fox's continual demands that it stop. It has coverage of every episode and short and tells you about the film references in each episode and a hundred little incidents.

Film

Through the internet you can find out which films are on near you at what time, how far away the cinemas are and the contact details. As with many areas, internet practice does not yet match up to internet theory. It is perfectly possible for a site to do this, but as yet we have not found one to do so reliably for the UK. Naturally the US has long since solved this one. The site that loves cinema, **www.popcorn.co.uk**, has an easy-to-use site. You enter your postcode and it tells you what is on at your local cinemas and how far they are from your door. But there are two problems: the links to cinemas never worked when we tried to test the site and the details of the films are sketchy. For example, if there are two films of the same name (there are around ten films which have been made with the title *The Wild West*) you will not know which one it is. So you can try the site of the *Financial Times*, **www.ft.com**, which has comprehensive listings for the country and you can search the site by cinema or film. Again, two problems: the listings are only for the day you search (you can't look up what will be showing next Saturday night) and we found that the site regularly made mistakes, for example seeming to think that Brixton was Bristol. Other resources that are useful in other areas also yield little help. For example, **www.countyweb.com** does not recognise film or cinema in its search, and **www.fish4.co.uk** only lists the contact details of your nearest cinemas.

If you live in London you are saved by the listings on **www.timeout.com** and **www.thisislondon.com**, but otherwise you have to make to with the offerings from Popcorn and *FT*, until somebody comes up with something better.

With the same Real Player software that you need to play the output from radio stations through your computer (see above) you can view short films that have been put on the internet and trailers for upcoming blockbusters. The site **www.ifilm.com** has a huge number of short films, ranging from arty to bizarre, while **www.filmzone.com** has a small number of generally better indie films, such as a parody of the latest Star Wars film, which was on the site at the time of writing. The site **www.movies.com** enables you to watch trailers for the latest blockbusters, but you need to have a quicker modem than a 56Kb standard home modem in order to have uninterrupted transmission.

Other than watching films online you can search through a number of movie databases to find information about or views on films. The oldest film buff site is **www.imdb.org** which was set up by a group of friends from Swansea University before the days of the internet and then transferred to the web to become the largest film database on the net with 200,000 films. Here you can find views, notes on the film and ratings. But beware that most people find the ratings less helpful than you might think. There are a number of other film database sites, including **www.filmbug.com**, which covers only a small number of films, but shows the complete screenplay for them.

Reviews

The largest film review site on the web was just about to be launched at the time of writing, **www.coppernob.com**. The owner of this site has bought the online rights to the famous *Halliwell's Film Guide* and intends to run it alongside another guide, *The Complete Film Guide*, and compile a database of 310,000 films. If all goes according to plan, you should be able to access reviews of all these films for free. Otherwise, you can start with views from the film database sites above or look at the sites dedicated to amateur reviews, such as **www.aintitcool.com**. For the views of professionals, go to **www.go2flix.com**, which links you to reviews of films from many different magazines.

Fan sites

If you are a fan of a particular film or actor, you can track down a great deal of information from the numerous film fan sites. Portals such as **www.yahoo.com** have huge lists of film fan, news and gossip sites and fan sites such as **www.countingdown.com** link you to coverage of every kind of film issue. Alternatively you can visit the sites of the major film distributors such as **www.warnerbros.com** or **www.foxstudios.com**.

Don't miss moviecritic.com

If you want to work out whether you might like a particular film, you can of course read the reviews, ask people in chat rooms their views (or indeed people on the street) – or you could try **www.moviecritic.com**. This site uses preference matching technology to try to work out, based on your views on a number of films you have seen, how you will like films you have not seen. You begin by rating twelve films you have seen, and then ask the site to rate a new film for you. Provided you were honest in your ratings, you are likely to find the results surprisingly accurate. We certainly found it a better predictor than each other's views. The site is a little difficult to find your way around and to understand, though; for instance, it tells you that you have to become a member, but in fact this only entails rating twelve films – but do persevere.

Selected sites

Radio
www.webradios.com ○○○○○
Provides a list of and links to thousands of radio stations from all around the world, – choose by jazz, rock, etc. It is hard to search for a specific radio station in the US, because they are not listed alphabetically but within other countries, e.g. the UK, they are.

www.internetradio.about.com ○○○
Slightly confusing site which claims to have a complete list of and links to all online radio stations.

Film news and short films
www.ifilm.com ○○○○
Enormous film site, with news and gossip where you can view a huge number of short films.

www.filmzone.com ○○○○
News, gossip, and short indie films shown in full, such as a parody of the latest Star Wars film. (You need to download Real Player to view them.)

www.movies.com ○○○
Lots of news and gossip, and you can view the latest trailers, provided you have downloaded Real Player and have a quick enough modem.

Film reviews and views
www.go2flix.com ○○○○
This site will find you reviews by different magazines on any film you can mention.

www.allmovie.com ○○○
Good directory of current films, old films and on present-day actors but the features are not fascinating.

www.imdb.org ○○○○
Entertainment crossword, find out stars' most obscure roles, short plot summaries, and user comments, message boards with film talk and TV talk and a mega database site.

www.filmsite.org ○○○○
Primarily for American films, this site has records of and views on, the world's greatest films.

www.britfilms.com ○○○
Database on the latest British films, and vital resource for amateur film-makers.

www.aintitcool.com ○○○○
Funky site majoring in amateur film reviews.

Film fan sites
www.filmbug.com ○○○○
Great site with almost the whole screenplays for some (although not that many) films.

www.warnerbros.com ○○
Substantial site, focusing on the latest releases. Good section for kids with games.

www.foxstudios.com ○○○○
Links you to dedicated film sites that are often good, with a great deal of information on current films and sample soundtracks.

www.countingdown.com ○○○○
This says it is the ultimate fan site, and it may not be lying. Votes on which are the best sites for every film issue.

www.disney.com ○○○○
The wonderful world of Disney. Great site for Disney pictures and sounds, if you like that kind of thing.

TV sites
www.channel4.com ○○○○
News, chat and live scorecard feeds for sporting events covered, such as cricket and racing.

www.bbc.co.uk ○○○○
Huge site with news, weather, etc. and background on programmes, interactive chats, and the *Archers* fan site.

www.itv.co.uk ○○○○
News updates and more on your favourite programmes.

www.channel5.co.uk ○○○○
Catch up with the gossip and background on your favourite Channel 5 soaps and dramas if you have any.

www.sky.com ○○○○
World news, business updates, games, background information on, for example, Harry Enfield's characters. Huge section on sports with interactive question and answers on football, changing room interviews and all upcoming fixtures.

TV fan sites
www.snpp.com ○○○○○
Brilliant site that tells you everything you could want to know about all the *Simpsons* shorts and episodes ever! Keeps going despite Fox's demands for the site to stop.

www.walford.2y.net ○○○
Good *Eastenders* fan site.

www.hignfy.com ○○○○
Website by Hat Trick for the show *Have I Got News For You*. The site is fun and filled with features and jokes.

www.thexfiles.com ○○○○
Spookily, it's just like the real thing . . .

Listings for TV, radio and cinema
www.unmissabletv.co.uk ○○○○○
Full listings of every channel, BBC and commercial, terrestrial and satellite. Very easy to use and to see. Click on TV listings on the homepage.

www.ft.com ✪✪✪
Excellent, clear listing of what's on at your local cinemas and with information of their websites (if any), or more usually phone numbers and address. On the homepage, go to Going Out about, then UK entertainment guide. But you can search only the day you are looking at the site.

www.popcorn.co.uk ✪✪✪
Enter your postcode and the film you want to see and the site will show you the nearest cinemas, with the distance from you. But the links to the cinema itself do not generally work.

www.thisislondon.co.uk/html/hottx/film/top_direct.html✪✪✪✪
Good cinema listings with addresses and phone numbers, allowing you to check what films are on and where they're showing. Only snag is that it only covers the London area – check out **thisislancashire.co.uk, thisisthenortheast.co.uk** or your local part of the Associated Newspapers web empire for slightly less comprehensive but still useful listings.

www.timeout.co.uk ✪✪✪
Online version of the popular London listings magazine. Difficult to navigate.

Music

Sometime during 2000 the term 'MP3' overtook 'sex' as the most popular search term on the web, demonstrating the importance of music on the internet. MP3 is the best-known type of compressed computer file that allows music to be manageably sent down old-fashioned telephone lines and stored on modest-sized computers – unlike films and television, which will have to wait for greater bandwidth. MP3 has ushered in a world where consumers can search for the songs they want on the internet, download them for free, and email them to their friends, regardless of whether the material is copyrighted or not.

The big recording companies are trying to hold the line against MP3 by developing encrypted versions of compressed music files, but the case involving Napster (a US website that enables file swapping of 500,000 tracks by some 38m users) has highlighted the difficulty of enforcing copyright laws on the internet: at the moment it is largely up to the individual to decide whether they want to respect the laws of intellectual property.

While the internet is transforming the method of delivery of music to consumers, it has also brought greater convenience for consumers wanting to track down obscure CDs. You can also take advantage of the unbelievable wealth of background material about music online. Almost every band has its website and its fanzine.

Downloading music

Listening to music or downloading music from the internet is easy. All you need is some software, such as Real Player, Winamp, Sonique or Media Player, all of which can be obtained for free at **www.downloads.com**. Otherwise copies can be obtained direct from companies such as Nullsoft (**www.nullsoft.com**) or Microsoft (**www.microsoft.com**). For the Macast package, you go to www.macamp.net. You then visit one of the many sites offering music on the net such as **www.emusic.com**, **www.peoplesound.com** or **www.icrunch.com**. After that, you can choose whether you want to listen to a sample immediately (so-called 'streaming') or whether you want to download the music in the form of an MP3 file for listening later.

'The only people scared of Napster are people who have filler on their albums.'

Courtney Love

> ## Music Jargon
>
> *MP3*: a compression technique invented by the German-based Motion Picture Experts Group (MPEG) that shrinks music files to about a twelfth of their original size, thereby allowing them to be sent over the internet in minutes rather than hours. Also the name used by a US website from which you can download MP3 files.
>
> *Liquid Audio*: a company making distribution software that protects copyright material using encryption and audio watermarks.
>
> *Streaming*: listening to a track directly from a website.
>
> *Burning*: recording a CD from a digital master.
>
> *Players*: software for downloading and playing MP3s.
>
> *Ripping*: transferring tracks from a CD into a basic (uncompressed) computer file.
>
> *Skins*: an alternative appearance for an MP3 player's user interface.
>
> *Encoding*: compressing a basic digital file (WAV) into a format such as MP3.
>
> *Bitrate*: a measure of the detail (and therefore quality) when transferring a digital recording. The higher the bitrate, the higher the quality – and also the larger the computer file.
>
> *Napster*: US web site that allows users to swap music files over the internet for free.
>
> *WAV*: uncompressed music file (bulky predecessor to MP3).
>
> *Watermark*: an inaudible code that identifies the original buyer of an MP3 – and which can be used to trace the origin of illegal copies.
>
> *Playlist*: option on an MP3 player that allows user to choose order of tracks.

Streaming appears attractive because it is usually free (for short tracks). The disadvantage is that the quality of the music sound can be adversely affected by the busy-ness of the net. If the net is really busy or if you don't have a fast modem, the sound grinds to a halt. However, you can store your favourite MP3s online, which means they don't take up valuable space on your hard disk and you can access them anywhere. If you download an MP3 file, the quality is nearly as good as a CD; and if you are using a cable modem or ADSL, then you can scoop up a track in a few seconds. But if you are working from fairly modest equipment, which home equipment often is, downloading a song may take up to twenty minutes.

At the time of writing, Napster appeared to have agreed to start charging users about US$5 a month in return for Bertelsmann dropping its court case, unspecified investment in Napster and access to Bertelsmann's tracks.

It's unclear whether the other big labels will follow Bertelmann's lead or whether Napster users will simply migrate towards more advanced sites such as Gnutella.

Once you have downloaded the MP3 file onto your computer, you can choose whether to listen to it directly from there (through built-in or attached speakers, or through headphones). You can email it to a friend or you can transfer the music to an MP3 player. This relatively new piece of hardware (not to be confused with the specialist software mentioned above) is smaller and more robust than Sony's Mini Discman – you can go jogging with it if you like because there are no moving parts. The memory is solid state. Cheap MP3 players cost about £100 and hold about an hour of music. The more expensive players have twice that capacity.

The attractions of internet music for consumers are considerable: you can sample a track without the risk of having to buy a whole album and then finding that you don't like most of it. Moreover sites like **www.MP3.com** and **www.peoplesound.com** offer the chance to listen to new bands who don't yet have recording contracts.

Copyright disputes

The ease of downloading and copying music files has encouraged the emergence of sites like **www.napster.com**, which enables the consumer to search for music files on computers belonging to other people that are also registered with Napster. Napster is the subject of a huge legal case in the US in which it is accused of encouraging illegal copying of copyright material. It is vulnerable because it keeps lists of registered users on its server. But a more advanced site, Gnutella (**www.gnutella.wego.com**) which uses a decentralised network and does not keep records of users on its servers. This type of system may be impossible for the authorities to monitor. Another decentralised system called Freenet is also under development.

The music industry is hostile to these sites because if everyone downloads Madonna tracks for free, record companies will not get a

> 'Napster pointed everyone in the direction of the best business model for music on the web. It works and it will probably be the primary way people access music in the future.'
>
> **Internet music executive**
>
> 'The internet distributes music cheaper and faster [than the big labels]. Their primary purpose will be replaced.'
>
> **Ian Clarke, Freenet**

> 'Where are the great MP3 discoveries we have been promised? I don't know of one act that has crossed over.'
>
> **Garret Keogh, iCrunch**

> 'There are 10 times the number of CDs released compared to 10 years ago and it's a £15 gamble that doesn't always pay off.'
>
> **Ernesto Schmitt, Peoplesound.com**

> 'Consumers have spoken. Regardless of whether they [the big labels] consider Napster right or wrong, they must beat Napster at its own game.'
>
> **Forrester Research**

return on their huge investment in artists. But the statistics are confusing. Sales of CDs are still rising, and Napster supporters point to the big sales of CDs when groups have decided to release the albums first on the internet. They point out that online CD stores have stimulated sales of CDs from backlists. Companies such as Peoplesound argue that being able to sample tracks from a CD – whether pop or classical – makes it easier to decide whether you want to buy a whole album, and that this may stimulate CD sales.

After a complex legal case between the record companies and MP3 in which the company's My.MP3 system (which makes about 5–10,000 tracks available online) was found to have breached copyright laws, the big labels are now softening their stance and making tracks available online. Sony and Bertelsmann have put tracks on **www.imix.com** (where you can select tracks and make up your own CD and even design the cover). EMI has put free tracks on Peoplesound and is using the new technology to test consumer reaction to new groups more thoroughly before backing them with really big money.

All of the big labels are experimenting with encryption and watermarking techniques that may prevent some types of illegal copies, and other companies such as Liquid Audio are offering encryption software for the same purpose. But it is hard to see how these moves will hold back the explosion in the use of MP3: the technology is increasingly popular offline as well as online. People can make perfectly legal MP3 files from their CDs to listen to on an MP3 player; and you can also now buy MP3 equipment for hi-fi systems. The next generation of MP3 players is likely to be even smaller and even more convenient. So it looks more and more as if the debate about MP3 is a re-run of other technological advances in the music business (such as audio tape) which the industry initially resisted and finally embraced.

The question is not whether music distribution switches to the internet but how the major labels will be able to manage the transition and still make money. The two main options appear to be charging much less for songs and albums. (a PriceWaterhouseCoopers study suggests that labels will only be able to charge 30 cents for a song or US$7.50 for a downloadable album) or moving to a subscription service where users pay, say, US$10 a month for unlimited music.

Buying CDs online

For consumers still interested in buying CDs, the web has brought major benefits. Tracking down estoteric CDs through sites such as Amazon (**www.amazon.co.uk**) or **www.bol.com** (which is backed by Bertelsmann, one of the big record labels) is far easier than calling round different music retailers, which are usually strong on new titles but pathetic about getting hold of other items. An online music retailer can list at least ten times the titles that a shop can stock. Amazon in the UK lists well over 200,000, and the site also offers a wealth of background information and reviews.

> 'Record companies need to make money [from electronic distribution], but I haven't figured out how.'
>
> **Larry Kenswil, Universal Music**

The only potential problem for consumers is delivery dates. You need to check delivery details carefully, particularly with a large order. If one of the CDs comes from a slower wholesaler, then you may have to wait for the whole order. Although it lacks the depth of Amazon, UK consumers should consider **www.hmv.co.uk** because it is one of the few CD sites that allows you to return any unwanted CDs you ordered online to any of their high street stores.

If you are a cheapskate, you go to **www.shopsmart.co.uk** and punch in the record you want and Shopsmart's 'bot' (price comparison search engine) will find the site which is selling the item at the lowest price, including delivery, and in the shortest time. This is a very real example of the internet's famous ability to create price transparency, and may change the strategy of retailers of easily comparable items.

For those buying from foreign websites (for example, the main Amazon site in the US), CDs are liable to import duty of 3 per cent and VAT if the invoice total is greater than £18. So in theory it is usually worth splitting larger orders. (For more details on import duties, see Shopping.)

Information

The wealth of online information about music is formidable. It includes official sites dedicated to big artists (often hosted by their record companies), fan-club sites, online magazines such as Miller Freeman's **www.dotmusic.com** and the online sites of established offline magazines, such as **www.nme.com**. There are useful resources whether you are interested in obscure types of dance music or opera. You can also track down people with similar tastes via chat rooms and forums. The best way to track down individual sites is to go through either a general search engine or a specialist music search engine such as **www.clickmusic.com**. The ultimate band listing (**www.ubl.com**) also has a vast range of links and covers recording companies as well as artists. However, when you actually click through to pages on some artists they are empty.

Selected sites:

Downloadable music

www.mp3.com ⚫⚫⚫⚫
Leading site offering legal MP3s.

www.napster.com ⚫⚫⚫⚫
US site providing access to MP3s on other Napster users' computers.

www.peoplesound.com ⚫⚫⚫⚫
Unsigned bands site. Currently has 8,000 artists. Best known for search facilities that allows you to hunt for groups that 'sound like' another band. Shortly to introduce an advanced search facility that will be suitable for classical music.

www.emusic.com ⚫⚫⚫⚫
Legal MP3s: 125,000 tracks and 7,000 artists.

www.icrunch.com ⚫⚫⚫⚫
Downloadable music from independent record labels, especially dance and alternative music. Well-designed site.

www.gnutella.wego.com ⚫⚫⚫⚫
More sophisticated technology than Napster.

www.vitaminic.com ⚫⚫⚫
Unsigned bands site.

www.gmn.com ⚫⚫⚫
Web casts and downloads of classical music.

www.onlineclassics.net ⚫⚫⚫⚫
Online videos of operas, concerts and plays.

www.mcy.com ⚫⚫⚫
Legal webcasts of big names (for a fee).

www.besonic.com ⚫⚫⚫
Downloads some free and some at a cost.

www.ejay.com ⚫⚫⚫
Radio/magazine/downloads.

www.musicmaker.com ⚫⚫⚫
Innovative US-based site offering customised CDs: you choose from a selection of 150,000 tracks across many genres. Also offers 100,000 downloadable tracks.

Music retailers

www.amazon.co.uk ●●●●
Lists more than 200,000 CDs. Useful reviews and information but postage charges are higher than on some other sites.

www.amazon.com ●●●●
Has deeper listings than the UK site but there is import duty and VAT to pay on orders worth more than £18.

www.boxman.com
CD retailer now in receivership.

www.bol.com ●●●●
Good levels of service but lacks the number of reviews offered by Amazon.

www.cdnow.com ●●●●
Big US site (now owned by Bertelsmann).

www.clickmusic.com ●●●
CDs and other music products plus useful music search engine.

www.hmv.co.uk ●●●
Navigation can be slow but you can return CDs to high-street stores.

www.whsmith.co.uk ●●
Solid site but slow to load and light on news and reviews.

www.jungle.com ●●●
Launched with £10m of free gifts in 1999 but recently bought by GUS for a knock-down price. Free delivery.

www.audiostreet.infront.co.uk ●●●
Free delivery and selection of MP3s. Popular but cluttered site.

www.countdownarcade ●●
Slow to load (with irritating video clip). Few reviews.

www.101CD.com ●●●
Simple site, competitive mailing costs, especially on larger orders. Like many other CD retailers, games, videos and books also available.

www.imix.com ●●●●
Site offering customised CDs from 250,000 tracks and 250 labels including Sony and Bertelsmann.

Music software

www.downloads.com ●●●●
Comprehensive software site.

www.real.com
Free downloading software and improved versions (for a fee).

www.nullsoft.com

www.microsoft.com/windows/mediaplayer/downloads

Music News, Reference and Magazines

www.billboard.com ❂❂❂
Music news and streaming. Also has "hits of the web" feature.

www.countrycool.com ❂❂❂
The world of country music, news, music, video and much more.

www.dotmusic.com ❂❂❂
The usual mix of news and music with UK bias.

www.nme.com ❂❂❂
Online version of offline magazine. Respected contents but buying CDs is more straightforward from specialist CD retailers.

www.rollingstone.com
Online version of magazine, also offers tracks and webcasts.

www.opera.co.uk ❂❂❂
Excellent links to opera houses world-wide. Site from Opera magazine.

www.rootsworld.com ❂❂❂
Online version of magazine with wealth of content covering folk and pop.

www.spin.com ❂❂❂
Another online magazine.

www.ubl.com ❂❂❂
The Ultimate Band List: source of links to bands, fanzines and record companies.

www.grove.music.com
Subscription-based online version of huge music dictionary available November 2000 (similar versions for Jazz and Opera).

www.roughguides.couk ❂❂
Tasters of books on music (but full text is not available, unlike the travel guides).

Restaurants

You worked late and you can't face the idea of cooking, and there's nothing in the fridge anyway. You say to your boyfriend, 'Let's eat out.' He says: 'Fine, I've got a yen for Japanese this evening.' Suppressing a groan, you say to your computer, 'Where's the nearest Japanese restaurant where we can eat for less than a hundred euros, and we won't have to book or queue?' A few seconds later, a mellifluous voice replies, 'Sorry, you'd have to go to Edinburgh for that. I can get you a table for 9.30 at the Osaka on Brompton Road, but the bill will be a little higher than you requested.'

Well, we're not there yet. There isn't a comprehensive directory of all the restaurants in the country, and the search engines on even the best sites leave something to be desired. But the interactivity of the internet and the ability to store and retrieve vast amounts of data is making it a little easier to answer that old question, 'Where shall we eat?'

Portals

A reasonable starting-point for national restaurant information is **www.waitrose.com**'s 'restaurant guide' section. It solicits reviews from users in order to build up its database but also incorporates reviews from a number of other guides and booking sites. In London it leans heavily on *Hardens* (see below). But it has major holes in its geographic coverage – for example, there are no listings for Maidstone, Kent. Now Maidstone may possibly be a pretty dreary place, but it is the county town of Kent, after all.

Most of the major search engines/directories have entertainment or lifestyle sections. Hunting around normally reveals a food and drink section, but they are not necessarily very useful. For instance **www.excite.co.uk/lifestyle/** makes you click through numerous pages to find your own area, and then yields a pretty limited selection of restaurants. You then have to click through to the site of each one individually to find information about location, price and so on. Yahoo's **www.yahoo.co.uk** is slightly better, as it simply clicks you through to guides put together by other people.

Traditional guides online

A number of traditional restaurant guides are setting up online. The excellent *Harden Restaurants* guide can be found at **www.hardens.com**. You have to register, but the process is free and brief, and the site offers a no-nonsense rating and price guide for restaurants by location and cuisine. If you only use one guide to London restaurants, use this. A national version of the guide is available through the Waitrose site at **www.waitrose.com/food_drink/hardens/hardens_home.htm**.

The AA's restaurant guide can be found online at **http://theaa.co.uk** under their hotels section. The site claims to list 8,000 hotels and B&Bs, and most entries include an extensive write-up and plus a map locator. The folk at the AA are pretty demanding: there are apparently no outstanding restaurants in the south-east of England. The AA's great rival the RAC (**www.rac.co.uk/services/hotelfinder/**) has only 3,000 hotels and pays less attention to restaurants.

The doyenne of restaurant guides in the UK, of course, is the Consumer Association's *Good Food Guide*. The Association doesn't seem to like the web culture of free information, and the *Guide* has no online presence.

Internet-only restaurant directories

Apart from these well-known offline guides, the internet also offers many specialist directory sites that serve up various types of national or regional coverage and restaurant information. However, no website (as far as we know) offers comprehensive nationwide listings.

www.baltipot.co.uk/, part of the **www.countyweb.co.uk** national directory service, gives a listing of Indian restaurants and take-aways by region. The restaurant listings are basic, giving address and telephone information, with the addition of a call-back service (although the usefulness of this feature will depend on the efficiency of the restaurant, of course). Users can request to be contacted immediately or within the hour. The site also has listings for other cuisines, from Japanese to 'Fish and Chips'. Countyweb's bigger competitors fared less well in our test. **www.scoot.co.uk** brought up twenty-five restaurants as a response to the London postcode entered, most of them a long way outside the area. Upmystreet (**www.upmystreet.com**) has a useful feature that will list restaurants by distance from your front door.

www.foodndrink.co.uk is a good-looking site providing restaurant guides for London, Leeds, Manchester, Edinburgh and Glasgow, and restaurant listings for a number of other cities. The directory is searchable by name, location, price and food type. Its coverage is less good than some of its rivals, but its reviews are frank and forthright.

www.placetoeat.co.uk/ is a garish, even ugly, site, but it claims to contain links to 40,000 restaurant sites across the country, categorised by location. There are pictures of many of the restaurants included. It has some major holes in its coverage and is far from comprehensive in the areas it does cover. **www.local-restaurant.com** claims to list 22,354 restaurants, and is reasonably clearly laid out.

www.where-to-eat.co.uk is a fairly good, if curiously liberal, search engine: a query about French restaurants in one London postcode district brought up 162 options. Top of the list was the only French restaurant in that code, then came some Spanish and Indian contenders in the district, and then a long list of French restaurants from all over London. It claims to have 2,000 restaurants listed.

www.restaurants.co.uk has a terrific URL, and is trying to leverage that asset by charging restaurants £99 for a listing. But its search engine's categories are too broad to be of real value: throwing up all the restaurants in south-east London leaves the reader with too much work to do. Trying to refine the search by entering say, French in London SE11 in the search box yielded Indian, Greek, Spanish, British and seafood restaurants – anything but French. Restaurants.co.uk will have competition. **www.cuisine.net** is still building its database of restaurants, but is only charging them £2 per listing. Maybe this fee will rise as the site gets bigger.

www.simplyfood.co.uk/eatingout/ offers listings/reviews of a claimed 25,000 restaurants nationally. It is powered by Yell. The reviews it contains are candid and helpful, but the coverage seems less extensive than other sites.

Where to eat in London

The *Evening Standard's* **www.thisislondon.co.uk**, reasonably enough, only covers London. But even within London its coverage is disappointing, although the standard of the reviews of the restaurants it does cover are perhaps the best on any web-based directory.

Time Out's site **www.timeout.com** has neat, simple design, but the navigation is poor. It is a struggle to find information about restaurants, and the search engine is very disappointing: a search for French restaurants in Central London yielded no results.

Specialist directories

Given the difficulties (illustrated by the previous sites) of putting together a comprehensive directory to a subject as vast as all the restaurants in the UK, the way forward may be a series of specialist directories. One excellent example is **www.currypages.co.uk**. Apparently created by a talented programmer in Bath as an experiment in WAP programming, it does not reveal how many Indian restaurants it covers, but a search on my area revealed most of the ones I know. The site can be accessed from PCs as well as WAP phones.

http://happycow.net/europe/england/ is the place for vegetarians, with basic information on 147 vegetarian restaurants in England, 51 of them in London.

Pot luck

The internet should be a great place to shop for last-minute tables at exclusive restaurants. **www.lastminute.com**, dealer in all things last minute, has a restaurant section. A number of 'exclusive' restaurants are listed under their 'Fully Booked' service, but the benefits of this service are dubious: the table availability listing on the site one night in September 2000 for Spoon at the Sanderson in central London had free tables listed until only 18.30. Actually phoning the restaurant revealed that tables were available throughout the evening. Booking is available online, though failure to turn up makes you liable for a £10 charge.

Lastminute.com is seen by many people as essentially a travel site, but as its name suggests, you can also use it to generate ideas for a quick booking if you are relatively time-poor, cash-rich. As I found out, however, the pot-luck approach can be a bad idea if you are booking for an important evening, like Valentine's Day. Following a very disappointing evening, the customer service from Lastminute was exemplary, though. Lastminute.com also has links with restaurants in Amsterdam, Paris, and with US restaurants via **www.opentable.com**. The site has tables listed at a number of restaurants in both European cities, and again booking is available online, ideal for those arriving late in a city who would like to be assured of somewhere to eat.

WAP Guides

Online restaurant guides are also starting to appear for WAP-enabled mobile phones. The mviva mobile portal (**www.mviva.com**) offers Citikey for London and Edinburgh in the UK, which offers listings of restaurants and bars as well as lastminute.com. The portal also explains how to set up a WAP-enabled mobile phone to access these guides.

Booking and ordering online

Booking services are useful if you want results quickly or if you are going to be visiting an unfamiliar city. With an ordinary directory you have to phone round the restaurants your search finds and find out if they have tables available. With these sites you are taken only to restaurants that have tables. The drawback is that the selection is narrower. For example, **www.book2eat.com/** offers one of the best booking services on the web. For one of the restaurants listed, surfers can view table availability, menu and restaurant information. A reasonable number of restaurants are listed on the site, but unfortunately coverage is limited to London.

The 'booking service with bite', **www.toptable.co.uk/**, claims to be Britain's largest booking and advisory service. The site offers a good list of 800 restaurants from around the country. Booking online is a painless process. On completion of a booking the user is given a confirmation code, and a number is provided for cancellations. For online booking for French restaurants try **www.gourmetsociety.com/**, a simple, good-looking site.

More ambitious than this is **www.menunet.com**. It allows you to order food for home delivery, and then 'to track, in real-time, the status of your order – in much the same way as you can track parcels! We also tell the customer immediately if the restaurant is unable to complete the order for you and we tell you why.' To overcome fears about credit card fraud on the net, the site announces 'We do not just pass your credit card details on to the restaurant. We collect the payment from your credit card directly, using the most highly secure methods available today. The security precautions we take mean it's more likely that you could have your credit card stolen in the restaurant if you went there yourself.'

Selected sites

Restaurants
www.osatsuma.com ✪✪✪
Overall: the site of the popular 'modern Japanese' London restaurant. Smart, simple design offering menu information and a guided tour.

www.belgo-restaurants.com/ ✪✪✪
Overall: the website of the Belgo chain of Belgium restaurants is a good example of a site that has had some effort put into its design.

www.holne-chase.co.uk/index.html ✪✪✪✪
Another good site which shows how to do it: attractive and informative.

www.waterside-inn.co.uk ✪✪✪✪✪
Overall: information about the Michelin-three-star-rated Bray restaurant. Online booking and enquiry.

Directories and guides
Harden's ✪✪✪✪
Access the London guide from **www.hardens.com**, and the UK one from **www.waitrose.com/food_drink/hardens/hardens_home.htm**.

www.countyweb.co.uk ✪✪✪✪
Beats the major directories like Scoot and Yell on restaurants.

www.foodndrink.co.uk ✪✪✪
Partial coverage, but good reviews.

www.where-to-eat.co.uk ✪✪✪
Good coverage, but an erratic search engine.

www.currypages.co.uk ✪✪✪✪
Overall, perhaps the best restaurant directory we found – if you like curry!

happycow.net/europe/england/ ✪✪✪✪
Top resource for vegetarians.

www.toptable.co.uk/ ✪✪✪✪
Go straight to a restaurant with an available table.

Nightlife

Pubs

One of the wonderful things about surfing the internet is the people you come across who are engaged in magnificent, heroic, and probably quite futile enterprises. In the last century people used to race to be first to the North Pole. Now they race to be the first to list and rate online all the pubs in London. A splendid chap called John Adams is engaged in this Sisyphean task, and you can see the results at **www.ucl.ac.uk/~ccaajpa/pubs-listed.html**.

The nearest thing to an equivalent for the whole of England seems to be **www.pubs247.com**, whose search engine lets you look for a pub in or near a particular postcode, with options like a real fire, a pool table, satellite television, and even baby-changing facilities. The site is a little delicate and seizes up too often, but perhaps time will stabilise it. Its rival, **www.pubsguide.co.uk**, is a long way behind in terms of coverage.

Far from trying to be comprehensive, the Campaign for Real Ale is very choosy about which pubs it puts on its national inventory at **www.camra.org.uk**, with only twenty-two pubs in the whole of London, for instance. But those it does include get a picture and a useful write-up. Another site which sticks to 'good' pubs is **www.real-ale-guide.co.uk**, but it has only six in London, and the reviews are provided by visitors, of whom there seem to have been three.

Clubs

The single best guide to clubbing to look at is **www.ministryofsound.com**. It covers clubs all round the country, with details of resident DJs, capacity, dress codes, number of dance floors and whether there is any food. Among other things, visitors can review clubs they have been to and buy VIP tickets. **www.clickmusic.co.uk** is a portal with links to all manner of great-sounding places. You'll find mailing lists and WAP services for regular updates on tickets, special offers and general information. The sites offer to send details of a club to a friend and let you exchange news and views with fellow clubbers out on the town. You can often buy tickets to sought-after clubs such as Fabric or Home in London from **www.lastminute.com**, but not if you wait until the last minute. They have to be booked at least a day in advance, but if you do this you can save yourself having to queue.

Even for those with no interest at all in clubbing, these sites are interesting places to wander around, as their owners are keen to experiment with Flash and other clever software to animate their pages.

General guides

The site **www.whatsonwhen.com** is a user-friendly US-based events directory covering special events around the world. At the time of writing it carried a surprisingly detailed and informative piece on the celebrations of Guy Fawkes Night at Lewes in Sussex. The site also offers links to travel guides, flights, tickets and hotels.

More locally, **www.ananova.com/whatson** has a reasonable search engine/directory of events in the UK, but it doesn't allow you to refine the search, so you end up with huge unwieldy lists. Another general listings site is **www.ents24.com**, which is less comprehensive, but nicely designed.

More locally still, **www.timeout.co.uk** and **www.thisislondon.co.uk** are the main contenders for the title of essential listings site for London. Neither is anything like comprehensive, but both are improving all the time. Like its offline parent, **www.timeout.co.uk** is aimed at a younger, trendier audience.

Selected sites

General guides
www.ananova.com/whatson ❶❶❶
Search for what's going on in art, dance, jazz, clubs, etc.

www.timeout.co.uk ❶❶❶
Reviews, listings and world city guides for all entertainment.

www.ents24.com ❶❶❶❶
Search by postcode for listings, addresses, web links and maps. Also, up-to-the-minute listings direct to your phone.

www.thisislondon.co.uk❶❶❶
The *Evening Standard* online; plenty of information but not comprehensive, and not all that easy to search.

www.whats-on-guide.co.uk ❶❶
Covers all sorts of leisure categories but far from comprehensively.

www.ukevents.net ❶❶
A limited selection of clubs and venues.

www.night-out.co.uk ❍
A selection of venues around the country.

UK Clubs
www.ministryofsound.com ❍❍❍❍❍
Great site with a flexible search facility for all clubbing events, top tens, reviews and webcasts. Also forums to ask all those questions you can't ask your mother.

www.clickmusic.co.uk ❍❍❍❍❍
The clubs and venues section has links to the best sites for club info.

www.clubbersguidetotheuk.co.uk
Soon to be re-launched as www.clubsuk.co.uk. Plans to include links, chat rooms to compare nights out, and a message board in case you've lost that babe's number.

www.clubbed.com ❍❍❍
General club life news and stuff.

www.ponana.co.uk ❍❍❍
Worth visiting once for the flying carpet introduction.

www.klublife.co.uk
Yet to be launched.

www.out2club.com ❍❍❍❍
Minimal but instant listings for club events in London for the week, and links to all London's clubs.

www.cream.co.uk ❍❍❍
Trendy enough site looking like it will offer much more than it actually does.

www.fridge.co.uk ❍❍❍❍
Full and easily accessible pitch of all forthcoming events, and you can search the deep freeze.

Music
www.nme.com ❍❍❍❍❍
Live music gigs around the UK, easy to search. Budding webmasters can add *NME* music news to their sites.

www.music365.co.uk ❍❍❍
More music news, reviews and features.

www.virgin.net/music ❍❍❍❍
News, reviews and popular gigs around the UK, topical and lively discussions too.

Comedy
www.sceneone.co.uk ❍❍❍
Good for comedy, also plenty of reviews, recommendations and detailed listings.

www.funny.co.uk ❍❍❍❍
Great for comedy listings, sign up for email updates.

Casinos
www.british-casinos.co.uk ❍❍❍
Casino addresses and numbers but no maps or web links.

Sport

If you want to be kept abreast of the latest state of play in a football, tennis or cricket match, there are sites on the internet which will the keep the score permanently updated on your computer screen. Whichever sport you are interested in, it is bound to be covered somewhere on the internet. And you can access more information, gossip, rumours and commentary on sporting subjects than you can find in all the daily newspapers combined. It is also possible to watch some sporting events on your computer, as they are 'webcasted' over the internet. But unless the sites offering the service have generous bandwidth, they tend to fall over when a significant number of people attempt to access them.

If you are interested in particular sporting teams or events, the internet provides the perfect resource to exercise your tribal affiliations: you can choose to have news covering just the sporting events that you care about emailed to you, or you can subscribe to specialist newsletters. If you have a credit card, you can bet online and make a 9 per cent tax saving, because betting on the net is tax free. Online betting sites also have an advantage over phone betting in that you don't have to listen to the bookies going through a list of odds: they are on the screen in front of you.

Live sport news

The major TV channels have significant sports sections on their websites (for example, **www.bbc.co.uk/sports** and **www.sky.com/sports/home**), which show up-to-the-minute news on sport, and whether they are broadcasting the event live or not. The sites feature audio and video clips, discussion forums and other interactive features – for example, football fans have the opportunity to put questions to television pundit Andy Gray on the Sky website.

The majority of internet portals, such as Yahoo, have sport sections, but you can also go to a dedicated sporting portal, such as the very aptly named **www.sportal.co.uk**. Again, you will find news on all the sports you can think of, along with extra features such as games, interactive chat with stars and the latest sporting gossip, or 'sossip'.

As well as the generalist sites, there are numerous sites dedicated to individual sports, with live news, commentary, editorial and, of course, the score. **www.cricket.org**

caters for all your cricketing needs when Channel 4 is not covering the events at **www.cricket4.com**, or indeed even when it is. One company that covers a range of individual sports well is the 365 brand, such as **www.cricinfo365.com**, **www.football365.com**, **www.rugby365.com**, etc.

Personalisation

One of great things you can use the internet for is to customise the sports information you receive. So, if you don't want to have to log on to the BBC's web site in order to find out the latest score in the cricket or football game you care about, you can instead personalise sporting sites to bring up the information you request. For example, if you only care about the England cricket score (wherever the team is playing) and the latest Man U game, then this is what you will be given news on. One of the best sites to personalise your sport interests is Yahoo, at **www.my.yahoo.com**.

Football

Football has a huge internet presence. Most professional clubs now have their own sites, although some (such as Liverpool FC, at **www.liverpoolfc.net/home.html**) have only recently got online. With club sites you get pretty much what you would expect: slick sites with match and player information, all toeing the party line. Club sites also have shopping areas with all manner of branded gifts.

A better starting-point for information and gossip are the many independent sites. A premium-rate phone call company, **www.teamtalk.co.uk**, has news and gossip from all UK league clubs, while **www.football365.com** is a news service with an quirky slant. For example, the following commentary was posted explaining Manchester United's defeat at Arsenal in October 2000: 'Arsenal were missing Patrick Vieira, but United missed him more. They were devastated to find the leggy linkman suspended – having only prepared a strategy to play against ten men.'

For "fossip" – football gossip – the best places to visit are often the unofficial fan-maintained sites. Put the name of your favourite club into any search engine. A good example of what such sites can do is
www.timespin.free-online.co.uk/womble.htm, a Wimbledon FC fan site that provides links to a huge number of Wimbledon sites on the web.

Live Sports Broadcasts

Live sports broadcasts are also starting to appear on the web, but webcasting is not yet proving a great success because the sites tend to crash when a great number of people try to access them at the same time. You can catch sporting events live on the radio over the internet at BBC's Radio 5, **www.bbc.co.uk/fivelive**, and also from a great number of stations in the US, covering, for example, baseball games (see Radio, TV and Films).

The BBC is also starting to show live matches on its web site. The latest FA television deal, which runs for the 2001–2 season, allows clubs to show highlights of their matches on their websites.

Keeping up-to-date

The internet, and specifically the 'mobile internet', are great for keeping informed of how your favourite sports teams are performing. Vodafone have an SMS football service with news about goals, half-time and full-time scores for Premiership and Division One matches in England and Premiership matches in Scotland. Sportal.co.uk has a mobile site at **wap.sportal.co.uk/** in addition to its SMS update service.

Participating

Using the internet can be a good way to find out about minority sports, and whether or not facilities and clubs exist in your area. For example, the Scottish Windsurfing Location Guide at **homepage.ntlworld.com/windsurfing/** provides details of a number of windsurfing clubs around Scotland, and **www.padi.com/**, the Professional Association of Diving Instructors (PADI), is a great site for divers, giving access to dive centres around the globe. The site offers reordering for the vital PADI card, although the reorder form has to be downloaded and posted.

For team sports, individual club sites allow club members easy access to team and match information. But many of these sites, such as **http://www.richmond-hockey-club.com/** are visually dull and of little relevance to non-members.

Betting

Betting online is fast becoming one of the most popular ways to gamble because it is free of the 9 per cent tax levied on bets placed by phone or in person. (The tax is payable either on the stake or winnings.) In addition, online betting sites give you a whole range of odds on your screen which are updated in real time, provided that you refresh your screen page.

Both Ladbrokes and Coral have strong online presences, Labrokes at www.ladbrokes.co.uk and Coral at www.eurobet.co.uk. Opening an account is quick, although the account forms could be improved. If you make a mistake when opening an account at Eurobet, the entire form needs to be re-entered. Minimum bets are £5. Of course, the drawback is that to bet you must either deposit money with a debit card (not advised, see Shopping) or use a credit card. So you not only need to have a credit card, and trust to the site, but also need to trust yourself with the dreaded plastic.

Selected sites

Live sporting updates
www.bbc.co.uk/sports ❍❍❍❍
Live news coverage of all sports.

www.sky.com/sports/home ❍❍❍❍
Great, visually appealing site with great sporting coverage.

www.yahoo.com ❍❍❍❍❍
Good sporting coverage, which you can personalise at www.my.yahoo.com.

www-uk.cricket.org/ ❍❍❍
Good site for cricket information, especially live scorecards.

www.cricket4.com ❍❍❍
Ditto.

www.athleticsnet.com/ ❍❍❍❍
Up-to-the-minute athletics news and analysis in a smart, easy-to-navigate site.

Sporting news, commentary and gossip
www.itv-f1.com/ ❍❍❍
Standard sport site features such as competitions and news and statistics.

www.sports.com/ ❍❍❍
Good sport site despite an annoying amount of pop-up adverts.

www.kitbag.com ❍❍❍
Clean, easy-to-navigate commerce site for all things sporting.

www.sportal.co.uk ❍❍❍❍
Vast site covering most sports and sporting events.

www.english.sports.gov.uk ❍❍❍
The site for Sport England, previously known as The English Sports Council.

Football sites
www.opta.co.uk ❍❍❍
Provides enough statistics to keep most football anoraks happy.

www.uefa.com ❍❍❍
The official site. Good for information on all European competitions.

www.teamtalk.co.uk ❍❍❍❍
Great site for football gossip.

www.fantasyleague.co.uk/ ❍❍❍
'The original Fantasy League'. Good site, but not the cheapest.

soccer.fantasysports.yahoo.com/premier ❍❍❍❍
Completely free fantasy-league service to all Yahoo account holders.

Useful search engines
www.sportquest.com ❍❍❍
Sport-dedicated search engine, but coverage is not great.

www.zdnet.com/searchiq/subjects/sports/ ❍❍❍❍
Lists a number of sports-specific search engines and directories for individual sports.

www.altavista.com ❍❍❍❍
Major search engine with good sport coverage.

Other sports
www.padi.com/ ❍❍❍❍
Good site, giving details of international dive centres and details of PADI courses.

http://www.wsf.org.uk/ ❍
Information from the Women's Sport Foundation. Ugly site which is not updated frequently.

www.golfcourses.org/ ❍❍❍❍
Great easy-to-use course finder. Contains latest news and course reviews.

Betting
www.eurobet.com ❍❍❍❍
Well-organised site, structured by sports.

www.ladbrokes.com ❍❍❍
Ladbrokes has great plans for this site but it has a tendency to crash.

Genealogy

Introduction

Pursuing an interest in genealogy on the internet can be frustrating. There are tens of thousands of sites focusing on different aspects of the subject, but you cannot use the internet to establish whether you are related to one of Charles II's illegitimate children – or even when your ageing aunt was born. Despite the net's ability to store and sort vast amounts of data, most genealogical information remains offline. The best online resource is (oddly enough) from the Mormons, and they don't go further back than the nineteenth century, and they don't include people unless they can be sure they are dead.

If you do want to start researching your family history, you generally have to start offline because most of the searchable online resources cover the period between 1850 and 1920 (although if you have Scottish roots or ancestors who died in one of the two World Wars, the online facilities are better). However, using a combination of off- and online resources, it should be fairly straightforward to track down a significant number of your ancestors back to the middle of the nineteenth century.

The main use of the huge range of genealogical information available on the web, then, is to make offline research more efficient. You can use the web to locate where records are kept and when they are available. Moreover, rising interest in family history means that the resources available online are getting better year by year, with much of the new information keyed in by volunteers.

Getting started

The starting-point for locating internet genealogical resources in the UK is Genuki (**www.genuki.org.uk**), a web-based library and information base, which is maintained by volunteers from various family history societies. The range of information is vast (more than 20,000 pages) and covers everything from national resources to cemeteries and parish records. It contains the details of local family history societies in the area you are researching and tells you if other researchers have already done some work on the family name you are investigating.

Another potential starting point is the UK section of the WorldGenWeb project (**www.worldgenweb.org**), a charitable organisation. On the BBC website there's a well-written introduction to family history research at **www.bbc.co.uk/history/programmes/blood/family_1.shtml**. And the Public Record Office also has a useful introductory leaflet **www.pro.gov.uk/leaflets**.

Talk to granny

Even before you go online, most genealogical researchers agree that the best way to start any research is to ask existing relatives what they can remember about their families and work backwards from that. Relatives may not be able to remember all the details accurately, but this is still likely to be a more fruitful start than manic digging on the internet. In the course of this research you may become aware of relatives that you did not know about, and the internet makes contact with distant or lost relatives much easier (see the section on 'missing persons' in Getting Started). Old family photographs or letters are also useful sources.

You need a plan

You should decide on a plan of research. Are you going to trace back your father's family name as far as you can go, or are you more interested in detailed information about the last few generations of your family? Some people aim to identify all their great-great-great-grandparents. Everyone has 16 great-great-grandparents and the size of many families in the nineteenth century means that you could be swamped with information if you do not decide where to concentrate.

US resources

As in many other areas of the web, developments in internet genealogy are more advanced in the US than in the UK. Two of the biggest genealogy sites there are **www.rootsweb.com** and **www.cindislist.com**. Both sites are relevant to you if you have family links to the US, or to countries that provided lots of immigrants to the US, such as Ireland or Poland. Cindislist boasts as many as 30,000 links with other genealogy sites, which cover everything from obscure aspects of Catholicism in Louisiana, to the area that was known as East Prussia before the Second World War and much, much more.

What official records are where?

The internet is invaluable for finding out which records are kept where. Many people waste a good deal of time and money on genealogical research by rushing off to libraries and record offices without checking whether they are heading for the right place and whether they have the right information to make use of the search facilities. In England and Wales the key resource for checking information about family history is the Family Record Centre (FRC) in London (which has a link to the Public Record Office website **www.pro.gov.uk**). These pages explain the procedures and costs of obtaining copies of the birth, marriage and death certificates going back to 1837, when civil registration began.

In England and Wales the indexes to these documents are still in leather-bound tomes, whereas in Scotland the indexes can be searched online – for a fee – at **http://wood.ccta.gov.uk/grosweb/grosweb/nsf/pages/home**, as can the details of the 1.7m UK and Commonwealth citizen killed in the two world wars (**www.cwgc.org**). Once you start locating certificates, the extra details shown on these papers (such as parents) should help you find other certificates. Before 1837 research gets trickier because most records were kept at parish level, and these records are now in county record libraries. Look at **www.genuki.org.uk**, and also at Familia (**www.earl.org.uk/familia**), a web-based directory of family history resources held in public libraries in the UK and Ireland.

Enter the Mormons

One of the oddest aspects of investigating family history online is that many of the advances in genealogical research have been achieved by the Church of Jesus Christ of Latter-day Saints (the Mormons). The Mormons have put a huge effort into developing systems and resources that can be used for tracking down ancestors because it is an important tenet of Mormonism that members should try to baptise their ancestors before the Day of Judgement. Non-Mormons can access the web-based information for free at **www.familysearch.org** and can also use the Family History Centres set up by the Mormons around the world, where you can order and consult the vast archive of microfilms. The web site provides access to the International Genealogical Index (IGI), a database of several hundred million records copied from parish records, which can be searched to identify either parents or children. Although this facility is invaluable, the data is neither complete nor 100 per cent accurate, and information retrieved from here should to be verified with offline methods.

The other main achievement of the Mormons is to transcribe the 1881 census of England and Wales onto CD-Rom (available for £30). Other censuses of the nineteenth century (which took place every 10 years) are available at the FRC, but the information is organised by location, so you need to know the address of your ancestors. On the CD-Rom version you can search by name and by birthplace. Census information provides useful details about a household – particularly from 1851, when the exact ages and place of birth of the occupants of each house were recorded. The FRC is putting the 1901 census online at the start of 2002, and for about £5 it will be possible to make several searches. Scottish census records are available at the General Register Office for Scotland and those for Ireland at the National Archives in Dublin.

For those pursuing research further back than the mid-nineteenth century, the Society of Genealogists (**www.sog.org.uk**) has the biggest selection of copies of church registers, but the records of many other religious groups such as Jews, Quakers and Baptists are at the Public Record Office.

Maps and places

The last 200 years have seen major shifts of populations away from the country into cities, and cities have swallowed up whole villages and hamlets. You should become acquainted with the geography of the area you are researching – so you can recognise adjoining villages and towns that might crop up in the course of your research. Map websites such as the Ordnance Survey's **www.ordsvv.gov.uk** are discussed in the Getting Around chapter of this book. From the Ordnance Survey site there are links to **www.old-maps.co.uk**, which puts up chunks of late nineteenth century maps on your screen. However this service does not cover London. You can order a large range of old maps of the UK and Ireland from **www.rallymap.demon.co.uk.**

For place names that have disappeared you may have to consult a gazetteer. For example on the Genuki site you can trace place names listed in the 1891 census for England and Wales on **www.genuki.org.uk/big/census_place.html**. There is also a parish search facility on Genuki (**www.genuki/org.uk/big/parloc/search.html**) and on the British section of the WorldGenWeb. Both parish searches provide extra background information when you have located the relevant parish. There is also a site (**www.lost-london.inuk.com**) that covers streets in London that have changed name or disappeared.

Family Trees

Computer programmes allow the construction of much more elaborate family trees than pen and paper. Initially you may prefer to use a simple Excel spreadsheet and add boxes as appropriate, but commercial software allows you to incorporate pictures, newspaper records and other information within one tree. Packages such as Family Origins and Ultimate Family Tree cost £20-40, although there are also some simpler free packages such as Gendesigner. If you become a really fanatical researcher, you may want to start exchanging information in the form of GEDCOMs, a format for storing genealogical information that was also developed by the Mormons.

Selected websites

General genealogy sites
www.rootsweb.com ❂❂❂❂
Huge US site with a battery of search engines.

www.cindislist.com ❂❂❂❂
Claims 30,000 genealogical links.

www.ancestry.com ❂❂❂
US-oriented website with index of 20,00 genealogical sites.

www.earl.org.uk/familia ❂❂❂
Lists resources in public libraries for family history research in UK and Ireland.

www.genuki.org.uk ❂❂❂❂
Good starting-point for research in the UK.

www.genuki.org.uk/big/EmeryPaper ❂❂❂❂
Useful A-Z of genealogy for new researchers.

www.lds.org ❂❂❂
Main Mormon (Church of Jesus Christ of Latter-day Saints) website.

www.familysearch.org.uk ❂❂❂❂
Invaluable Mormon search website.

www.ffhs.org.uk ❂❂❂
Association of Family History Societies – useful introductory material and lists of contacts.

www.pro.gov.uk ❂❂❂❂
UK Public Record Office – you can search the catalogue online, but only a fraction relates to genealogical research.

www.pro.gov.uk/leaflets ❂❂❂
Public Record Office leaflets – and link to information on the Family Record Centre.

www.bbc.co.uk ❂❂❂❂
Useful Family history with introduction to research and useful genealogical links.

www.statistics.gov.uk ❍❍❍
Office for National Statistics. Also with links to the FRC.

www.sog.org.uk ❍❍❍
Society of Genealogists – some information for new researchers and details of SoG's collection of parish records

Specialist sites
www.gro-scotland.gov.uk ❍❍❍
Site for General Register for Scotland – information about how to search online for Scottish records.

www.nisra.gov.uk/grohome.htm.❍❍❍
General Register Office for Northern Ireland.

www.nifths.org ❍❍❍
Northern Ireland Family History Society.

www.jgsgb.ort.org ❍❍❍
Jewish Genealogical Society of Great Britain – links to other Jewish archives and resources.

www.one-name.org ❍❍❍
Site for researchers into particular family names (rather than individual families).

www.nationalarchives.ie ❍❍
National Archive of Ireland – guide to offline research in Ireland. Little online material

www.ellisisland.org ❍❍❍
Currently a museum site but from early 2001 it will provide a searchable database covering the 17m immigrants into the US through Ellis Island between 1892 and 1924. For a modest fee it will be possible to order a copy of relevant shipping records.

Weather

Maybe it's because it's so bad here or because we try to avoid other subjects, but the British – and perhaps especially the English – do talk a lot about the weather. It is fitting that there is a lot of weather about on the internet.

There are short-term (1–3 day), medium-term (up to a week) and long-term (up to a month) weather forecasts, plus details of day and night temperatures, humidity, wind speeds, UV indices and so on. There are also specialist sites for sailors and flyers, and sites for hay-fever sufferers. And there are sites for those fascinated by the science of meteorology itself.

The internet is strong competition to TV, radio or print for weather information because it is available round the clock, and you can call up the precise detail and pictures you want when you want, rather than waiting for the end of the news or calling premium-rate phone numbers.

General weather forecasts

Many weather pages are powered by the Met Office, whose own site (**www.meto.gov.uk**) is one of the best. Another good all-round weather site is the BBC's **www.bbc.co.uk/weather**. Most of the major news publishers and broadcasters have a weather feed, as do the major portals – for instance, **uk.weather.yahoo.com**.

Specialist information

Skiers, fliers, sailors and others need specialised weather forecasts, some of which can be found at the BBC and Met Office. On **www.uk-weather.co.uk** you can find more detail, including synoptic charts (whatever they are) plus avalanche information for climbers and skiers, and tidal information for surfers and sea kayakers, including tides and wave predictors. An amateur site for fliers and gliders is at **www.weatherjack.co.uk**, run by an ex-RAF pilot.

All sorts of local groups offer geographically specific services too, as testified by Eddie Phillipps, a surfer on Hayling Island in Sussex: 'On a breezy summer's evening I can check out the surf at the bottom of the island using the live webcam at **www.haylingisland.net** before getting my board out.'

If you suffer from hay fever, the National Pollen Research Unit has a detailed UK pollen map at **www.pollenuk.worc.co.uk**, with short-term and outlook forecasts.

Weather where you're not

You can easily find out from a newspaper what the weather is like for skiing in Chamonix or sunning in Chile, but using the internet you can do this and see the weather too, from webcams. Most of the major travel sites have good weather sections or link to someone else who does – try **www.firstresort.com**. Plus there are a huge number of webcams around the world, mostly overlooking cities, although for planning a trip you should consult forecasts as well because you can't always tell from them what a foggy Mexico City looks like. Start by looking at **www.earthwatch.com**.

Education

If you want to know more about the weather than whether you should take an umbrella to work, or can you go sailing at the weekend, there are several sites with in-depth educational and research resources. The Met Office site has an education section (**www.met-office.gov.uk/education/index.html**) designed to let teachers and pupils explore historic events or weather phenomena and measurement in more detail. An amateur site run by two Davids, **www.weather.org.uk**, has links to lots of research groups, technical data and local reporting stations. If you're a high-flyer, the British Atmospheric Data Centre, **www.badc.rl.ac.uk**, provides stratospheric and atmospheric chemistry data.

Going further afield, **www.accuweather.com** provides detailed weather forecasts for everyday life in the US and also for various outdoor activities. It covers a range of international locations too.

Finally, if you need a minute-by-minute update on the local weather, sign up at **www.onlineweather.com** for weather news delivery to your WAP phone, or text messaging to an ordinary mobile phone.

Selected sites

www.meto.govt.uk ✪✪✪✪✪
The official UK Government Met. Office. High-quality information, well presented, easy to navigate. Excellent for education and research.

www.bbc.co.uk/weather ✪✪✪✪
Weather information for UK regions and world cities as well as a magazine-style menu featuring gardening, holiday destinations and historic events.

www.pollenuk.worc.ac.uk ✪✪
This site provides the useful UK pollen map.

www.weatherjack.co.uk ✪✪✪
A useful resource for gliders in England.

www.onlineweather.com ✪✪✪
A nicely presented site, where you can set up mobile weather updates.

www.weather.org.uk ✪✪
Straight to the point, no graphics, but tons of weather information and data and lots of links.

www.accuweather.com ✪✪✪
Weather in the USA, and around the world.

www.earchwatch.com ✪✪✪✪
Easily see a view of the weather and the scene from hundreds of places around the world.

5 Organising your life

Money

If telephone banking made money management a good deal easier, the internet offers consumers even greater convenience and the possibility of saving money by making well-informed financial decisions. The web makes it very easy to compare what is on offer from many different providers at the click of a mouse. With major banks citing increased use of the internet as a reason to close branches, it is only a matter of time before many more of us will have to change the way we manage our money – whether we like it or not. Moreover, the arrival of WAP phones (which allow you to check your bank balance on the move or before making a major purchase) is likely to push the penetration of internet banking faster and further.

That's the theory, but although there are some significant advantages, in practice the benefits of the internet in money management are patchy. Some online financial products such as savings accounts and credit cards offer much better value than offline products. Online investment in the stock market costs a fraction of old-fashioned brokers. But there are significant drawbacks with some internet-only bank accounts, and the online insurance offerings appear to be well behind the rest of the financial services industry.

Shopping around

One of the most attractive tools offered by the web is the ability to search for the best financial products available. In the past the only way to do this was to scan the personal finance supplements of weekend newspapers. But the increasing variety and complexity of savings accounts, investment products, credit cards and mortgages has undermined that route. The most useful personal finance sites such as Moneynet (**www.moneynet.co.uk**), Interactive Investor (**www.iii.co.uk**) Moneyextra (**www.moneyextra.co.uk**) and Moneysupermarket (**www.moneysupermarket.co.uk**), offer interactive tools that allow you to choose criteria for narrowing down the vast range of accounts and products on offer. For example, you can search for the best credit card deal, or the best savings account for £1,000. If you have an existing account or mortgage these tools also help you decide whether it is worth going through the hassle of switching providers to save money.

These comparison engines are at their best when you hunt for the cheapest deal. They may be less reliable if you are trying to combine several different factors in a search. For example, if you were looking for a mortgage that was cheap and allowed a degree of flexibility with payments, the search engines might not point you in the best direction because flexibility is hard to quantify. One solution to the problem of comparing different financial service products is to consult Gomez, a US company that rates online financial services (and some other products) and measures factors other than price in its ratings system. It currently covers online banking, broking and credit cards at **http://uk.gomez.com**.

As well as sites such as Moneyextra, there are many other personal finance portals such as **www.ftyourmoney.com** and **www.uk-invest.com**, which offer introductory articles to many aspects of financial services. Many sites also offer glossaries of financial terms. Motley Fool (**www.fool.co.uk**) is quirkier than most; it has an interesting range of articles and doesn't pull its punches about where the consumer gets ripped off.

Banking

Savings accounts

Savings accounts have been one of the big attractions of online financial services for consumers. Banks were quick to launch online savings accounts because they are cheap and simple to operate. Customers are only interested in the rate of interest and how easily they can withdraw their money, and to recruit investors, these accounts have been offering loss-leading rates of interest, far higher than the comparable rates from branch-based accounts and slightly higher than those from telephone-based accounts. Egg (**www.egg.com**) led the way and is estimated to have spent £150m on paying out generous interest on its savings accounts. At the time of going to press, Egg offered tiered rates up to 6.8 per cent; Nationwide (**www.nationwide.co.uk**), offers 7 per cent on amounts as little as £1 and other online operators such as Smile (**www.smile.co.uk**) which is the online arm of the Co-operative Bank, are almost as competitive.

Apart from higher interest rates, some of the best operators are offering innovative products on the web. For example, Halifax's Web Saver (**www.halifax-online.co.uk**) enables the customer to place money in up to fifty different pots with different time horizons. This allows a customer to save money for a mortgage deposit alongside another pot for a holiday while still receiving competitive interest rates.

However, there are some drawbacks associated with online savings accounts. Opening an account can be just as time-consuming as a traditional postal account because you have to prove your identity (with passport copies and utility bills) and the process of registration itself is often bone-crunchingly frustrating, First-e (**www.first-e.com**), a Dublin based online bank, even resorted to offering vouchers because so many customers lost interest in completing the tortuous process.

Getting money out of an online account is far from instantaneous. Usually it takes two to three days to transfer money to a current account (no faster than telephone accounts that pay almost as much interest). Also, some banks such as Nationwide and Smile insist that savings account holders hold a parallel current account to take these transfers whether they want to or not. On top of these drawbacks, some banks have had well-publicised problems with their computer systems. So before opening an account it is worth checking to see what telephone back-up is available if you need to move your money when the computer is down. But for many people the attractions of high savings rates are likely to far outweigh the disadvantages.

Current accounts

Current accounts are the heart of most people's financial affairs, and the arrival of online banking has brought the biggest improvement in services for consumers since the arrival of telephone banking. The advantages of online banking are clear: you can get access to your account and can set up payments and standing orders not just at your convenience, but also when you are far away on business trips or holiday.

The arrival of WAP banking (currently available at First Direct, Woolwich and Egg) allows even greater ease of access – you only need a phone rather than a computer. There are also significant practical advantages to internet banking: you can see a full set of recent entries on the screen, not just the limited amount a clerk reads out to you over the phone. Moreover you can access this information at any time, rather than having to wait for a statement at the end of the month.

Although there is a substantial difference between the interest rates offered by online banks, First Direct (5 per cent) Smile (4.5 per cent), and those on the high street where you are lucky to get anything at all, there is not a great financial incentive to use online current accounts because few people are foolish enough to keep significant amounts of money in their current account. On an average balance of £1,200 a year, the gain from using an internet bank over Barclays or Lloyds is only about £60 a year. Plus, Halifax's move to offer 4 per cent on its offline current account may force the traditional high-street banks to begin offering meaningful rates of interest.

An online current account may bring you more significant benefits if you run an overdraft. For example Smile offers a "fee free" overdraft of £500 at 9.9 per cent. This compares with a rate of 18.8 per cent at Lloyds TSB and a further £60 in charges. In a full year the savings achieved by switching to Smile would be well over £100. Moreover Smile offers a no-fee and no-interest overdraft of up to £2,000 to students who fulfil certain criteria.

One problem facing users of internet banks is the lack of a branch network. Most people use branches occasionally to pay in cash, convert currencies or pay in the odd cheque. Smile and Cahoot (the online unit of Abbey National) have solved this problem by allowing customers to deposit cash at post offices. For most people in employment and with relatively little branch business, an internet-only account might be attractive. But for others, particularly the self-employed or those with small businesses, a branch-based account with an internet service will be far more appropriate.

The internet also opens up the possibility that customers will be able to pay for the level of service that they need. For example, Cahoot offers a tiered interest rate depending on whether customers opt for an internet-only account, an internet-plus-telephone service or whether a cheque book is required as well.

How to choose an internet bank

If you do want to pick an internet account there are several aspects that need to be considered. It is far easier to enable your existing account to be accessed on the internet than it is to open a completely new account (although Smile is bending over backwards to make it easier, and a new improved system of transferring direct debits is due to be introduced in 2001). Most traditional banks don't even allow you to open up an account online and often their sites are clunky and irritating (NatWest's is an appalling piece of work, a case study in how not to do it). You also need to make sure your computer and software are fully compatible with that of the bank. Some sites do not work with Apple Macs (Woolwich) and many others restrict the types of personal finance software you can use. So you might find that your bank prevents you transferring data to your own computer if you use it for drawing up accounts or a tax return.

Unfortunately you can't really see how well an account operates unless you open one. But it is still worth testing a demonstration of

'I have never come across a website from a large company that was anything like as bad as NatWest's. I do believe the thing is run by a competitor, and they are trying to force me to move my account. Or maybe their IT department has been infiltrated by anarchists.'

NatWest customer, London

an account on the computer you are most likely to use to operate it because some sites (such as Nationwide) make particularly generous use of graphics. These might work well on a fast office computer but could slow access at home to a crawl if your computer is modest. You should also consider how quickly you can get into your account. The need for visibly tight security has encouraged the use of multiple passwords on some sites (such as Barclays), which makes a mockery of the idea of speedy access.

Some internet accounts are very slow to set up details of a new payee account (someone you might want to pay). It takes several days at some online banks (such as NatWest) – which undermines the point of internet banking, especially since these payments can be set up quickly at call centres. Finally, different sites offer different amounts of account information on screen. The Bank of Scotland shows only thirty days' worth of transactions, whereas the Woolwich shows the entire transaction history on screen. This kind of feature is invaluable if you have to complete a tax return and have incomplete records; high-street banks charge heavily for reprints of statements.

Offshore accounts

Offshore banking accounts offer some advantages over UK-based accounts because they can pay interest gross of tax. The internet allows much easier and cheaper access to these accounts than in the past. For non-residents or non-taxpayers they may offer significant advantages, and there's a website (**www.moneynetoffshore.com**) to help track down the best rates. The best-known offshore internet banks are **www.first-e** and **www.fsharp.com**. Traditional banks are set to follow, but at this stage most only offer information rather than online accounts. At **www.Lloydstsb-offshore.com** even the information was out of date.

However, depending on the location of the bank, protection for depositors may be less robust than that offered under UK jurisdiction – or non-existent. It is particularly important to beware of banks with plausible but unfamiliar names in strange or exotic locations. (See Regulation, below p. 179)

Mortgages

It has been a long time since people had to curry favour with a building society in order to secure a mortgage. But the introduction of online mortgages is helping swing the balance of power even further towards the borrower, although online prices are not significantly lower than those offline. The main advance achieved by the internet has been the arrival of mortgage supermarket sites that offer a wide range of loans from a variety of lenders. Search software matches the requirements of the borrower with the most competitive product.

E-loan (**www.e-loan.co.uk**), the UK arm of a US operation, and John Charcol (**www.charcolonline.co.uk**) are the leaders in this field. E-loan boasts 1,700 mortgages from around fifty lenders and Charcol, the online arm of the traditional mortgage broker, offers around 400 loans from forty-five lenders. Both sites are well designed and offer a wealth of information as well as the ability to apply online, a facility that many banks and building societies are still struggling to offer. You can also track the progress of your mortgage online and take advantage of online conveyancing (see Law for more on online conveyancing).

However, neither E-loan nor Charcol is entirely comprehensive, and it may be worth looking at some of the less advanced sites such as **www.creditweb.co.uk**, **www.moneysupermarket.co.uk** and **www.virginmoney.co.uk** to see if they come up with more attractive loans. For example, Creditweb lists more than three times the number of mortgages than E-loan; but you can't apply online, and the information is not displayed in such an attractive way.

Most online mortgages are no cheaper than those bought from branches (although John Charcol offers some special deals that cannot be obtained direct from lenders). But the mortgage supermarkets are excellent for researching where to find the best deal – perhaps at a smallish building society. You can then go direct to this provider. The big mortgage sites are also an invaluable source of information for both novice property buyers and for those wanting explanations of the more exotic types of mortgage. Most also offer a range of calculation tools that allow the potential borrower to experiment with different loan/repayment combinations. If a mortgage search engine leads you to a cheaper mortgage or shows that you could profitably remortgage, the savings could be substantial: a half of one per cent saving on a £50,000 mortgage would be worth about £250 a year or £1,750 over seven years, the average length that someone holds a mortgage.

The US is already seeing the logical conclusion to developments in the mortgage markets where borrowers can put their requirements up on the web for lenders to bid for in a reverse auction. There is nothing like this available yet in the UK. On **www.ftyourmoney.com** there is a very rudimentary matching service with a restricted list of lenders. But bids are not individually tailored and there is no real auction process.

Credit cards

If you consistently pay interest on your credit card balance, an internet-based credit card could save you a significant amount of money. As with savings accounts, banks like Egg have used loss-leading rates of interest to tempt people to transfer their credit cards. Most of the online operators offer tempting introductory offers for customers who transfer their credit card balances: For example, Egg charges transfer balances only 2.5 per cent for six months, although the rate then goes up to a slightly uncompetitive 10.9 per cent. However this is still well below the 19.4 per cent charged by traditional card issuers such as Barclaycard. Switching a £500 balance to Egg from Barclaycard would save about £70 in a year.

Online applications are relatively straightforward and, as with bank accounts, you get much better access to statements than with traditional card companies like Visa. Moreover for those who are worried about online security, both Egg and Marbles (a credit card specialist) will cover any online fraud.

Loans

By contrast, online personal loans do not offer significant savings over some offline sources. For example, Smile charges 9.9 per cent on personal loans, but you can undercut that significantly by more than 1 per cent by going to LloydsTSB Direct. But this could change if online banks decide that personal loans are a priority area for competition.

Insurance

The fragmented insurance industry is ripe for transformation by the internet, but the changes are only just starting to get under way. In theory, insurance supermarkets ought to be able to scan the market for the most competitive deals for an individual, removing the need to approach many different firms and brokers and fill in multiple forms. But there are only two insurance supermarkets: **www.screentrade.co.uk** and **www.inspop.com**, at the moment and they have restricted lists of insurers, so they may not be competitive on an individual quote.

For example, in our test Inspop could provide only one insurer to quote for car insurance, and it did not provide a quote at all for house insurance. Screentrade, which takes a commission like a broker, fared little better, providing a single quote for buildings insurance that was far from competitive. Even many of the direct insurance sites (such as CGU) only provide quotes online; applications still have to be made offline.

Insurance web sites are also well behind the best standards offered elsewhere on the internet. One insurance site, **www.insurancewide.com** was so slow that we gave up testing it. Some companies require huge amounts of detail before offering a quote, and payment systems can be long-winded. Some sites, such as Egg's car insurance section, offer a fairly quick quote. But it turns out this is only an initial estimate: you have to fill in pages of further forms before the quote is either confirmed, modified or withdrawn.

In some specialised areas of insurance such as travel insurance, it is possible to find a good deal on the internet. Moneyextra (**www.moneyextra.co.uk**) offers a smooth service with plenty of different deals to compare (you can click to remove or add cover for business equipment, cash or winter sports). Moneyextra could be worth watching when its home and car insurance operations get going.

If you are looking for insurance, the web may produce a reasonable quote, but a traditional offline insurance broker can usually come up with a better deal, especially if the requirement is for non-standard cover. In some areas you may even find buying direct from an insurance company is cheaper than a broker. On Direct Line (**www.directline.co.uk**) you get a 5 per cent discount on policies taken out online (compared with the telephone service), but you would have to go to another site to check whether this deal was competitive. By way of consolation, Screentrade and 1stquote offer to refund any difference if a customer finds cheaper cover elsewhere.

Investments

Investment fund supermarkets have already changed the face of private investment in the US, and they are starting a similar process in the UK. Although there are currently only three UK fund supermarkets selling Individual Savings Accounts (ISAs) and unit trusts (**www.fidelity.com**, **www.egg.com** and **www.virginmoney.co.uk**), many more are likely to be launched soon.

The best supermarkets provide: background information for novice investors; comparison tools to help customers select funds; and lower prices than are available from financial advisers or direct from fund providers.

But there are drawbacks to fund supermarkets because they are more expensive than discount brokers they are not fully comprehensive. Fidelity and Egg do not carry all fund providers. Egg offers seventeen fund providers and Fidelity slightly fewer. Some of the biggest fund managers (such as M&G, Theadneedle and Jupiter) refuse to sell through Fidelity. However, Virginmoney at least allows you to search all existing funds, including ones not available through Virgin itself.

Despite these disadvantages, investors will probably find the simplicity of fund supermarkets very refreshing. On the better sites (like Fidelity), jargon is avoided where possible, and explanations are provided throughout the website. Some commentators are concerned about the matching process used by fund supermarkets. Fund supermarkets help investors refine their choice of funds by using an online questionnaire that directs investors towards certain funds depending on their attitude to risk. This gives a spurious scientific gloss to the selection of funds. Funds are selected, as usual, on the basis of past performance, but of course this is not necessarily a good guide to future performance. But at least the selection is being made across a bigger range of products than that offered by a traditional financial adviser.

Stockbroking

The internet could transform share ownership from an expensive pastime for the few into a cheap, accessible activity for the many. Stockbrokers used to charge at least £60 to trade a share (and much more for bigger deals), but the internet has reduced costs dramatically, with some online brokers offering dealing for as little as £2.50 minimum per trade (**www.sharecentre.co.uk**), and with an average cost of about £12. Moreover the internet has made it possible for the private investor to access much of the up-to-date news and comment that used to be restricted to professional investors.

If you don't have a broker, the internet has demystified the process of finding one. A glance at **www.investorschronicle.co.uk** or **www.iii.com** will help you identify a suitable broker, which will largely depend on how much you want to trade. These online websites can keep up with different charges and deals more effectively than any printed source. If you have a broker already, then the most obvious step is to see if it has an online facility and then compare that with the competition.

The biggest online brokers are mostly American: Schwab, E★Trade, DLJ Direct and TD Waterhouse. However, Virgin and Egg are now competing in this area, and big European players such as Comdirect, E-cortal and Selftrade are setting up UK sites. There are also a handful of independent web brokers such as Sharepeople and iDealing, although whether these can match the resources of larger groups remains to be seen. (see Selected Sites for their web addresses and charges).

The best broker sites such as **www.etrade.co.uk** have a financial news service and data on companies to help you research you potential stock purchases. But on this site, as on several others, you have to be a registered user to get access and you have to pay an extra £5 a month to get a full news and analysis service. Other tools on offer include email alerts, delayed trading facilities and portfolio tracking options. But sometimes you get better news and information, and sometimes better research, from non-broking sites. The best approach is to combine the use of several sites for trading and research.

A good source of free initial information on companies is Hemscott (**www.hemscott.net**). It covers not only big companies but also provides material on companies on the Alternative Investment Market (AIM). Hemscott provides a brief overview of a company, summary accounts, profit forecasts from brokers and details of shareholdings. You can also download the latest report and accounts. If you register with Hemscott (also free) you can get access to more detailed forecasts, email alerts and other enhancements. The *Financial Times* (**www.ft.com**) also provides free annual reports and presents brokers' forecasts in an attractive way.

It is also becoming easier to get access to some research from city analysts directly from investment banks such as Merrill Lynch (**www.ml.com**). The public still does not get access to the cream of the research or company meetings with brokers, as the key information from these exchanges goes straight to big institutional shareholders before it seeps out onto the web. But you can sometimes pick up tips from general investment sites such as **www.uk-invest.com**.

The internet also makes it far easier to do research about foreign companies, particularly those in the US. Finding out what is going on the US is vital, particularly in areas relating to technology. Good starting points for research are Bloomberg (**www.bloomberg.com**) and the Dow Jones site (**www.dowjones.com**), although you have to pay to get access to the archives of the Wall Street Journal (**www.wsj.com**) You can see extracts of interviews with leading US business men on **www.twst.com** (*The Wall Street Transcripts*), but again you have to pay to obtain full transcripts.

For following stock market developments, one of the best sites is the *FT's* **www.ftmarketwatch.com**. Many sites offer the London Stock Exchange's Regulatory News Service, which covers price-sensitive announcements companies release via the Stock Exchange. It is sometimes just as useful to look at these relatively brief items (and their exact wording) rather than the much longer press reports. You

MONEY

can get company announcements as they come out from many financial news sites such as **www.sharepages.com**.

One relatively new source of comment on financial stories is London-based **www.breakingviews.com**, with some of the analysis written by former *FT* journalists. Note, however, that 'real-time' in online financial services means different things on different sites. On some of the big broking sites, it means up-to-date prices which are constantly updated, but on some websites it means after a fifteen-minute delay.

For news about new issues or initial public offerings (IPOs), the obvious source is the London Stock Exchange (**www.londonstockexchange.co.uk**). For developments in Europe a good source is **www.europeaninvestor.com**, and on **www.epo.com** you can subscribe to issues online. In America, Bloomberg (**www.bloomberg.com** and **www.co.com**) or **www.ipo.com** are the best sources of IPO news. For finding archives of newspaper reports and comments on companies, the *FT* (**www.ft.com**), the *Daily Telegraph* (**www.telegraph.co.uk**) or the Guardian's **www.newsunlimited.co.uk** are good sources. The *FT* has the best daily coverage, but only the *Telegraph* puts the entire offline paper on its site, and it also has the longest archive (see News).

Although online share dealing is much cheaper than the traditional route, there are some restrictions. Although most sites allow you to trade the bulk of UK-quoted shares, few sites allow trading in all UK-quoted shares (i.e. including AIM and Ofex). A minority of sites (such as Sharepeople) allow trading in both the UK and US shares from one account, but many insist on separate accounts. This situation is likely to change because of consolidation between European online brokers. Within a couple of years it should be possible to hold one account and deal in European and US shares from one account. For the time being, if you want to deal cheaply in Germany, it is best to go to a local online broker such as Consors (**www.consors.com**), which allows you to trade in German equities for DM19 per deal.

One of the ways that brokers have been able to cut the cost of online dealing is to insist that investors use nominee accounts. This removes the need to issue and despatch share certificates. Many brokers make up for low dealing charges with a fee of £50 (or more) for obligatory use of nominee facilities. However, some, like Virgin, DLJ and Selftrade do not. Nominee accounts mean firstly that you do not possess the physical share certificate, and, more significantly, that you cannot vote on the shares. You can ask your broker to vote for you, and if they are set up to do so they will. Another limitation of online brokers is that they often restrict the size in which you can deal. So substantial private investors are thrown back on offline resources.

But do not let the ease of buying and selling seduce you into forgetting the underlying risks of owning shares. You can still lose (as well as make) money quickly. Moreover, despite the publicity given to daytrading, stockmarket investment is usually more profitable over the longer term when purchases are properly researched and held for months or years rather than hours or days. Novice investors should beware rumours and recommendations in chat rooms and discussion groups. Despite the best efforts of regulators and site operators, 'pump and dump' scams abound. For example, the *Industry Standard* reported in October 2000 that two Californians had been arrested after spreading a rumour that a small publicly-traded car dealer had bought another company that just happened to possess a cure for AIDS. The stock had risen sharply, proving that some people will believe anything.

Fraud/Regulation

Although the press continues to hunt hard for fraud on the internet, to date there has been no serious breach of a financial services website. The only significant problems have been caused by banking staff errors and attempts at multiple credit card applications. However, regulators still worry that security between different parts of banks is not sufficiently robust: the fear is that once hackers have penetrated one area of a bank, they might be able to move to another.

You can minimise the risk of fraud by

o checking that any site you use has 128-bit security (this encodes transactions and makes hacking difficult) – if the site does use this, and it absolutely must to be secure, it will say so prominently somewhere, such as in the security section;

o checking that the password you are expected to type in is of a good length, at least eight digits, and is not easily changed by you or anyone else;

o avoiding dodgy financial firms that offer improbably spectacular returns. Beware sites operating from obscure, unregulated locations: if in doubt, check with the Financial Services Authority (FSA), which has a register of all regulated firms.

The FSA has a good website (**www.fsa.gov.uk**), and has links to its register (**www.thecentralregister.co.uk**), which contains the names of companies authorised to do investment business. (There have been some complaints that the search facilities on the central register are slow.) If you are still concerned about security, read the guide on the Motley Fool (**www.fool.co.uk**)

Tax

Although most people don't have to grapple with a tax return because their income tax is deducted at source via the PAYE system, the self-employed or those with more complex financial affairs have to steel themselves for the annual task, or pay an accountant, or both. The recent arrival of self-assessment has not made things easier for these unfortunates. The forms are still complex, and more than a quarter of tax calculations made by tax inspectors were incorrect in 1999 (according to the Inland Revenue's own figures. It is rather charming that the Revenue reports some of its own mistakes.) In addition, errors made by individuals lead to millions of pounds of overpaid tax each year.

The internet offers the potential both to make the process of filing a tax return much easier, and to reduce the room for error on behalf of you and the Revenue. In time it should also cut the costs of tax accountancy. The Inland Revenue (**www.inlandrevenue.gov.uk**) now offers the possibility of filing a tax return and submitting it online. It is even dangling the prospect of a £10 tax discount for those who file the return and pay their tax bill electronically.

However, there have been considerable teething problems with the system. First the software took up to two hours to download, and then were problems with the software that was sent out (by post) on a CD-Rom. A further difficulty with the system is that you have to wait for the Inland Revenue to send you a user number, a process that takes about a week. This seems to undermine the point of using a medium like the internet. You also cannot make a tax return online if you have an Apple Mac. That said, the Inland Revenue claim to have improved the software and continue to promote it aggressively.

Companies offering simple free tax calculation software include Forbes **www.tax.co.uk**, Digita (**www.digita.com**) and the Consumers Association **www.taxcalc.com**. These packages assist you to enter the right number in the right box. However, individuals with more complex affairs (for example, involving capital gains tax) would probably need a package costing about £25. However, this is still good value compared with filling in the tax return unaided or paying an accountant. Ironically, those with yet more complex financial affairs (including partnerships or foreign earnings) are currently debarred from the online tax filing system.

Of course, the Inland Revenue's website (**www.inlandrevenue.gov.uk**) is not aimed just at individuals but also at companies and tax advisers. Part of the site provides information – for example, you can download a comprehensive range of Inland

Revenue leaflets that cover subjects as diverse as inheritance tax and 'non-resident entertainers and sportspersons' as well as some leaflets in Welsh. For an individual with a particular tax problem, there may be straightforward information available here that would obviate the need for an expensive meeting with an accountant or solicitor.

The site also covers National Insurance both from an employer's and employee's perspective. In addition there are also reports of 'news' developments that affect particular aspects of taxation – for example, relating to self-employed consultants (IR35). For companies, there are leaflets covering basic information on starting up companies as well as more complex tax issues.

Other online resources relating to tax include **www.virtuallyanywhere.co.uk**, which offers the services of former tax inspectors. This is a slick site and offers tax advice by email or more traditional home consultations (at a cost). Like Digita, the site offers a number of tips for saving tax as well as tax-related news stories. A list of accountants that can be searched by postcode can be found on **www.tax.co.uk** (which engagingly claims to be 'the most exciting tax website in the world'). Several personal finance websites such as **www.moneyextra.com** also have tax calculators and tax guides for individuals where you can check whether you are being taxed correctly (even if you are in the PAYE system).

Although the internet is likely to affect the tax affairs of the self-employed (and their accountants) first, the impact of the technology will eventually spread much further. From 2001 the Inland Revenue is offering a £50 discount to small companies that file their PAYE forms and VAT returns and make the appropriate payments online. Eventually the Inland Revenue wants to use internet technology to send out tax returns to many more people. So even if the initial response to the Inland Revenue's initiative has been cool, the number of electronic returns is likely to rise as the technology becomes more reliable. In the US already a quarter of tax returns are filed electronically.

The future

Although developments in internet financial services are still moving fast, the focus of developments is shifting to the television. The arrival of digital television will allow so-called 'sofa banking', enabling customers to transact during advertising breaks. HSBC already has 100,000 TV banking customers and Abbey National and Woolwich are also offering full banking on Sky's Open. Digital TV may end up being the focus of simple financial transactions given the UK government's decision to move all television broadcasting to digital within the next few years. The other likely development is that people will run their financial affairs from their mobile phones – given that they are more portable and cheaper than computers. But this is still some way off.

Selected sites

General Finance Sites
www.moneynet.co.uk ❂❂❂
Allows you to search for the best deals.

www.moneysupermarket.co.uk ❂❂❂
Greatest strength is in mortgages.

www.iii.co.uk ❂❂❂❂
Interactive Investor International. Sound personal finance and investment site.

www.moneyextra.co.uk ❂❂❂
Personal finance portal with some comparison tools.

www.ftyourmoney.com ❂❂❂
FT's personal finance site. Good design.

www.fool.co.uk ❂❂❂❂
Quirky financial advice site. Down-to-earth guides to investment and online services.

www.find.co.uk ❂❂❂
Lists virtually all UK personal financial services sites and their links.

http://uk.gomez.com ❂❂❂
Quarterly reviews of online banks, credit cards and brokers.

Banks and building societies
www.lloydstsb.com ❂❂
Confusing site because of all the competing brands; no support for credit cards.

www.ibank.barclays.co.uk ❂❂
Poor navigation and low interest rates.

www.natwest.com ❂
Poor demonstration; customers appear to have been drawn in by free ISP rather than banking service.

www.hsbc.co.uk ❂❂❂
Good design but you have to go to a branch to open an account.

www.rbos.com ❂❂❂
Poor demonstration despite the fact that RBOS has one of the longest records in internet banking.

www.bankofscotland.com ❂❂
Limited functions, site navigation not always reliable.

www.citibank.com ❂❂❂
Website is well designed, but citibank requires £2,000 deposit and a salary of £20,000 to open an online account.

www.nationwide.co.uk ●●●●
Rich in background information and some of the best interest rates available. But it takes ages to open accounts.

www.halifax.co.uk ●●●
Much-improved site – both in terms of navigation and content. Interest rates are now highly competitive. But site is not compatible with most personal finance software.

www.abbeynational.co.uk ●●●
Good record on customer service and colour scheme works well. But rates are uncompetitive.

www.woolwich.co.uk ●●●
Useful feature such as multiple saving pots and Open Plan features are excellent (see below) but you can't set up standing orders.

www.alliance-leicester.co.uk ●●
Limited features: you can't set up standing orders and you have to telephone to set up new payments.

Internet/telephone banks
www.cahoot.com ●●●●
Abbey National's internet bank; good design, competitive interest rates.

www.egg.co.uk ●●●●
Much promoted bank from Prudential, good design but losing the edge on interest rates.

www.first-e.com ●●
Problems with opening accounts.

www.if.com
Halifax's Intelligent Finance has yet to launch properly.

www.smile.co.uk ●●●●
Well-designed, simple site from Co-op, high interest rates.

http://secure.openplan.co.uk ●●●
Woolwich's Open plan. Barclays thought it was so good that it bought Woolwich.

www.firstdirect.co.uk ●●●
Good design but not particularly competitive interest rates.

Fund supermarkets
www.fidelity.co.uk ●●●●
Restricted choice of funds but otherwise excellent site.

www.egg.co.uk ●●●●
Good site, but closes for part of the night.

www.virginmoney.co.uk ●●●
Slightly unreliable website but more comprehensive than Egg or Fidelity.

Mortgage sites
www.e-loan.com ●●●●
Leading online mortgage site, good background information.

www.charcolonline.co.uk ❂❂❂❂
Leading online mortgage site, very clear design.

www.ftyourmoney.com ❂❂
Modestly useful reverse auction.

www.virginmoney.co.uk ❂❂❂
Wide choice of lenders but system not always reliable.

www.moneysupermarket.co.uk ❂❂❂
Less slick than e-loan and charcolonline.

www.creditweb.co.uk ❂❂❂
Less sophisticated design but large choice of products.

www.fredfindsmortage.com ❂❂❂
New mortgage service; easy navigation.

Insurance
www.screentrade.co.uk ❂
Slow and very uneven results.

www.inspop.com ❂❂
Restricted list of insurers.

Stockbroking and investment
www.idealing.co.uk ❂❂❂
Execution-only online service with very few frills. Share trading costs £10 per deal (plus £20 p.a. admin charge).

www.comdirect.co.uk ❂❂❂❂
Good broker site from Commerzbank. Charges £12.50–£14.50 for trades plus £25 annual fee. Access to AIM shares but not foreign equities.

www.dljdirect.co.uk ❂❂❂❂
Good US-owned broker site; good navigation. Individual dealing charges are on the expensive side at £14.95 but there is no annual fee.

www.e-cortal.com ❂❂
Rather slow site from Paribas.

www.schwab-europe.com ❂❂❂❂
European site for Charles Schwab dealing in UK and US shares. Good 'Education Centre' but poor navigation and relatively expensive.

www.stockacademy.com ❂❂❂
New venture from Globalnet Financial and Freeserve. Quick to open an account but no foreign markets as yet. Some pages slow to load.

www.sharecentre ❂❂❂
Slow to load, but currently cheapest dealing (£2.50) for buying shares (plus £5 p.a. admin charge).

www.etrade.co.uk ❂❂❂
£50 p.a. admin charge; extra research available at £5 per month. Lack of background information about investment.

www.selftrade.co.uk ❶❶❶❶
£12.50 fee per trade (Franco/German operation). Easy to use but no alerts and no foreign dealing.

www.stocktrade.co.uk ❶❶❶
Broker site from Brewer Dolphin offers research but poor navigation.

www.sharepeople.com ❶❶❶
Offers one account for trading in UK and US. Offering all trades at £5 at time of going to press (normal price £14.50-£17.50). Recently scrapped its annual fee.

www.tdwaterhouse.co.uk ❶❶❶
Access to new issues but not foreign or US stocks.

www.equityinvestigator.com ❶❶❶
New tech-focused site from city analysts. Small amount of free analysis. Subscription of £200 buys research coverage of 54 companies. The number of companies covered will increase and so will the subscription charge.

www.breakingviews.com ❶❶❶
Comment on breaking financial news stories from former FT journalists.

www.smartmoney.com ❶❶❶
Investment-related technology news from US.

www.eo.com ❶❶❶
Online IPO service for private investors.

www.eonews.net ❶❶❶
News on IPOs and internet-related development.

www.carol.co.uk ❶❶
Free annual reports from Asia and US as well as Europe (although the coverage outside the UK is patchy).

www.corpreports.co.uk ❶❶❶❶
Downloadable reports on about 3,000 companies including AIM, OFEX, EASDAQ and the top NASDAQ companies. Access to full accounts costs £50 a year although more basic information on individual companies is available for free.

Tax

www.inlandrevenue.gov.uk ❶❶❶❶
Huge resource of tax-related information.

www.tax.co.uk ❶❶
Helps you to find an accountant (but little more).

www.digita.com ❶❶❶
Tax software specialist (writes software for Microsoft and Inland Revenue).

www.taxcalc.com ❶❶❶❶
Practical software for filing online tax return.

www.virtuallyanywhere.co.uk ❶❶❶
Tax services from ex-Inland Revenue inspectors.

Health

> 'People tend to think that the information is accurate and up-to-date just because it is on a computer, but often it isn't'.
>
> **NHS patient**

The biggest impact the internet has so far had on health is to give us, the patients, quick access to a huge amount of health information. The kind of information that even five years ago either could only be obtained by gatecrashing a hospital's medical bookshop or could not be obtained at all. You can use the net to look up the results of clinical tests on drugs and treatments, view the entire list of drugs prescribed on the NHS and their cost, side-effects and contra-indications, and find out the latest breakthroughs achieved with medicines only available on private prescriptions.

This information explosion has the potential to make patients very much better informed, and the evidence is that we are using it – about 30 per cent of internet hits access health information. Some doctors are resisting this development which makes patients more able and likely to question their diagnosis or prescribed treatment. But many more see the upside: a more informed patient can make for a better doctor–patient discussion.

Find people in the same boat

The internet has also brought us new ways of dealing with health problems. Patients who suddenly discover they have a serious illness no longer have to feel isolated and alone, because there are chat rooms for most illnesses where you can link up with those who are suffering from similar conditions.

> 'It's great if you can meet your doctor with some background knowledge because you can have an informed discussion – otherwise you just do what they say'.
>
> **Nuala Corry, NHS patient**

Diagnosis

If you are at an earlier stage than that, and trying to understand what your symptoms might mean, you can answer a set of online questions and have an online diagnosis in an instant. This can even be followed up by an online consultation.

But beware. Not all health sites on the net have good information or give good advice. And even on the official sites where the information is usually very accurate and where the advice has been produced by highly trained doctors and nurses, online communication cannot always replace a personal consultation where the doctor or nurse can actually see your condition. To get around this problem the good sites are always ready to suggest (when appropriate) that you visit your doctor or in an emergency phone 999.

Tips to picking out good healthcare sites

- Stick with reputable names. You do not want to take risks with health, and there are some sites with inaccurate information as well as a fair number of quacks. The way to avoid them is to use sites that are well-known offline organisations. Don't be taken in by sites ending in .org, they are not necessarily official sites. There are also some excellent sites that are purely online enterprises, and commercial enterprises, but you can tell they are of good quality by the fact that they have been endorsed by government or other official sites. For example, look out for sites that display the logo of the excellent Swiss non-profit health site **www.hon.ch**. This means that they subscribe to its code of practice.

- Beware any site that claims to offer miracle cures. This may seem obvious, but it always needs to be repeated. Successive surveys by the Office of Fair Trading, **www.oft.gov.uk**, have found several sites offering Japanese 'slimming soap' that 'washes away fat'. If you haven't heard about a product from your doctor or from other sources and if it sounds too good to be true, it nearly always is. Of course, the point is that by the time you find out, you have already paid for it.

- Beware sites that demand cash before offering advice.

Where to start

There are a large number of health portals on the net, populated with news, discursive articles, illness-specific content, separate sections for men, women, children and seniors, an 'ask the doctor' facility, and links to a mass of other sites. The best places to start are **www.bbc.co.uk/health**, and the well respected **www.netdoctor.co.uk**. Three other sites with comprehensive content are **www.healthinfocus.co.uk**, **www.surgerydoor.co.uk** and **www.wellweb.com** although they are somewhat cluttered. Two good US sites are

'You have to learn how to distinguish the good medical sites from those put up by nutters.'

Internet user

'I'm all in favor of health information on the internet because people who are better informed about health know how to look after themselves properly.'

Dr. Albert Yeon GP

www.drkoop.com and www.webMD.com but these have recently been rescued from financial difficulty.

When you are trying to interpret symptoms

Diagnosis: There are many sites that offer self-diagnosis tools. Start with the online presence of NHS Direct, **www.nhsdirect.nhs.uk**. The site has high quality, unbiased, free medical advice on a great range of symptoms and conditions, and for self-diagnosis guides you through a series of yes/no questions, and depending on your answers the site advises a particular treatment, calling NHS Direct, or calling 999. But note that there is no database on the site enabling you to find your local GP or hospital – because NHS Direct has been set up precisely to try to limit GP visits. The site **www.netdoctor.co.uk** is also very good. Use the self-diagnosis to create a 'second opinion', read the chat from experts, look up anything in the comprehensive encyclopaedia reference section, and post a question to 'ask a doctor'. Note that you may have to wait up to 72 hours for a reply. The online pharmacy **www.allcures.com** has a reasonable amount of content and another 'ask the doctor' option.

Consultation: Many sites offer online consultations. If you are considering this option, you should be aware that an online consultation usually costs £15–30. Be sure to use a reputable site to ensure confidentiality and good advice, but if you need a quick response, or if your condition should be seen with better clarity than a web camera allows, it may be a better idea to visit a doctor rather than use the net. The most reputable UK site is **www.e-med.co.uk**, run by Dr Julian Eden. His service can use a web camera to offer medical advice remotely (provided, of course, that you have a webcam!) with the option of a face-to-face consultation. There is a small joining fee (£20) and then a charge for each consultation.

'Individuals sometimes go online deliberately to provide misinformation about their own medical and personal histories.'
Dr Marc Feldman, University of Alabama

'I often see all kinds of stupid, immature and downright offensive replies.'
Anonymous user of a health chat room

Finding local healthcare providers: There are a number of excellent directory sites that can be used to find your nearest health services including **www.nhs.uk**, or the Department of Health's site **www.doh.gov.uk/dhhome.htm** or **www.patient.co.uk** (which is edited by two GPs). The site **www.upmystreet.co.uk** is very user-friendly – you merely have to type in your postcode and local providers appear – but its listing are currently incomplete.

When you know what subject you want information on

Illnesses: Many illnesses have official sites dedicated to them such as www.asthma.org.uk, www.aidsmap.com, www.cancerweb.org, or cancernet.co.uk, and these are good places to start for information, links and chat rooms. But do beware that you may find extensive narratives of difficult cases distressing. Also beware that everyone who has posted a message or to whom you 'chat' may not be genuine.

Treatments: Begin your search on the different forms of treatment and how effective they are considered to be at the comprehensive website of the National Institute of Clinical Excellence, www.nice.org, although note that much of the site is concerned with future plans for trials and reports. A very valuable health resource that the internet has brought us is the ability to see the list of all NHS-prescribed medicines, their cost, side-effects and contra-indications. To look up any drug, begin with the British National Formulary online at www.bnf.org. This is the twice-yearly publication that all GPs refer to when they prescribe treatments. Easier to use is the Electronic Medical Compendium, www.emc.vhn.net. This site also gives updates on drug news. . For a better understanding of medical terms, use the very good medical dictionary at www.graylab.ac.uk/cgi-bin/omd, sponsored by Cancerweb. Each definition allows you to link to related terms mentioned in the definition .

The place to start for real commentary on different treatments is the *British Medical Journal,* www.bmj.com. This is the most reputable British professional medical journal that is totally online and free (the *Lancet,* www.thelancet.com, has decided to open its pages to the online world but its offering is largely intended for doctors). The *BMJ* site has become known as a valuable resource for health professionals, researchers and patients alike for its editorials, reviews and a fully searchable archive for the *BMJ* and other journals going back to 1994. There is a very useful customised alert service for weekly emails of press releases and content listings. The site unfortunately lacks a links page. (If you are interested, you can view adverts of prescription drugs that are intended only for doctors' eyes. It is still theoretically illegal in Europe for drugs companies to advertise their wares direct to consumers, but this online version has escaped regulatory censure. Promotion to consumers is not illegal in the US, and US health sites are peppered with such adverts.)

A good place to find research literature is www.medlineplus.gov, which has free access to a substantial selection of material from the National Library of Medicine. Enter the subject you are interested in into the search facility. Many sites will link you to Medline itself (**www.ncbi.nlm.nih**) which contains the contents of the whole medical library, but while abstracts are free, you have to pay for articles. The *New England Journal of Medicine* (**www.nejm.org**) is a good place to start searching for material on current US medical research, although only titles, abstracts, and editorials are free. For statistical research on health issues such as the incidence of asthma in inner cities, go to the government's Office of National Statistics website, **www.statistics.gov.uk**. A lot of the data here is free, providing you have the patience to understand the search facility's terminology. Alternatively look at the facts and figures presented in the links section. Clinical trial recruitment has started moving online in the US, and some trials are even partially run via the net with participants logging on with personal details at regular intervals. The internet has the potential to revolutionise every aspect of clinical trial management from recruiting patients, improving the quality of data and the ease of collecting it, and improving the retention of trial patients, to providing the means to monitor vulnerable patients more easily. The UK is not as advanced in this area as the US, although there are likely to be many developments in this area as doctors, hospitals and the public become more net-savvy. For a flavour of things to come, look at the site of the US National Institute of Health (**www.clinicaltrials.gov**) which provides patients and the general public easy access to information on clinical trials covering a wide range of diseases and conditions.

Pharmacies

Using an internet pharmacy, you can buy everything that you would expect from a pharmacist in the high street – shampoo, Kleenex, nappies, vitamins, etc. There are a few UK online pharmacies including **www.allcures.com**, **www.pharmacy2you.co.uk**. Of these, Allcures is the only one equipped to deal with prescriptions – but you have to put your prescription in an envelope and actually post it to them. These businesses hope that the government's plans for e-prescriptions, whereby your doctor will be able to send your prescription directly to an internet server or to one of these companies will be delivered on target – by 2002. However, many are sceptical of whether this date will be hit. Boots, **www.boots.co.uk**, also has an online presence but is not yet equipped to deal with prescriptions and you cannot buy over-the-counter drugs from the site.

Pharmacy activities are strictly regulated in the UK, but the UK consumer can use the net to access sites from less strictly regulated countries. This has resulted in UK consumers easily obtaining drugs not licensed for use in the UK from abroad. Consumers are best advised to stick to UK sites that are regulated because this ensures that a UK doctor will have access to details on the drug. But of course you really want to buy Viagra . . . (If you do, use any search engine and typing in the name of the drug you are interested in will reveal a myriad of sites ready and willing to sell it to you. If you are considering this, carry out the common-sense checks of the site you are thinking of buying from set out in Shopping.)

Alternative medicine

Most major health sites, such as **www.bbc.co.uk/health**, **www.netdoctor.co.uk** and **www.wellnessweb.com**, as well the online pharmacies, have features covering alternative medicine. Whether you believe in these treatments or not, it is useful to have access to information. More and more people are considering using alternative techniques as they become disenchanted with conventional medicine and you may find friends or family members embarking on such treatments.

For detail on homeopathic medicine try **www.homeopathyhome.com**, an American site with links to suppliers in the UK as well as discussion forums. For mostly positive views on potent Chinese herbal medicines and a listing of registered practitioners, as well as a good set of links, see the register of Chinese medicine, at **www.rchm.co.uk**. And finally, the site **www.allayurveda.com**, claims to be the world's first ayurveda portal. The site has been launched in India by a group of ayurveda practitioners but aims to attract an international audience.

Private healthcare and insurance

Private healthcare provision in the UK is gaining more attention as the strain on NHS budgets increases and patient access to treatment information drives demand for newer and more expensive treatments. The drugs and clinical treatments provided by the NHS are available to patients at a low fixed price, but there is a restricted list of such treatments, and for some you can only receive an NHS prescription if you suffer from a certain complaint – this is the case for so-called lifestyle drugs such as Viagra. By choosing a private healthcare provider you may avoid long waiting lists and unpleasant hospital wards, and you may also be able to gain access to other treatments and drugs only available abroad, of course for a hefty fee.

Private healthcare providers tend to have good web presences. For general information on private health services see **www.privatehealth.co.uk**, which has contact details and websites of healthcare providers, insurers and associated private services. Bupa is the UK's largest private provider and **www.bupa.co.uk** is a portal-style site with content of general interest, although it can be tricky to navigate. Nuffield Hospitals, **www.nuffieldhospitals.org.uk**, provides healthcare on a fixed-price basis if the

> 'The internet is a paradise for hypochondriacs and there are plenty of sites out there that try to take advantage of them.'
> Dr. Crosbie, Dentist

patient is not covered by an insurance scheme. The site is easy to use and provides essential information on available services (including alternatives like homeopathy), hospital locations, press releases and patient information on hospital referrals and treatments.

Travel health

There is substantial information and advice on travel health on the internet. See Travel chapter.

Dental

Portals and directory sites are more than adequate for locating your nearest dentist. A few dentists have websites with links from Scoot if you want to know more about the practice before visiting. But while dentists themselves are not in the vanguard of internet developments, there are plenty of sites with useful information about dental care. For a comprehensive yet comprehensible look at teeth then the BBC's site **www.bbc.co.uk/health/teeth** is a good starting point – and it does not have any gruesome pictures.

The British Orthodontics Society has a user-friendly site at **www.bos.org.uk** with a separate section for patients. For links to UK and US dental organisations, follow the dental health links at **www.patient.co.uk**.

> 'As a single father working long hours in the city, I found it hard to find reliable and readily available childcare information, so the idea of Smallfolk.com was born out of need. Great Ormond Street Hospital was the ideal partner.'
> Ilesh Kotecha, co-founder of Smallfolk.com

Children's health

All the portal sites have sections on children's health, largely targeted at parents. These sites tend to offer plenty of general heath advice as well as information on childhood diseases and other problems. Netdoctor is good for general health advice, patient.co.uk has good links to support groups and networks while the BBC also tries to answer those difficult questions that children ask about 'how things work'. For example, you can tour a rather more anatomically correct body than the one in the Millenium Dome. One of the best sites is **www.smallfolk.com**. It is a high quality, comprehensive and authoritative source of online information on childcare, development (focused on 0–5 year olds) and related topics. The site's partner is Great Ormond Street Hospital Children's Charity.

Sites aimed at children are usually colourful and wacky but

sometimes heavy on graphics — which makes them slow and so not very suitable for impatient children. In addition, some sites use language that may be too difficult for the average seven-year-old. For example, **www.healthykids.org.uk** has been set up by three primary school teachers to provide information for children between the ages of three and eight. Visitors select their age and then choose one of several topics to find out more, but adults will still be needed for reading some of the text. The more adventurous may want to try **www.yucky.com** for reports from Wendel the Worm, revolting (but edible) recipes and a teacher centre.

Disability

People who are housebound or unable to use voice communication will find email and internet resources excellent for keeping in touch with friends and family, receiving news and information specific to individual needs and linking with support organisations. Most of these resources are also useful for carers. However, websites from specialist equipment and device manufacturers are not widespread yet. The Disability Living Foundation at **www.dlf.org.uk** is a comprehensive resource for help with equipment selection, training and also has plenty of links. For carers, the Department of Health's site (**www.carers.gov.uk/index.htm**) has several separate sections including links for parents and young carers. There are also links to the relevant government agencies.

For rare or unusual conditions, support groups and organisations specific to your needs may be a useful way of finding further valuable resources on the web. US health portals are good starting-points when searching for these types of groups. Other sources of support are specialist web magazines. For example, **www.fromthewindow.org.uk** is edited by teenager Joy Nightingale, who is unable to walk or speak. The site covers topics such as travel and also includes a guest column by Stephen Hawking.

Mental health

For mental health information, research and support begin with **www.mind.org.uk**. Mind is a leading UK mental health charity and this portal-style site contains useful information and links to other web resources as well as details of local offline facilities. The National Schizophrenia Fellowship (**www.at-ease.nsf.org.uk**) has designed this site for 15–24-year-olds but it has a wider audience. The layout is stylish, and the content is useful. There are also links to other relevant organisations.

Sexual Health

The internet is excellent for finding information on delicate subjects and health topics of an embarrassing nature (see **www.embarrassingproblems.co.uk**). Even knowing where to go for advice offline can be an awkward problems – for a solution look to **www.lovelife.co.uk** run by Health Promotion in England. This is a bright, young-looking accessible site with advice on sexually transmitted diseases, emergency advice and clinic locations as well as links. The Society of Health Advisers in STDs at **www.shastd.org.uk** has content for the public and professionals as well as discussion rooms, news and FAQs.

Nutrition

The subject of nutrition is increasingly important for people of all shapes, sizes and ages. Modern lifestyles and eating habits are driving people to look for healthier diets and ways to keep fit. The internet offers all sorts of reliable, practical information about balanced diets that previously only food allergy sufferers, those on restricted diets or very fussy eaters might have bothered to search out. For issues concerning food safety the European Food Information Council **www.eufic.org/open/fopen.htm** covers nutrition and biotechnology issues too. For advice on balanced diets and specific groups try **www.nutrition.org.uk**, run by the British Nutrition Foundation. This is a nicely laid out site with factsheets about healthy eating through various lifestages, facts about different foods, and related sites. Another source of dietary advice is **www.eating4health.co.uk**, a site run by a group of registered dieticians. There are also hundreds of American nutrition-related sites but they may recommend foods or brands that can only be obtained in the US.

A growing trend in the US and increasingly in Europe is the consumption of functional foods or so-called nutraceuticals. These claim to provide improved health or a reduced risk of disease, so reducing the need for pharmaceuticals or treatment later. US-based **www.nutraceuticalsworld.com** provides a taster of what the US has been up to in this field. Another website to look at covering nutritional and food issues is that of the Center for Science in the Public Interest, **www.cspinet.org** which aims to educate the public and policy-makers about the importance of nutrition and food safety. The site is a little clunky but if you cut through the American veneer you will find pages on topics such as food additives, resistance to antibiotics and even tips for lunchboxes.

Before seeing your doctor

Say you suffer from severe headaches which you suspect might be migraine and plan to visit a GP. How could you use the internet to learn more before the appointment?

- Diagnosis: go into NHS Direct, **www.nhsdirect.nhs.uk**, and describe your symptoms and see what it suggests.

- General information about the ailment: look at some general health sites, such as **www.bbc.co.uk** and **www.netdoctor.co.uk**.

- Treatments and side-effects: look at the Electronic Medical Compendium, **www.emc.vhn.net** or the British National Formulary (**www.bnf.org**).

- Alternative treatments: try portal sites.

- Nutrition/diet related: see **www.nutrition.org**.

- Support: find other sufferers from migraine by typing the word into a search engine such as **www.google.com**.

From this brief example it is easy to see that the internet provides a lot of useful information and advice. Using the internet, you can locate much more specific material than is available offline unless you have friends who are doctors. Even if you do, no individual doctor has comprehensive up-to-date research from around the world sitting on the shelf. Plus you can also find resources that a doctor may not provide, including information about support groups, details of side-effects of certain drugs and news about new treatments.

To set against these advances there are some basic practical problems. To obtain a NHS prescription in the UK, you still have to visit your GP until e-prescriptions become available, which may not be for several years. Moreover, the internet also provides access to information that some people don't want or need. It also provides a perfect platform for quacks, and sometimes these operations are hard to spot. In addition, some patients report that linking up with support groups may not always be helpful. Support groups can attract particularly troubling or tragic cases, and this might be distressing to someone doing initial research into an illness that may or may not have been confirmed by an offline doctor.

Selected sites

Portals and directories
www.patient.co.uk ○○○○
Comprehensive UK listing of medical services, contact details and search facility.

http://dir.yahoo.com/health ○○○
Good if you know exactly what you are looking for, but lacks opinions on individual sites.

www.bbc.co.uk/health ○○○○○
Excellent site with clear, up-to-date information and content.

www.netdoctor.co.uk ○○○○
Easy to use and full of information but 'ask the doctor' feature could be improved.

www.surgerydoor.co.uk ○○○○
Rather overpowering front page but information, rich site with links to UK and US sites for greater coverage.

www.healthinfocus.co.uk ○○○
Another portal bringing together contributions and information from various healthcare providers.

www.reutershealth.com ○○○
Slightly more technical and commercial news; Search and view some health articles free.

www.achoo.com ○○○
American gateway to consumer, professional and business content on health.

www.nhs.uk ○○○
Limited but accurate and helpful content and information.

www.nhsdirect.nhs.uk ○○○
Online version of the NHS phone service.

www.doh.gov.uk/dhhome.htm ○○○
News about the Department of Health, its activities and publications.

www.drkoop.com ○○○○
US site with all the usual content and handy risk calculators for various conditions.

www.webmd.com ○○○
Slick site with US specific content, good topical discussion articles.

www.wellweb.com ○○
Straightforward site with content on general health and fitness.

www.healthy.net ○○○
American site favouring alternative health treatments, prevention rather than cure.

Professional bodies, publications and research
www.nice.org.uk ○○○
National Institute for Clinical Excellence. It is excellent itself.

www.ncbi.nlm.nih ○○○○
The National Library of Medicine online. Abstracts are free but you have to pay for articles.

www.bmj.com ❺
Excellent site for UK world-wide medical research, news, views, policy and reviews.

www.nejm.com ❸
New England Journal of Medicine online with limited free access to abstracts and editorials.

www.thelancet.com ❸
Access to search and selected full articles following free registration.

www.statistics.gov.uk ❸
Public health and government statistics, but difficult to use.

www.graylab.ac.uk/cgi-bin/omd ❺
Great medical dictionary.

www.medline.gov ❸
Useful for in-depth medical research.

www.who.int ❹
World Health Org. site for big, global health content.

www.gmc-uk.org ❹
General Medical Council, good for GP guidelines and best practice info.

www.eudra.org/emea.html ❸
European agency for the evaluation of medicinal products. All pharmaceutical products must be approved here before being sold in the UK or Europe.

www.open.gov.uk/mca/mcahome.htm ❷
UK medicine's regulatory body.

www.medical-devices.gov.uk ❷
Medical devices regulatory body.

www.hon.ch ❸
Organisation that endorses internet health sites. Also provides some content.

www.abpi.org.uk ❷
Association of the British Pharmaceutical Industry.

Pharmacies and medicines
www.allcures.com ❹
Good content and with a facility to process private and NHS prescriptions, although you have to post them your prescription.

www.pharmacy2u.co.uk ❷
Limited site of this online pharmacy.

www.boots.co.uk ❸
Colourful, but tricky to navigate.

www.rxlist.com ❸
Good site for dosage and side-effects on alternative medicines.

www.bnf.org ❹
GP handbook now accessible online for all medicines available for prescription in the UK.

www.emc.vhn.net ❍❍❍❍
Similar to the *BNF* but easier to use.

Private healthcare
www.bupa.co.uk ❍❍
Pretty but difficult to use, with no contact numbers to view.

www.nuffield.org.uk ❍❍❍
Practical information.

www.privatehealth.co.uk ❍❍❍❍
Private healthcare portal.

www.iha.org.uk ❍❍
Professional association for independent healthcare providers.

Alternative health
www.homeopathyhome.com ❍❍❍
Good starting-point.

www.thinknatural.com ❍❍❍❍
Good site aimed at the UK market.

www.allayurveda.com ❍❍❍❍
New Indian site comprehensively covering all things ayurvedic.

www.rchm.com ❍❍❍❍
Register of Chinese medicine practitioners.

www.nfsh.org.uk ❍❍❍
National Federation of Spiritual Healers.

www.int-fed-aromatherapy.co.uk ❍❍❍
International Federation of Aromatherpaists.

Specific diseases
www.tht.org.uk ❍❍❍❍❍
The Terrence Higgins Trust's very user-friendly, welcoming site.

www.aidsmap.com ❍❍❍❍
The British HIV Association's site has more news and general health advice.

www.avert.org ❍❍❍❍
Focused on prevention and education relating to HIV.

www.bhf.org.uk ❍❍❍❍
British Heart Foundation. Start here if you are interested in heart health.

www.heartlink.org.uk ❍❍❍
Basic site with information on cardiac care with its own web TV.

www.americanheart.org ❍❍❍❍❍
American Heart Association with stacks of content on prevention through to treatment.

www.heartpoint.com ❍❍❍
More heart-related news and views.

www.asthma.org.uk ○○○○
Excellent, informative, unpatronising site.

www.cancerweb.org ○○○
Resource for coping with cancer. Details of experimental drugs for breast, colon and lung cancer.

www.cancernet.co.uk ○○○○
Straightforward information in a plain format.

www.embarrassingproblems.co.uk ○○○○○
A quick and easy site with good summaries and links.

www.lovelife.uk.com ○○○○
Bright, no-nonsense with essential facts and contacts.

www.shastd.org.uk ○○○
More chat rooms and content on sexual health.

www.mentalhealth.com ○○○
Canadian site with an international flavour.

www.mind.org.uk ○○○○○
Less intimidating site aimed at the individual in the UK.

www.samaritans.org.uk ○○○○
Samaritans online service.

www.at-ease.nsf.org.uk ○○○○○
Aimed at younger people with mental health problems.

Disability
www.dlf.org.uk ○○○
Disability Living Foundation for equipment selection and use.

www.carers.gov.uk ○○○○○
Essential information from the government on caring.

www.fromthewindow.org.uk ○○○○
Inspirational online magazine .

www.codi.buffalo.edu ○○○
Covers all aspects of disability from the US. Slow to load.

Dental
www.bbc.co.uk/health/teeth ○○○○○
About as fun as teeth and dentists can get.

www.bos.org.uk ○○○○
British Orthodontics Association with matter-of- fact content on all aspects of dentistry and treatments.

www.toothinfo.com ○○○○
Practical information to help people understand and obtain good dental healthcare.

www.dentalfear.org ○○○○
For those afraid of visiting a dentist.

www.dentalpath.com ○○○○
Information covering everything from prevention to treatments, together with dental products

www.thesmilestones.com ○○○
US site for kids with cute characters.

Kids
www.yucky.com ○○○○○
Hugely entertaining yet educational American site.

www.smallfolk.com ○○○○○
Great Ormond Street Hospital provides the content on this not-for-profit site that concentrates on child development issues.

www.healthykids.org.uk ○○
Limited content, good for 5–7 age group.

www.kidshealth.org ○○○
American site aimed at parents, kids and teens.

www.fda.gov/oc/opacom/kids ○○○○
Lots of colour and facts, written by adults for children.

Nutrition
www.eufic.org/open/fopen.htm ○○○
Multilingual information on food and nutrition.

www.nutrition.org.uk ○○○○
News, facts, education and events.

www.eating4health.co.uk ○○○
Hosted by dieticians offering diet programmes and resources on healthy eating.

www.nutraceuticalsworld.com ○○○
American site with its eye on new foods.

www.cspinet.org ○○○○○
US site with strong opinions on food safety.

Getting around

The internet is a great help in getting you the information you want to get around the country. First there are maps – street maps, route and country maps – a great number of which you can download for free. Then there are the timetables – you can quickly and easily access timetables for almost every bus, coach and train in the country. And finally the tickets – you can purchase special offer and standard price train tickets and tube and bus travelcards without having to speak to anyone at Railtrack or queue at your local station.

There are a few travel sites that are continuously updated, and these convey the same information about delays that the company would tell you if you spoke to them on the telephone. However, as yet these are the exception, and for most journeys you still need to resort to the phone. But this should change over time as travel companies put more attention and resources into managing their sites.

Maps

There are a few key sites for maps, from the excellent National Ordnance Survey's site, **www.ordsvy.gov.uk**, to new internet-only map companies. Although the Ordnance Survey aims to sell you its specialised maps, such as a 2.5inch scale map of footpaths in the Lake District, it provides maps of the whole country at a variety of scales for free. All you have to do is enter in the name of a village, town or city, or a postcode, and the map appears. You can then zoom in on an area by double clicking on the location you want to see in more detail.

Another excellent map provider for the UK is **www.streetmap.co.uk**. Here you get a larger area of map as a default than with the other sites. Again, you can zoom in on the area you are interested in, and this changes the output from a relief map to a road map. Another very good online map provider for the UK is **www.multimap.com**, which has an easy search facility and a clear site. The maps go down to a scale of 1:10,000. The site is sometimes a little slow to load. The **www.netlondon.com** site has excellent user-friendly maps of London and a map search using a postcode for anywhere in the UK. Both features are easily zoomable.

The site **www.mapquest.com** is an American site specialising in America and Canada. It covers some of Europe and increasingly the rest of the world.

Getting directions

Three main sites provide free route directions for driving in the UK (and some parts of Europe), but all have drawbacks. Perhaps the most comprehensible are those provided by the AA, **www.theaa.co.uk**, but the search facility does not let you put in entire postcodes so the directions cover only main routes and not the streets within towns. The **www.multimap.com** site gives full directions from a street in Aberdeen to another in Andover, but they are pretty difficult to follow, and they do not yet take account of one-way roads, although this is planned. The RAC's site, **www.rac.co.uk** gives good directions but the site very often gets jammed, and even when it does not it is very slow to load.

As yet no one has come forward with a website which suggests the best route incorporating a range of possible transport modes – maybe bus then tube, or car then park-and-ride. But no doubt John Prescott is on the case.

The sites **www.a2travel.com** and **a2airport.com** are reportedly excellent, but at the time of writing had been withdrawn for a redesign.

Traffic information

There are only two places to go for up-to-date road travel information for the whole country: the AA, **www.theaa.co.uk**, and the RAC, **www.rac.co.uk**, and of these two we recommend the AA. It is far easier to access the area of the country you wish to see information on, by clicking on to a map. For both sites, the information on the website is constantly updated, and is identical to that on the telephone line. Apart from these two sites, you may be able to get information from some local radio websites, but these may not be kept as up to date as the information given out over the air.

Traffic information for London is available at the excellent section on the BBC's website **www.bbc.co.uk/londonlive/travelandweather**. Here they show the latest news on traffic jams, but also a map of London displaying the locations of roadside traffic cameras. You click on the image of one of these 'jam cams' and it shows you the scene there and then, very regularly updated. A great service if you want to know how the A40 is looking after that lorry spilled its load, again.

As yet, no one has picked up the images from all the jam cams around the country and put them on a centralised site. There are a few random ones around, such as the views of the traffic on the M5 and other roads in Devon which you can see on **www.devon.gov.uk/environ/webcam**. To find out if there are any for a route near you, try a search engine such as Google and type in 'webcam' and the name of the road.

Train timetables

The place to start for rail information is the Railtrack site, **www.railtrack.co.uk**. Here you can quickly and easily find accurate timetable information for all the train companies. You can specify how many changes you are prepared to make, and choose to find the train you want by departure time or arrival time. The site used to be plagued by errors and was slow to download, but Railtrack has managed to sort out the leaves on the phone line, and now the site is quick, complete and rarely falls over. However, the site has no information on delays, other than those caused by the engineering works listed on the site.

The individual train companies all have different websites and some are worth a look because they have good route planners.

Buying tickets

You can now buy tickets for train journeys online, and sometimes get better deals than from the station. However, you cannot use any of the cards which give you reductions, such as a young person's railcard or a network card, and this can easily make the ticket more expensive than it would be from the station. In addition to the offers available from the train companies' websites, you should check out **www.thetrainline.com** which offers good deals and a reliable record for posting tickets to reach you on time. Although it is jointly owned by Virgin and Stagecoach, thetrainline provides impartial advice on train travel.

Buses

There is nothing desperately exciting you can do on the internet regarding buses, but you can find out timetable information easily and quickly, which is more than you can often do by phoning them up, so it is an advance, of sorts.

Transport in London – buy travelcards, find out about tube delays

There is already a goodly amount of information on the net on transport in London and more is on its way. They key site is **www.londontransport.co.uk**. This is developing detailed bus timetables and what is being billed as an interactive journey planner. It currently shows details of river services, DLR trains and links you to the website of Croydon's trams. You can also buy monthly or annual travelcards from the site and have them delivered to you for free.

For tube timetable and delay information, downloadable tube maps and purchasing tickets look no further than **www.londontransport.co.uk/tube**. The best thing about this site is that it shows real-time travel delays which are regularly updated, at **www.londontransport.co.uk/tube/rt_home.shtml**. Be sure to go to this section of the site for information on long-standing delays such as broken escalators, because the information on the home page is not complete. You are meant to be able to sign up to be sent emails informing you of travel delays, but the process often generates an error message. You can also download a tube map from the site.

The site carries timetables of the tubes, including last and first trains from central stations, but beware – the timetables are not complete and the site confesses that it is just a guide and you should phone for detailed information. The site is also expecting a journey planner soon.

'We are applying to the EU for £1 million cash to set up a project to map all the cycle lanes in the UK so they can be downloaded from the internet for free. But we are at the early stages of it now; the earliest we could get it up and running would be mid-2001.'

Paul, www.sustrans.org.uk

Cycling

Through the internet you can link to cycle organisations, download suggested route maps, and find out the latest information on cycle lanes, all for free. And if you are fed up with the National Rail Enquiries office giving you contradictory advice on which train companies will let you take your bike on which services, you can get this information too – but you have to pay for it by joining the Cyclists' Touring Association (**www.cta.org.wtc**).

The streets where you live

The site **www.streetmanagement.org.uk** lets you report a faulty traffic signal to the relevant authority, but not a pothole. Nor a set of cones which has outlived its welcome. Nor the fact that NTL has just started digging up a piece of road which was dug up and repaired last week by Transgas. And the week before that by BT. Ho-hum. When, oh when, will public authorities start charging contractors for the use of roads they dig up? They introduced this on motorways, and guess what, the time that lanes were shut fell dramatically. The internet could be a brilliant tool to get the public to help police schemes like this, but no doubt it will take the powers that be a while to catch up.

Selected sites

Maps
www.ordsvy.gov.uk ✪✪✪✪✪
Appealing site with zoomable maps for anywhere in the country.

www.streetmap.co.uk ✪✪✪✪✪
Extremely easy-to-use site with instant maps for anywhere.

www.multimap.com ✪✪✪
Slightly cluttered site with maps and directions for everywhere.

Getting directions
www.theaa.co.uk ✪✪✪✪
Easy to use but no directions through towns.

www.multimap.com ✪✪✪✪
Good directions with realistic time projections, although one-way streets not yet accounted for.

www.rac.co.uk ✪✪✪
Good directions if you can find your way around the site and wait for it to load.

Rail timetable information
www.railtrack.com ✪✪✪✪
Good, easy-to-use site for an instant full timetable.

Buying rail tickets
www.thetrainline.com ✪✪✪✪
Quick, easy site which lets you buy tickets for all train journeys in advance. For special offers, see the relevant train company's website.

Railway company sites
www.gner.co.uk ✪✪✪✪
For timetable info it will transfer you to the Railtrack website. Has special offer tickets, and instant real-time info on delays expected for arrivals and departures.

www.angliarailways.co.uk ✪✪✪
Good route planner with information on engineering updates. The timetable has to be downloaded using Adobe Acrobat.

www.eurostar.com ✪✪✪
This easy-to-use site shows the full timetable and availability, but we have had reports of the site suddenly changing the details you input!

www.great-western-trains.co.uk ✪✪✪✪
This good site shows the full timetable, fare information and ticket promotions. The site pushes you to **www.traindirect.co.uk** for buying tickets.

www.scotrail.co.uk ✪✪✪
Easy to navigate around this site, which has fare offers, and shows the timetable limited only to when you plan to travel.

www.rrne.co.uk ✪✪✪✪
This site for Northern Spirit has an excellent interactive map for a journey planner as well as full timetable information.

www.virgintrains.co.uk ✪✪✪
Very good fare offers for booking online. Its timetable facility is simple, but limited – it does not tell you the train company or give times for trains which have already left. And there is no information about multi-hour delays, which is what you really need to find out from Virgin.

Real-time updates on delays

So far only a few train companies have updates on delays posted on their site. Hopefully the numbers will increase.

www.ger.co.uk (Great Eastern trains) ✪✪✪✪
The real-time train information is kept well updated. Note that timetable information is under the 'your journey' section.

www.thamestrains.co.uk ✪✪✪✪
Has real-time information on delays from the starting station you choose, but the site appears to admit to delays about as often as the Thames Trains staff do.

www.connex.co.uk ✪✪✪✪
Publishes apologies as well as expected delays and long-term delays due to engineering work. Timetabling information provided by Railtrack. The 'train service at-a-glance' facility is excellent, with a coloured map showing where delays are, although as you might expect it does take a little while to load.

Transport in London

www.londontransport.co.uk. ✪✪✪✪
Clear and easy-to-use official site for the bus and tube network in London. Here you can find out about delays and can buy your bus and tube travelcard. Note that for delay information you need to go to **www.londontransport.co.uk/tube/rt_home.shtml**

www.bbc.co.uk/londonlive/travelandweather ✪✪✪✪✪
Constantly updated news on delays and you can instantly see images from London's traffic cameras – 'jam cams'.

Bus timetables

www.busweb.co.uk ✪✪✪✪✪
This great site links you to all the bus companies of Britain.

www.ukonline.co.uk ○○○○○
Great site, with information on many bus and trains services and the website addresses for all bus companies.

Cycling sites
www.ctc.org.uk (Cyclists' Touring Association) ○○○○
If you join this organisation you will receive the latest bikes-on-trains information. The well-organised site has chat rooms and a very good set of links.

www.sustrans.org.uk (sustainable transport) ○○○○
This site wants you to buy its cycle route booklets, but it also lists the national cycle network and you can locate the part of the network near you.

www.lcc.org.uk (London Cycling Campaign) ○○○
Brings you the latest in developments to establish new cycle lanes.

www.cycleweb.co.uk ○○○○
Perhaps the best cycling portal, with a fantastic list of links.

www.hikebiker.co.uk ○○○○
This cycling portal has sample cycling routes mapped out with decent instructions, and incorporating lists of B&Bs and camping sites *en route*.

Politics and Government

Whether or not the internet was invented by Al Gore as he sometimes seems to imply, politicians and governments have made ringing statements about the New Economy and the Information Superhighway. The UK government is no exception. In order to give some substance to the polemical statements enthusiastically embracing the net, almost every organ of UK government has a website of some sort, but, like other points of contact between citizens and bureaucracy, they vary widely in their helpfulness and user-friendliness. As well as government sites, the web is permeated (polluted?) by a vast array of political viewpoints and organisations, from the established political parties and news organisations to the fringe groups on all extremes of the political spectrum. And then there is the wild and crazy world of online political discussion . . .

Government departments

At present, no British government site lets you make transactions. Although you can file taxes online at **www.inlandrevenue.gov.uk**, you can't pay fines or receive benefits online. Most sites are simply downloads of what is already available offline: leaflets and advisory documents, White Papers and brochures. Not much effort is made to use the specific advantages of the web as a medium; they basically use it as a big filing cabinet.

'The government doesn't understand the net, and neither do its advisors.'

Marcus Austin, Editor of Business 2.0

Having said that, there are some honourable exceptions. NHS Direct (**www.nhsdirect.nhs.uk**) affords a high degree of interaction, allowing you to contact nurses directly and to get responses to a variety of common questions more or less instantly (see Health). The Land Registry (**www.landreg.gov.uk**) has the usual variety of policy information, but its main attraction is the comprehensive database of house prices gathered from transactions around the country. The Companies House website, **www.companieshouse.gov.uk**, provides a certain amount of useful and free searchable information about registered companies; the process of actually getting the official accounts of a company from the web is somewhat tortuous and costs £6.50, but anyone who has tried to dig things up in the physical Companies House will know that 'somewhat tortuous' is a big step forward.

The websites providing statistical information, the Central Office of Information at **coi.gov.uk**, **www.statistics.gov.uk**, and the Office of National Statistics at **www.ons.gov.uk** also have useful searchable databases, though many of the most popular and useful data series are quite difficult to get hold of.

The government's portal, **www.open.gov.uk**, links you to all government departments, provided you know the name of the department you want and so can find it in the alphabetical directory, or provided you can guess the exact keyword the site creator has chosen for the 'search by topic' facility. Frankly you are generally better off with a good search engine, such as **www.google.com**. At the European level, things are not much better – although **www.europa.eu.int** is a better and more navigable portal than **www.open.gov.uk**, the information is somewhat scanty.

Local government

No local authority yet allows transactions to be carried out over the web, but some of them do provide a means of getting in touch, or monitoring the queue of planning applications, or calculating one's liability for council tax, (**www.wandsworth.gov.uk**, for example). The site **www.gwydir.demon.co.uk/uklocalgov** has information on local government issues and provides links via a map interface to the web sites of local government across the UK, while **www.lga.gov.uk** provides links to all government assocation web sites.

Contacting your MP

In theory, the net provides an easy method to contact your local MP, although it cannot make them responsive. First of all you need to know who your MP is. You can identify which constituency you are in by your postcode at **www.locata.co.uk/commons**, and then who your MP is. Many MPs are efficient in replying to emails, in the sense of replying as quickly as they do to a letter. To contact your Conservative constituency MP, you are best off going to the Conservative Party website, **www.conservativeparty.org.uk**, which guarantees a response from MPs to emails sent from constituency members. Of course, because of the anonymity the web allows, they cannot actually tell if you are from their constituency, which gives you an excuse to badger John Major with emails about cones in the roads of Huntingdon if you so wish. (Sounds like a good idea to us.) Alternatively you could go directly to **www.johnmajor.co.uk** or a number of other politicians' own sites, such as **www.charleskennedy.org.uk**.

Political parties

All three of the main parties have at least some presence on the internet, as do the nationalists in Scotland and Wales. Political parties appear, for some reason, to like complicated, browser-specific and slow-loading web designs; in contrast to **www.open.gov.uk** with its proud boasts of compatibility with all international internet standards. Assuming you manage to navigate your way through the site and don't come up short for lack of exactly the right plug-in, you will find that the central sites for the parties are not very informative anyway; they tend to offer more vague propaganda than hard information and often suffer from a bad case of spin-doctoring.

By way of aggravating a bad situation, the sites are not frequently updated. The Liberal Democrats (**www.libdems.org.uk**) are probably the best of the bunch. The sites will allow you to join the party or pay membership fees online, but instead of one-off credit card payments over the web, you have to pay by recurring direct debits which require you to print out and post a form with a physical signature on it. Apparently this is a requirement of the banks rather than the parties themselves (and a politician would surely not dissemble), but it breaks up the continuity of the experience.

Many local parties have their own websites, and you may find that your local branch of a political party has a site which is of more use or interest to you than the national one. You can usually find the web address from a query in a search engine, or from your local government website, see above.

Other political sites

Of course, the established political parties are by no means the end of the story as far as the web is concerned. Quite the opposite; the growth of the internet has made it easier for new political movements to spring up and prosper, such as the Countryside Alliance, **www.countryside-alliance.org.uk**, and notoriously, the fuel protesters of autumn 2000.

The more established campaigning organisations like Greenpeace also have sites, as do a number of influential think-tanks like the Adam Smith Institute and the Institute for

Public Policy Research. The publishing-driven design of these sites appears tame after the interactive, frequently updated sites of the new political movements. And that's without considering the genuine lunatic fringe of political belief, who have also sadly made their way onto the net – if you really want to see what these groups look like, a directory is kept of them at **www.hatewatch.org**.

Political news

You can keep up with political news from a variety of sources on the net – see News. Other than reputable sites, such as **www.bbc.co.uk** or **www.cnn.com**, or **www.newsunlimited.co.uk** (the *Guardian*'s site), political news on the net needs to be taken with a pinch of salt. It is comparatively easy to set up a convincing-looking website, and to fill it with news that is slanted, biased or just not true. A lot of political misinformation exists on the web; for example, a list of *Dan Quayle's* malapropisms shows up attributed to both candidates in the 2000 US Presidential elections!

Developments

The government is committed to increasing internet use in the country and increasing access to government services via the internet. The latest initiative is a substantial £3bn project, to be disbursed over the next three years, which aims to give access to all parts of the country, through computer give-aways and communal access points and make available online all the government services (457 in total) which have been selected for electronic access. The aim is to move from the mostly informational sources that currently exist to transactional sites. You should be able to pay your council tax online, receive your benefits online and calculate your pension. The government is clearly serious about making the new economy central to Britain's growth, and is requiring senior civil servants to go on courses to educate them on the potential of the internet. All they have to do now is to stop passing laws which make it harder to run internet businesses in the UK.

Selected sites

Government sites

www.landreg.gov.uk ❍❍❍
Average prices of residential properties in your area.

www.companieshouse.gov.uk ❍❍❍❍
Details from Companies House for £6.50, much easier than actually visiting Companies House.

www.dss.gov.uk ❍❍
Information on benefits and entitlements. Locate your nearest benefit office.

www.dfee.gov.uk ❍❍❍
School performance records and Ofsted reports and news of job creation schemes.

www.foc.gov.uk ❍❍❍❍
Good clear information on safety advice when travelling and health advice.

www.maff.gov.uk ❍❍
Government policy on the latest food scares, as well as information on fishing licences.

www.dag-business.gov.uk ❍❍❍
Directory for business to access regulatory information.

Contacting government, parties and politicians

www.number-10.gov.uk ❍❍❍
News, broadcasts and speeches.

www.parliament.uk ❍❍❍
Explanations about how Parliament works, and some publications.

www.gwydir.demon.co.uk/uklocalgov ❍❍❍
Ugly but functional entry point to finding local government websites.

www.locata.co.uk/commons ❍❍❍
Find your constituency and local MP.

www.lga.gov.uk ❍❍❍
Links to all government association websites.

www.the-commons.com ❍❍❍
Links to parties and MPs online.

www.london.gov.uk ❍❍❍
The mayor of London's site with where you can read Ken's monthly speeches or, as a treat, hear him make them.

www.libdems.org.uk ❍❍❍
Detailed information on policy and news which is kept well up to date, MPs' biographies and details of their electoral results.

www.conservative-party.org.uk ❍❍
Good feature guaranteeing a response from your constituency MP, but with poor navigation.

www.labour.org.uk ❍❍❍
Party news and political information following the government line.

www.freespace.virgin.net/raving.loony ✪✪✪✪
If you are fed up with official party lines, try those of the Monster Raving Loony Party.

www.party-register.gov.uk ✪✪✪✪
A listing of registered political parties in the UK.

www.trytel.com/~aberdeen/ ✪✪✪
This site provides the websites and other contact information for the government and royalty for 195 countries.

Government portals
www.open.gov.uk ✪✪✪
Clear site with directory of government sites.

www.ukonline.gov.uk ✪✪
Links to the best government sites, such as Companies House, and full details of the government plans for the internet.

www.europa.eu.int ✪✪✪
Extensive site which is often slow to load. Links to some EU government sites and EU policy information.

www.ukstate.com/portal.asp ✪✪✪
Quick and easy links to a range of governmental and parliamentary sites.

Policy institutes
www.fabian-society.org ✪✪✪
Searchable site with summaries of Fabian publications.

www.fabian-society.org.uk/yf ✪✪
The minimal site of the Young Fabians with more to say about the history of the Fabians than anything else.

www.ippr.org.uk ✪✪✪
Clear site with some publications from the Institute for Public Policy Research for free online.

www.cepr.org ✪✪✪✪
Downloadable publications from the Centre for Economic Policy Research and details of forthcoming events.

www.demos.co.uk ✪✪✪
Trendy site, as you would expect from this Third Way think-tank. Some might say more style than content.

Political expression
www.publicopinion.org.uk ✪✪✪
Cast your votes on questions like 'Should the Queen abdicate in favour of Prince Charles?', as many times as you like.

www.yougov.com ✪✪✪
Answer a set of multiple-choice questions and this site will tell you which political party your preferences most closely match in a fairly simplistic way.

www.hatewatch.co.uk ✪✪✪
Combating online bigotry.

www.politicos.co.uk ✪✪✪
The online arm of the specialist bookshop Politicos is a great place to browse for political literature.

www.keele.ac.uk/depts/por/ukbase.htm ✪✪✪✪✪
The site of the University of Keele has a fantastic set of links to a huge range of political expression sites, political news sites and satirical sites.

The Law

Until recently lawyers would have been horrified at the idea of their services being sold in the same way as discounted cookery books or low-cost flights. But the scramble of solicitors to offer their services over the net is doing a great deal to demystify the legal process and lower prices, particularly for the more basic services.

For consumers there are particularly good deals to be had in the provision of basic documents such as wills, and simple services such as conveyancing, although you can also arrange a straightforward divorce online. Remember to shop around: there are big variations in prices, even online. However, whether you are a consumer or running a small business, for more complex legal work you should stick to old-fashioned techniques such as asking friends or colleagues to recommend a lawyer.

There is a huge variety of legal websites available and they are useful for different things. Some have been put up by entrepreneurs (usually in association with lawyers) to provide basic legal information online and then refer business on to (local) solicitors in return for a fee. Other sites have been put up by lawyers or groups of lawyers who provide certain services themselves and refer other types of business to specialists. Finally, there are document-only sites that may provide some of the same services available from solicitors' sites at a fraction of the price. It is worth identifying the kind of site you are in because it may affect the price you pay and what happens if you are dissatisfied. There is usually an 'about us' button that makes it clear who is behind the site.

Finding a solicitor

At **www.solicitors-online.com**, a site provided by the Law Society, you can hunt for solicitors by area or by specialisation in England and Wales. This is handy for rural areas, but the search engine produces too many names in some urban areas to be really useful. If you are looking for a solicitor with detailed local knowledge you can use Scoot (**www.scoot.co.uk**) or Upmystreet (**www.upmystreet.co.uk**), which lists solicitors by distance from your front door. The Law Society's site (**www.solicitors-online.com**) lacks general legal information and it simply advises you to contact a lawyer rather than directing you to a website that provides the same information at a fraction of the price. However, there are useful tips about how to get

> 'Lawyers ought to be moving upmarket and leaving the simple stuff to web sites.'
> Meriel Schindler, Withers

the most out of a solicitor. For information on Scotland, the starting-point is the Law Society of Scotland (**www.lawscot.org.uk**).

Perhaps to the chagrin of the Law Society, then, there is a wealth of basic legal information available on the web. For consumers, this is mainly going to concern employment, family, housing, personal injury, small claims and wills. One of the best legal information sites is **www.venables.co.uk**, because it provides links to solicitors with websites and a good deal of basic information. Some sites such as **www.lawrights.co.uk** from the Consumers Association offer law guides (including a free divorce pack), while others publish questions and answers (**www.legaladviceforfree.co.uk**).

A few sites such as Desktoplawyer (**www.desktoplawyer.co.uk**) combine both approaches. A small number of solicitors' sites (such as **www.pearsonmaddin.co.uk**) offer good online libraries of guides to different legal topics. The main attraction of these sites is that they provide reasonably well-written introductions to different types of law. For example, you can find comments on what to do about noisy neighbours.

Of course these guides may not offer the exact answer to a particular problem, and many sites offer a free query service in the form of email. For a list of providers of free email advice see **www.venables.co.uk**. If you don't get a prompt response from the email services, you could try the premium-priced telephone hotline from **www.lawrights.co.uk** at £1.50 per minute. But this works out at £90 per hour, so you would have to ask your question concisely to avoid running up a large phone bill.

For small businesses, similar types of basic information covering areas such as employment (and internet usage at work) are available from sites like Desktoplawyer. Inevitably these types of service would not cover complex contractual disputes, and for that you would have to approach a solicitor in the traditional way.

Big companies operate in a completely different market and city law firms such as Linklater (**www.blueflag.com**) and Clifford Chance (**www.nextlaw.com**) have designed big websites to service them. However, subscription costs thousands of pounds a year.

Identifying and tracking down the piece of legislation that covers a particular legal problem is not easy unless the legislation is recent. Since 1996 statutes have been published on the Stationery Office's website (**www.hmso.gov.uk**), but reading the material is hard going for the non-lawyer. For older laws you would have to resort to a search engine or even an old-fashioned library. For recent legal developments it may also be worth looking at the Home Office website (**www.homeoffice.gov.uk**), where you can see White Papers.

Legal documents

Basic legal documents such as wills are available very cheaply over the web. What you do on a legal website is exactly the same as what a secretary does in a solicitor's office: enter your personal details into a pre-designed form and press the 'print' button. The usual procedure is to choose whether you want your will emailed, faxed or posted. With this simple process you can undercut the high-street solicitor substantially. We found one will package for £10 (**www.diy-lawyer.com**), which compares with a high-street charge of £70 and up. But competition on the web is in its early stages, and another site charged as much as £40 for a simple will. However, for those prepared to do the writing by hand, it is still cheaper to buy a will package from W. H. Smith for £6.99.

In other areas we found the web offered convenience, but at a wide range of prices. For example, an Assured Shorthold Tenancy document cost between £20 and £50 but the basic legal stationery for this document can be bought for as little as £2.00 from Oyez the legal stationer, who will post out the forms for a £1 charge. You can't download these forms on the net, although a website is in the pipeline. To contact Oyez, see **www.oyezstraker.co.uk/welcome.htm**.

The best value online may be found in slightly more complex documents. For example, DIY lawyer offers a package covering 'how to bankrupt an individual or a company' for £49.99, which includes notes and background information.

Legal services

As well as information, the internet also provides lots of competitively priced legal services. For example, DIY lawyer undertakes credit checks on individuals for £10 and on companies for £20. Divorce packs are also available on-line (see the section on divorce in Dating, Marriage and Divorce).

Conveyancing is one of the most competitive areas of online law. Some online providers offer premium services that allow contact with a solicitor, but the cheaper deals assume no direct contact at all. You would have to assess the complexity of your property transaction before opting for an entirely no-frills approach. Some websites quote a final fee, and others provide a quote 'excluding disbursements'. (With lawyers you always need to check the fine print). Some of the financial websites such as

www.moneysupermarket.co.uk also offer online conveyancing. It is worth checking to see whether you will be able to track the progress of the conveyancing online because if you can't do that, you would still be left trying to call your solicitor when he's on the golf course.

Personal Injury

One of the most striking developments in consumer law in recent years has been the emergence of companies taking on personal injury claims on a 'no win no fee' basis. The most successful company is this area is Claims Direct (**www.claimsdirect.com**). Apart from saving the cost of a phone call, there is no particular advantage to starting off a claim on the company's website because claimants don't pay anything unless the case is successful. However, there is plenty of background information about how this company works.

Problems

While some solicitors are eagerly embracing the technology of the internet, others are much more conservative in their methods and stick to writing letters (expensive and slow) rather than emails (quick and cheap). Perhaps the latter type cannot or will not use a keyboard, and insist on having Miss Smith take dictation.

If you experience any problems with an online legal service, you can go to the Law Society's Office of Supervision of Solicitors (**www.oss.lawsociety.org.uk**) – although the Society does not have a strong record in following up complaints promptly.

Selected sites

Non-commercial legal sites
www.lawsociety.org.uk ○○
Main Law Society site. More use to solicitors than consumers.

www.solicitors-online ○○○
Law Society-funded site. Helps you to find a solicitor by area and by specialisation. The search engine produces uneven results.

www.justask.org.uk ○○○
Government-funded community legal service that provides search facilities for legal resources from Citizens Advice Bureaux to solicitors.

www.lawscot.org.uk ❂❂❂
Law Society of Scotland provides a search for Scottish solicitors and introduction to the world of Scottish law.

www.hmso.gov.uk ❂❂
Texts of all new acts of Parliament since 1996. But hard to follow for non-lawyers.

www.legalservices.gov.uk ❂❂❂
Advice about government-assisted legal support (not very extensive now Legal Aid has been scrapped).

www.courtservice.gov.uk ❂❂❂
Background information on UK court system and charges. Useful notes on how to obtain probate. Also useful links section at courtservice.gov.uk/lexicon/links.htm.

www.tradingstandards.net ❂❂❂
Consumer information on Trading Standards. Background information on weights and measures.

Commercial law sites
www.venables.co.uk ❂❂❂❂
Useful starting-point for online legal resources.

www.lawrights.co.uk ❂❂❂
Basic consumer and business services.

www.pearsonmaddin.co.uk ❂❂❂❂
Solictors' site but also a particularly good source of legal information.

www.family-solicitors.co.uk ❂❂❂
Covers all aspects of family law.

www.firstlaw.co.uk ❂❂❂
Aimed at SME (Small and Medium-sized Enterprises). Claims to be first legal website regulated by the Law Society. Not suitable for consumers.

www.kt.uklaw.net ❂❂❂
Good solicitor's site from Kaye Tesler, but prices for documents are high.

www.infolaw.co.uk ❂❂❂❂
Articles and listings relating to online law and new legal websites (on Nick's page). Aimed more at lawyers but useful for consumers too. Links to some online legal services.

www.out-law.com ❂❂❂❂
Legal service for new economy businesses from Masons. The focus is on 'how to' do something (like start-up a business) rather than showing lots of complex regulations.

www.desktop-lawyer.co.uk ❂❂❂❂
Good all-round site serving consumers and small businesses. Text written by barristers. Not the cheapest of services, but there is a useful glossary.

Religion

'Pascal's wager' is the name for the notion that a rational man will believe in Christ with all his might because if traditional Christian teaching is correct and you do not believe, you're going to feel mighty uncomfortable after the Second Coming. Of course the problem with this is that you have to be sure that all the other religions (including the myriad sub-divisions of Christianity) are wrong, because many of them say the same thing about their own belief system. So the question is how to be sure which one is right.

> *'Religious Groups Great and Small Reach Out to the Believer'*
> — Washington Post

If this sort of consideration keeps you awake at night, stay away from the net! It is chock-full of information and propaganda from people espousing more varieties of human religiosity than you would have believed possible. There is straightforward coverage of the major religions, curious titbits about minor religions, satire from confirmed atheists, and – mostly from America – quite a lot of downright weird stuff.

> *'God Is Everywhere on the Net'*
> — LA Times

If you are so minded, you can join online meetings, sermons, and religious gatherings twenty-four hours a day, seven days a week. You can find local places of worship and places of contact. You can educate yourself about world religions, and view translations of religious texts into many languages. And you can buy all manner of religious paraphernalia.

The internet obeys few moral or aesthetic codes, so you do need to approach religious websites with an open mind – or if you cannot manage that, then at least approach them with caution.

General information on religion

The major portals have extensive listings of religious websites. For UK sites, start with **uk.yahoo.com**. The US-oriented portals have even more on religion, so try **www.aol.com**, for instance.

There are portals specialising in faith and belief, and again the US ones are more numerous and more comprehensive. Beliefnet at **www.beliefnet.com** has an easy-to-use, approachable site with unbiased content. The site is trying to build an interactive, global, multifaith e-community to provide information and inspiration to all.

For spiritually neutral, information-only sites, try the 'people and beliefs' link at **www.bbc.co.uk/worldservice** for a neat summary of major world religions. For a more academic directory site, **www.academicinfo.net/religindex.html** is run by a Comparative Religion graduate, and is a good source of high-quality links with helpful comments on the sites' contents. Helpfully, the links are split into 'start with' and 'continue with' sections, depending on how much you already know.

To find out where to experience religion in the real world, **www.scoot.co.uk** or **www.yell.co.uk** will help find your local places of worship.

The major world religions

Christianity

Christianity is the most widely represented religion on the internet. A useful starting-point is the Bible Gateway, **www.bible.gospelcom.net**, where you can search a number of Bible versions by passage or keywords in nine different languages.

Sooner or later you will need to dig down into the individual denominations. The official Church of England site, **www.cofe.epinet.co.uk**, has a well-designed site, with practical information on finding your nearest church, information on special occasions, and news and views on hot topics. For Anglicans, **www.anglicansonline.org** is an independent site with basic information for non-Anglicans and country-specific news, events and resources. Then **www.anglican.org** offers a gateway to Anglican and Episcopalian sites around the world.

Sites for the various strains of Orthodox Christianity are rarer. One of the best is **www.orthodoxinfo.com**, which is content-rich while **www.goarch.org/access/orthodoxy** provides a detailed introduction to the faith and plenty of text on a long list of topics from baptism to exorcism.

Keying 'Catholicism' into a search engine serves up many sites eagerly discussing modernisation and the need for change in the Catholic church. For less polemical stuff, the *Catholic Herald* is online at **www.catholicherald.co.uk**, or the official Vatican site is at **www.vatican.va**. Most pages, but not all, are available in English. The site is extremely professional yet sedate with information on the Vatican City State, the Pope and his predecessors, and the Vatican's museums, libraries and archives. If you have Real Audio software you can listen to radio services and Sunday prayers.

The site **www.catholic.org** attempts to bring together Catholics from all over the world through online forums and international news links. It has a shopping channel for pilgrimage tours and articles. A popular site with a fun layout and easy style is **www.suite101.com/welcome.cfm/roman_catholicism**. Suite 101 also covers other religions and topics. For a more academic look at Roman Catholicism, its doctrines and practices see **www.carm.org/drc.htm**, while for a liberal view visit **www.natcath.com/ncr_onli.htm**, where you can view news and editorials on current events.

Islam

Targeted at a broad audience, IslamiCity at **islam.org** is a portal addressing everything from news and finance to online radio and media broadcasting information. You can search the Qu'rān (in Arabic and English) and visit a virtual mosque. To order a literal translation of the Qu'rān with no omitted or additional words, and with cross references to the Bible and Hadith, visit **www.qurantoday.com**.

For balanced Muslim news, **www.muslimnews.co.uk** is an independent commercial publication, and **www.ummah.org.uk**, is a non-profit news site that encourages discussion and debate, with opinionated news and features, cartoons, and links to the Qu'rān and further resources. The multimedia section offers a small selection of Islamic programmes, lectures and news videos.

Judaism

Jewish sites are above average in terms of style and appeal, with stacks of content and links. An excellent Jewish portal site (apart from the pop-up adverts) is **www.judaism.about.com**. You can access the *Jewish Chronicle* online at **www.jchron.co.uk**, or for more controversial news there is always **www.goodforthejewsnews.com**, which assesses news items in terms of whether they are good for the Jews. A cool-looking American site aimed at a young Jewish audience, **www.generationj.com** covers news and spiritual topics from yoga to poetry. Hang out in the café or check out the Jewish TV guide.

Then **www.jewfaq.org/toc.htm** is a basic site offering comprehensive content on several categories including the faith, people and language. Each link or page is given a basic, intermediate or advanced label to help users find the appropriate level of information.

Hinduism

Hinduism is not based on a sacred book in the same way as the major Western religions so its websites are often less formal and include lifestyle information and matrimonial ads.

A huge portal site, **www.hindunet.org**, covers all aspects of Hinduism. The homepage is a little cluttered and page loading is slow. With a little patience, you can link to classical texts, matrimonial listings, descriptions of gods, goddesses and famous people, and children-specific sections. A straightforward and valuable resource is the Hindu directory at **www.hindu.org**.

For fans of devotional music and songs in Hindi and Sanskrit (some with English translations) **www.bhaktisangeet.com** allows you to play music online. Children can learn about Hindu prayers, festivals, customs and culture through pictorial descriptions and forums at **www.hindukids.org**. Something to look out for is **www.eh.sc.edu**, an encyclopedic site on Hindu traditions in English.

Buddhism

The philosophy and teachings of Buddhism are covered at **www.theravada.net**, which includes summaries of Buddhist thinking on topics like marriage, women in society, etc. There is an online community, but with few postings, so try **www.buddhanet.net** instead, a sometimes humorous Australian site with deep content on meditation and art work, cartoons and an online magazine. An index of resources online and off can be viewed at **www.dharmanet.org**. For more spiritual humour head for **www.dharmathecat.com**.

Sikhism

A clear guide to the Sikh way of life and its scriptures is available at **www.sikhs.org**, as well the philosophy and history. The resource section includes a reading list, a glossary, and links to further sites. A very comprehensive directory is available at **www.sikhseek.com**.

www.sikhnet.com is a professional, well-presented site for Sikhs around the world, covering religion, news and live events. It provides a matchmaking service and advertises a handful of job ads from Belgium to Brazil.

Other religions

Sites about the Bahai faith cover all the usual aspects – community, teachings, chat rooms, etc. Start with **www.bahaifaith.net** or **www.bahaullah.net** and follow links from there.

If the Jehovah's Witnesses haven't visited recently then look them up at **www.watchtower.org** – an unimposing site with articles on the faith, discussions of pornography on the internet and descriptions of kangaroos!

For L. Ron Hubbard's teachings in depth, go to **www.scientology.org**. Nothing on Richard Gere and small furry animals, though.

For something a little more spiritual, visit the **www.holisticshop.co.uk** to read or buy something spiritually uplifting.

Agnosticism and Atheism

The official religions do not have it all their own way. A comprehensive site for atheists, with excellent content, detail and discussion, is the Secular Web at **www.infidels.org**. Daily news is pulled from sources world-wide on hot topics from cloning to the legalisation of marijuana. Worth a mention is **www.hereticards.com**, where you can buy greetings cards which proudly proclaim the non-existence of God.

The site **www.hti.net/www/atheism** tries to be comprehensive, but is also stronger in its views with a tendency to bash religions for the sake of it. There are some great cartoons and interesting history pages, though.

As you might expect, **www.godless.org** is loaded with articles about the importance of science and unimportance of god.

Humanism

The British Humanist Association can be found at **www.humanism.org.uk**. A low-key site, but good for the basics on humanist thinking and contact details. The American Humanist Association has an exhaustive list of documents fundamental to humanism, **www.humanist.net/documents**. An essay summarising humanism is available at **www.jcn.com/humanism.html**.

Internet religion

The internet doesn't just describe existing religions, it spawns new ones. One such is Cosmosofy which seeks to 'avoid the extinction of all mankind'. The site (**www.cosmosofy.org**) offers several hundred of pages of text to enlighten you on its philosophy. Claiming 1.3 million members, **www.digitalism.8m.com** expounds the unity of technology with Buddhism.

Humour

Don't visit **www.crucify.com** unless you are non-Christian, have an open mind or enjoy getting really angry. It is the only place we know of where Jesus talks directly to you, and the reactions of previous visitors (letters to Jesus) are every bit as funny as the discussion itself.

'Jesus hears us when we pray and when we talk to him, but he does NOT have a website.'

– Disapproving reader of www.crucify.com

Not primarily intended as humour, **www.exit109.com/~mcluff/bible.shtml** quotes some extraordinary passages from the Bible and proves that if any book should be censored, the Bible is it. What is funny on this site is the selection of reactions from previous visitors.

If you've been naughty, and feel in need of absolution, **www.nosin.com/good.htm** is the place for you. On the other hand, if you enjoy the odd guilt trip, indulge yourself at **www.nosin.com/evil.htm**.

If you enjoy these, visit **www.dir.yahoo.com/Entertainment/Humor/Religion** for a whole lot more.

News

Newspapers demonstrate perhaps better than any other service area what a strange and contradictory place the internet is. Online newspapers are better than offline newspapers, and they are also worse. Online newspapers are completely different from their offline parents and they are also exactly the same.

In praise of online newspapers

For those who like to have a glance at lots of newspapers or compare what they are saying about a particular issue, the internet is invaluable – you don't have to buy them all or go to the local library. All the broadsheets have followed the lead of the *Daily Telegraph* and have set up sites: www.telegraph.co.uk, www.thetimes.co.uk, www.independent.co.uk, www.guardian.co.uk and www.ft.com. Online editions reflect the political allegiances of their offline parents – although the format of the web (with its greater emphasis on breaking news) means that you notice the design, speed and organisation of the site much more than its political affiliation.

The major advantages of online papers are that you can customise your favourite paper so that the bits of news which interest you come up first, and you can arrange for those bits to be emailed to you every day. If you hate sport, you don't even have to bin it. You can also copy an article or an excerpt from an online paper and email it to a friend far more easily than cutting up the hard-copy version and putting it in an envelope. Just as easy, you can save it to an archive folder on your computer and build up your own database of reports on subjects of interest.

The online papers can lead you with hyperlinks down a trail of related articles until you have explored an issue as fully as you like. They can link you to pages in completely different websites, as well as to different pages (including articles from different days) in their own.

The online papers are more up-to-date. News is uploaded on them as soon as the editor has approved it, while the offline paper is printed late at night and starts becoming obsolete at breakfast. Finally, no more soggy papers, spotted with rain and chewed by the dog; no more ink that comes off on your hands.

In praise of hard copy

Most people would far rather read from paper than from a screen – many people print off anything longer than a page rather than read it on-screen. You can't very easily read a laptop standing in a train or a bus. Browsing online is less relaxing to most people than leafing through a paper.

On normal domestic modems, online newspapers take too long to load, so hopping between pages is full of frustrating delays. You need to have several browsers on the go at the same time if you're going to consume much news online.

Meet the new editor – same as the old editor

Obviously the internet is a different medium from the printed page, and at least for the moment people use the two media differently. But the editorial line doesn't change. So you will still find Little Englander small-mindedness with a cheeky grin and semi-naked women on **www.the-sun.co.uk**, and you'll still find a somewhat more serious approach to life on **www.ft.com**.

For serious political and business news, the place to go is definitely **www.ft.com**. Pearson, its owner, has spent a fortune on this site, and its importance to them is illustrated by the fact that an upturn or a downturn in its ad sales can move the whole group's share price. Ft.com offers free access to all surveys and reports produced in the paper version, a personal office (including email, calendar, address book, file storage facilities), and a first-class archive of articles with a search engine that trawls the *Financial Times* back issues, other websites and other online news.

Both the *FT* archive and the *Guardian's* select articles for inclusion in the electronic edition (so if you search for a particular item, you might not find it). By contrast the *Telegraph* includes everything from its offline edition online (and you can search for an article on a specific date). The *Telegraph* also has the longest archive (going back to 1994) whereas the *Independent's* goes back to only 1999. It is usually worth reading the notes attached to each site's archive search because the rules vary slightly (and are different from search engines such as Yahoo).

It is debatable whether *The Economist* (**www.economist.co.uk**) is a broadsheet, but it insists on calling itself a newspaper rather than a magazine, and it sure ain't a tabloid! As a non-subscriber you can read a selection of articles from current editions. Registration is free and allows you access to weekly politics and business emails and five retrievals from the archive. To get more, you must subscribe.

Local newspapers

There are literally thousands of local papers in the UK, and many of them have online versions. One of the main reasons people buy local papers is for the small ads. Six of the biggest local paper groups (Newsquest Media Group, Northcliffe Newspapers Group, Trinity Mirror and Guardian Media Group Regional Newspapers, Regional Independent Media, and Bristol United Press) have come together at **www.fish4.co.uk** to offer access to their combined classified ads.

For any local papers beyond this coalition, you could try **www.yahoo.co.uk**, either via towns and cities, or through links from news. Also worth trying would be **emedia1.mediainfo.com/emedia**, an intriguing site run by *Editor and Publisher* magazine in America, which seeks to be a directory to media all over the world.

For Londoners who haven't yet discovered it, **www.thisislondon.co.uk**, is the *Evening Standard*'s online site, and is jam-packed with London news and gossip.

American newspapers

US papers have front pages packed with information but with good layouts either based on drop-down menus or sub-sites that you link to from the front page. You can sign up for emailed news from a selection of categories. The *Washington Post*'s **www.washingtonpost.com** has a detailed front page and manages to avoid irritating, flashy ads alongside the title. The **www.nytimes.com** is also refreshingly free of distractingly flashy ads, which makes the leading story much stronger. Its archive search gives you the first couple of lines of each article free; for more than that you have to pay $2.50. **www.chicagotribune.com** has a similar layout and high-quality content, but they couldn't resist the flashing ads headlining the front page.

The *Wall St Journal* – **www.wsj.com** – is the US equivalent of the *Financial Times*, and is one of the very few newspapers in the world that has managed to sustain a paid-for web service. You can sign up for free trial access to the site's content and archive, but for regular use you will need to pay a subscription.

Broadcasters

The obvious place to start is **www.news.bbc.co.uk**, which has a hectic front page but is loaded with content, including foreign language options, TV features and audio/video clips. You can link back to the BBC's homepage, which is a portal to an enormous amount of material – almost an internet in itself.

www.itn.co.uk is the main alternative – don't make the mistake of looking for news at **www.itv.co.uk**, which in its fervour to treat you to enormous amounts of information abut *Coronation Street* doesn't even link to ITN. ITN offers a personalised news delivery service, in which you can choose the time of delivery, and how many stories you would like delivered from the categories of UK, World and Business. The delivery can include pictures, if your email software can handle them. ITN also has a news ticker service, but we've never seen any news on it.

If you are a radio fan, there are online audio news providers, including **www.bbc.co.uk/worldservice** and **www.npr.org**, an American site. For radio, you need the appropriate software, and you cannot usually receive radio online if you are behind a firewall, which you almost certainly will be if you are connecting from within a large company.

The venerable news agency PA has an innovative site at **www.ananova.com**. There is a mass of content, but the prize draw is Ananova, the world's first virtual newscaster. She bears more than a passing resemblance to Lara Croft, the male-fantasy heroine of the Tomb Raider video game.

If you think that living in the American century makes it sensible to turn to the American media for a take on world events, start with **www.abcnews.com**, a rich site with live video, audio and chat as well as detailed sub menus. ABC's great rival NBC also has a personalisable site at **www.nbci.com**, but the site is less oriented to news than ABC's. CNN (which according to some stands for Cheap & Nasty News) has a personalisable site at **www.mycnn.com** which allows you to see only what interests you. A European CNN site is on the way, headed up by ex-BBC chief political correspondent Robin Oakley.

News aggregators

Offline, aggregation of news is rare. *The Week* collects the best news stories from round the world each week, but there are few other examples. Online, aggregation of content is rife. Portals like Yahoo (**http://uk.news.yahoo.com/**) gather together stories from various reliable sources, but one of the better aggregators is **www.moreover.com**. It has stacks of content, and if you have your own website you can add Moreover headlines to it quickly, easily and for nothing.

'Ours is a special spider, trained to look just for headlines, not for rubbish. It has a nose for news.'

– Nick Denton, CEO, Moreover

Specialist publications

There are a million sites with news and views on specific areas of interest. Armed with a good search engine, some ingenuity and persistence, you should be able to find somebody somewhere on the net publishing stuff on the subjects that interest you.

To take just one sector, here's a quick overview of what's being published on the net about technology. For new technology products hitting the shops and all things internet-, software- and hardware-related, have a look at **www.zdnet.com** – or **www.zdnet.co.uk** for more UK specific content. The site has tech and stock news, product reviews, free software downloads, games and lots more. Jesse Berst's column is always informative and stimulating, and you can have it emailed to you daily.

For business- and investment-related technology news, analysis and discussion, visit **www.redherring.com** or sign up for regular emails. Red Herring has a laid-back American style and is not afraid to make statements and give opinions. **www.wired.com** has less of a business focus and a similar style.

A successful publication in America, recently launched in the UK, is *Business 2.0*, **www.business2.co.uk**. It has very readable content covering business in the 'new economy' with a critical look at what is and isn't working in the UK as well as in the US. Also, check out **www.silicon.com**, **www.thestandard.com**, and **www.tornadoinside.com**. Offline publishing giant CMP produces **www.techweb.com**, and the Stockhouse Media Corporation is behind **www.netimperative.com**.

The list goes on and on, but should not omit **www.theregister.co.uk**, a tiny outfit, which through imagination (and probably through sheer impertinence) often manages to break IT news before its bigger peers.

Selected sites

UK newspapers – broadsheets
www.telegraph.co.uk ❍❍❍
A popular site with regular readers, and the first of the UK broadsheets to take the internet seriously. But it has been overtaken in functionality and design by the rest.

www.newsunlimited.co.uk ❍❍❍❍
The site of the *Guardian* and the *Observer* has a crisp, trendy format. The webguides are good and and The Wrap is an excellent digest of what the other papers are saying – complete with links.

www.thetimes.co.uk ❍❍
Worthy, if a tad dull. You can choose whether it displays articles in web-style or straight text.

www.sunday-times.co.uk ❂❂❂
Like it or not, the *Sunday Times* is the UK's weekend journal of record. 'Reading it online at least prevents your arms dropping off because of the weight of the hard-copy version.

www.independent.co.uk ❂❂❂❂
A modern, tasteful design and layout with good interactive content and leisure sections. The search facility is reasonably flexible too.

www.ft.com ❂❂❂❂❂
Excellent site, which has had a lot of money spent on it.

www.economist.co.uk ❂❂❂❂
Arrogant, opinionated and magnificent.

UK newspapers – tabloid
www.anorak.co.uk ❂❂❂
Created by the Online Editorial Bureau, this offers a digest of the press along with satirical commentary.

www.mirror.co.uk ❂❂
Not a pretty site, but its news and views come in handy bite-sized chunks. You can sample some of Victor Lewis-Smith's spleen there, which is usually worthwhile.

www.the-sun.co.uk ❂❂❂
A bit more lively than its red-top rival, and most *Sun* readers will want to click through to www.page3.com for what comes naturally, and also for their daily joke, which is useful if you need to retaliate against a persistent joke-emailer.

www.dailymail.co.uk ❂
Takes you to a site which indicates that the traditional paper of the Tory woman does not yet have an online version, but points you in the direction of several other offerings from its parent company, Associated Newspapers.

Other newspapers
www.nytimes.com ❂❂❂❂
Heaps of content, and proves that flashy ads all over the place are not necessary.

www.fish4.co.uk ❂❂❂❂
Enormous classifieds resource.

www.thisislondon.co.uk ❂❂❂
An important site if you live in London, although the listings could be better.

Broadcasters
www.news.bbc.co.uk ❂❂❂❂❂
Auntie's put a whole world in here.

www.itn.co.uk ❂❂❂❂
Some interesting initiatives, and a lot of content.

www.ananova.com ❂❂❂❂
If the news is dull, Ananova will liven it up.